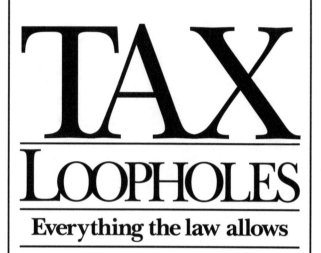

TAX
LOOPHOLES
Everything the law allows

BOARDROOM CLASSICS
55 Railroad Avenue, Greenwich, CT 06830

Completely Revised Edition
10 9 8 7 6 5 4

Boardroom® Classics publishes the advice of expert authorities in
many fields. But the use of this material is not a substitute for
legal, accounting, or other professional services. Consult a
competent professional for answers to your specific questions.

Library of Congress Cataloging in Publication Data
Tax Loopholes. Everything the Law Allows.
   p.cm.
   Includes index.
   ISBN 0-88723-116-0
   1. Tax Planning—United States—Popular works.
   2. Income tax—Law and legislation—United States—
   Popular works.
KF6297.Z9B6 1988
343.73 04—dc19   88-13935
(347.3034)   CIP

Boardroom® Classics is a registered trademark of
Boardroom,® Inc.
55 Railroad Avenue, Greenwich, CT 06830

Printed in the United States of America

TAX LOOPHOLES

EVERYTHING THE LAW ALLOWS

Contents

1 • SHREWD TAX PLANNING

Keys to the right resources

Really prepare if you really care

Early is best—most of the time

Before you file your return...

Tactics for itemizers and nonitemizers

Angles on a very, very special tax

All about estimated taxes

Advantages of overseas banking

Recordkeeping hotline

The magic of amended returns

Defenses, loopholes, and gimmicks

2 • TAX ANGLES FOR INVESTORS

Investment self-defense

x Contents

11 • AUDIT SECRETS

Ways to avoid an audit

Audit risks

Preparation is half the battle

Good news about audits

IRS audits—myths and realities

Secrets of dealing with auditors

Making a deal with the IRS

IRS audit tactics to know

Audit alert for companies

1

TAX LOOPHOLES

EVERYTHING THE LAW ALLOWS

Shrewd Tax Planning

Keys to the right resources

Picking The Best Tax Adviser

If you really want to save taxes, you must find a specialist who can...
- Help you rethink your tax situation in light of the new law.
- Guide you through financial transactions.
- Tell you which tried-and-true tax-saving strategies are still good, and which aren't.
- Inform you of new tax-saving opportunities.
- Alert you to dangerous new tax traps.

Where to Start

Use a checklist approach to methodically conduct your search for the ideal tax professional:

Get recommendations from friends, neighbors, members of clubs you belong to, and business colleagues. Word of mouth is by far the best way to find the right tax adviser. Give additional weight to recommendations from those whose financial circumstances are similar to your own. *The ideal tax adviser should be:*
- Familiar with your line of work. This is a key requirement, and it is especially important if you run your own business.
- Comfortable with your income level. You want someone who's familiar with the type of income and deductions that show up on your tax return. If you're not yet a millionaire, you probably don't need an adviser who has only millionaire clients.
- Neither overly conservative nor unreasonably aggressive. You want a professional whose financial philosophy is compatible with yours.

Ask your banker and attorney for recommendations. They are financial professionals who probably know some of the best tax people in the area. Ask them for the names of tax specialists whose work they have had a chance to evaluate.

Select no more than four possible candidates. Telephone for interviews. When you call to set up an appointment, ask about fees. Is there a charge for the initial meeting? Should you bring any particular papers with you, such as your previous three years' returns?

It's important to set up a fee structure immediately, to know what you're getting for your money, so there'll be no misunderstanding later. *Questions to ask:*
- What is the fee for preparing a tax return?
- How much is the fee for advice?
- Does that fee include visits throughout the year? How many?

A competent tax professional will want to see the income tax returns you have filed during the past few years.

Test the candidates' knowledge. You don't have to be an expert to do this, but you do need a working knowledge of taxes. *Areas of questioning:*

■ If you operate a business, ask what tax law changes mean to the particular type of business you run. Discuss how and when to buy and sell corporate stock, when to pay dividends, techniques to pull money out of your firm tax-free, how to share business profits with your children without paying tax.

■ If you are an active investor, or are involved in trust and estate activity, discuss how changes in the law can be used to your advantage and how changes will hurt if you fail to act.

■ Discuss the latest strategies in retirement planning and how to put money away to help finance your children's education.

If the tax professional you are interviewing seems to be knowledgeable, that's terrific. If not, look elsewhere.

Deciding Factors

Make a final decision after narrowing down the number of candidates. Professional qualifications and fees being equal, the final choice is strictly a personal one. Select the person whom you are comfortable with personally and professionally. *Other deciding factors:*

■ The adviser is in business on a year-round basis. You don't want a seasonal tax representative, one who just does returns, because you want tax advice as well as tax preparation.

■ The adviser will meet with you at least quarterly during the year. Saving taxes is an ongoing process—one meeting a year at tax time isn't enough.

■ The adviser can represent you before the IRS. Unless you're extremely lucky, you'll have at least one confrontation with the IRS during your taxpaying lifetime. It's worth the extra money to have someone who can represent you at audits.

Saver: The fee for tax planning and advisory services is deductible, provided your total miscellaneous itemized deductions exceed 2% of your Adjusted Gross Income.

Source: Former IRS tax-law specialist Paul N. Strassels, Box 8331, Rapid City, SD 57709.

Computer-Prepared Returns

Computer programs that assist in planning and preparing returns are becoming increasingly popular. *Danger:* When a program contains errors that result in an understatement of taxes due, the program's creator and seller may become liable for *return-preparer's penalties*—the same penalties that are imposed on tax professionals who are negligent when preparing a client's return.

Source: Revenue Ruling 85-189.

Free Filing Help From The IRS

An abundance of free help is available from the IRS...if you know where to get it.

Free information publications. The IRS has an in-depth explanation booklet on almost every topic. These publications usually contain related forms and schedules, with filled-in examples. *Necessary:* Every taxpayer should obtain a copy of IRS Publication 17, *Your Federal Income Tax.* It contains more than 200 pages of information to guide you in filling out your income tax return.

A partial list of other publications is included in the instructions to your Form 1040. A more complete list can be found in IRS Publication 910, *Guide to Free Tax Services*—and in Publication 17.

Where to get the free publications:

■ At your local IRS office.

■ Call 1-800-829-FORM and ask the IRS to mail the publications or forms that you request. During filing season, you can call this number during the week from 8:00 a.m. to 8:00 p.m. and on Saturdays from 9:00 a.m. to 3:00 p.m.

■ Use the order form included in your Form 1040 instructions. Mail it to the forms distribution center listed for your state (also in the 1040 instructions).

Free phone service. The IRS will answer questions regarding the preparation of your tax return over the telephone. Check the list in your 1040 instructions to find the number to call in your state. From most areas, the number is 1-800-829-1040.

Caution: The IRS is not always accurate when answering your telephone questions. You are ultimately responsible for errors on your return, even if you used incorrect information obtained from calling the IRS number. *Better idea:* Verify any information you receive from the IRS over the telephone by looking it up for yourself in one of the IRS publications.

Recorded tax information. You can call the IRS and listen to recorded tapes on any of about 150 tax topics. A list of tax topics and the phone numbers for your area are listed in the instructions to your 1040.

Walk-in services. Most IRS offices provide a walk-in counter to help you with information.

Help for handicapped, elderly, and low-income earners.

■ Deaf taxpayers who have access to TV/Telephone-TTY equipment can call 1-800-829-4059 for assistance.

■ Blind taxpayers can obtain braille tax materials at regional libraries for the blind and physically handicapped.

■ Elderly, handicapped, low-income, and non-English-speaking taxpayers can receive assistance in preparing tax returns from the Volunteer Income Tax Assistance (VITA) program. IRS-trained volunteers work in libraries, community centers, and churches during the filing season. To find the nearest VITA site, call your local IRS office.

Does Your Accountant Have The Right Stuff?

Far too many accountants are intimidated by aggressive revenue agents. Some even allow themselves to be pressured into giving damaging information about their clients. Any number of practitioners who profess to be capable of representing clients before the IRS are more nervous about a confrontation than their clients are. *Best question to ask your accountant before an audit:* "If I told you that I didn't report all my income, how would you respond to the agent when he/she asks?" The kind of answer you would want your accountant to give is a noncommittal one, such as: "Why do you think my client hasn't reported all his income?" or, "I'll get back to you later with an answer to that question." You don't want an accountant who lies, nor do you want one who would incriminate you by telling the truth.

Source: Ms. X, Esq., a former IRS agent who is still well connected.

When To Ignore Your Accountant

Higher ethical standards for tax return preparers has become one of the hottest topics at the IRS. The Service has proposed that tax advisers who steer their clients into taking positions that are not supported by substantial authority should be barred from practice before the IRS. Tax practitioners who are aware of the proposed new ethical standards are apt to overreact. *Advice:* Don't let your accountant talk you into filing an overly conservative return. Resist his/her effort to make you pay more tax than you really have to...just so *he* can sleep easier.

Source: Ms. X, Esq., a former IRS agent who is still well connected.

Really prepare if you really care

Getting The Most From Your Tax Preparer

Here are ways to maximize the value of your tax adviser's time and expertise.

Organize Your Records

Nothing dismays an accountant more than a client who comes in with a shoe box full of old bills, checks, and whatnot in no discernible order. Eventually the accountant can sort them out. But there are better, more productive uses for the accountant's time—and you're paying for it.

Act early. Don't wait until the beginning of April, when accountants are busy day and night and will have little time to devote to you.

Get organized. Around the end of the year, most accountants send their clients an "organizer"—a booklet explaining which records are needed and a questionnaire listing your marital status, dependents, salary, and other information needed for your return. Use the "organizer" to the full. If you're a new client, ask for one. If you have any questions, don't hesitate to phone and ask. In the long run, you'll save time and work for both the accountant and yourself.

Bring the necessary records. The more complete the information, the better the job your accountant can do. If information is lacking, the job will take longer, cost more, and run a greater risk of error. To do a good job, your accountant has to understand your situation thoroughly, so don't assume that anything is irrelevant. When in doubt, ask.

Get Help for the Future

You're not taking full advantage of your accountant's expertise if you just have him/her fill out your return. You should use the opportunity to plan for future years. Good accountants will offer help on their own. But never hesitate to ask questions and get advice on your own particular situation. Here are some ways in which your tax adviser can help:

■ *Proposed transactions.* Are you thinking of buying or selling your home? Investing in a business? Buying securities? Changing your marital status? Moving to another state—with different tax laws? You can't make an intelligent decision without knowing the tax consequences. Keep your accountant fully informed.

■ *Long-range planning.* Confusion about retirement plans is rampant. No matter what your age, you must know the laws and the rules in order to plan intelligently for the future. You may also want advice on estate planning. What will happen to your family upon your death?

■ *Keeping up with the tax changes.* Tax Reform was a sweeping revision of the entire tax structure. But every year brings additional changes that could affect you. Your accountant can keep you up-to-date on new laws, regulations, etc.

■ *Recordkeeping.* Many taxpayers don't know which records they should keep, how long they should keep them, or what can be safely discarded. It is complicated. Your tax adviser can tell you. And he may be able to suggest a good system to help you keep them in order without spending half your life doing paperwork.

Be Prepared...Very Prepared

Don't wait until April to start putting together what you'll need for your tax return. Start now.

■ IRS forms and publications. If the IRS hasn't already sent you these materials, pick them up at your local IRS office or order them by phone (call 1-800-829-FORM). Don't overlook the new forms, such as Form 8598 (home mortgage interest), Form 8582 (passive activity losses), and Form 8615 (the Kiddie tax).

■ W-2s. Your employer must mail these to you by February 1. If you don't get one, contact your employer. When you receive your W-2, check it for accuracy. If it's wrong, get it corrected immediately.

■ 1099 information returns. These, too, should be mailed to you by February 1. You should get 1099s from any persons, companies, banks, financial institutions, etc., who have paid you interest, dividends, free-lance income, etc., during the year for which you're filing. Again, double-check for accuracy and get all mistakes corrected.

■ Deduction data. Sort out your checks, credit-card statements, paid invoices, bills, etc., by category—e.g., medical expenses, charitable donations, travel and entertainment, and any other items that you need for your tax return.

Early is best— most of the time

Get A Jump On Tax Planning

The best way to save taxes is to work out a plan early in the year. *Begin with these strategies:*

Fill out your tax return for the current tax year as soon as you can. Even an estimate will help you project for next year. You'll see where your mistakes were and have plenty of time to set them right in the coming year.

Set up your recordkeeping for next year. Once you've figured out your tax bill for the current year, it will probably be all too obvious where you lacked sufficient records to substantiate your deductions. Set up or improve your recordkeeping system to accommodate your current needs and to make sure you get every deduction you're entitled to next year.

Convert your consumer-interest payments. Interest paid on consumer debt is nondeductible. However, your interest on home-equity mortgages of up to $100,000 on your principal residence (plus one other residence) and interest incurred in your trade or business generally remain 100% deductible. Instead of using your credit card or taking out a consumer loan to pay for purchases, remortgage your home or borrow through your business. Either arrangement means you'll be able to fully deduct the interest payments.

Reevaluate your rental real-estate investments. You can deduct $25,000 of rental real estate losses if your combined Adjusted Gross Income is $100,000 or less. If your combined AGI is $100,000–$150,000, the $25,000 loss limit is gradually phased out. Consider whether it's worthwhile to keep these real estate investments if you can't deduct the losses.

Contribute to your company's 401(k) plan. You were allowed to contribute up to $9,240 in 1995 (indexed for inflation in future years) to this plan. Taxes that you would ordinarily pay are deferred on that part of your salary and on the earnings in the plan until you actually withdraw the money. The earlier in the year you contribute, the more you can earn over the years.

Set up your Keogh plan now. Keogh plans are available to anyone who has self-employment income—e.g., from free-lancing, sideline activities, etc. A significant portion of this income can be contributed, and taxes on both the contribution and its earnings are deferred until you withdraw the money. The sooner you start to contribute, the sooner you'll be earning tax-deferred income for the future.

Set up a gift-giving program for your children. You can still shift a certain amount of your income to family members who are in a lower tax bracket, and the best time to do this is early in the year. Children under the age of 14 who have investment income below $1,300 in 1995 pay tax in their own lower tax bracket. Their investment income *over* that amount, regardless of its source, will be taxed in your higher tax bracket. Make sure you have $1,300 taxed in your child's lower bracket.

If you have children who are age 14 or older, consider shifting even more than $1,300 to them. The entire amount will be taxed in their lower bracket.

Caution: Don't forget that gifts are irrevocable. Once you part with the investment, it belongs solely to your child.

Source: Larry Axelrod, tax partner, Deloitte & Touche, 1900 M St. NW, Washington, DC 20036.

Help For Early Filers

If you have a refund coming, you may want to file your return early. If you owe money, of course, you should wait until April 15 and keep the money working for you as long as possible.

W-2s: You can file as early in the year as you wish, but you must include W-2 forms from *all* employers—and they aren't required to send them to you until February 1.

If you don't get your W-2 on time, check with your employer. As a last resort, you can file Form 4852 (substitute for Form W-2). Explain on the substitute form the source of your salary figures. (For example, you took them from your pay stubs.)

1099s: You'll also be receiving Form 1099 information returns from various sources, showing your income from interest, dividends, or other nonemployee compensation. You do *not* have to attach these forms to your return, so you can file even before you receive them—if you're sure your own records are accurate and complete.

Check all 1099s: Besides checking for corrections, make sure the income is taxable. Banks and financial institutions may sometimes mistakenly use 1099s to report income from IRAs or other accounts that are *not* taxable. Corporations may report both taxable and nontaxable dividends. *Don't pay tax on tax-free income.* Watch out, too, for typographical errors on Social Security numbers, which could cause someone else's income to be reported as yours.

Important: There may be a discrepancy between the 1099s you receive and your records if payments were mailed in late December but not received by you until January. The payer reports the payments in the year they're earned, but they are not income to you until the next year. You do not have to report these payments on this year's income tax return—but you should be prepared to explain the discrepancy if the IRS questions it.

Early-filing hazards: The only real danger in filing early is that you'll omit some item or items from the return, particularly if you file before receiving all of your W-2 and 1099 forms. If you do find an error after you've mailed the return, make sure you file an *amended* return by April 15 to avoid interest and penalties. Include a check for any additional taxes due (or a claim for a refund if you find you've overpaid).

Best Time Of Year To Plan

The beginning of the year is the time to assess your financial situation for the entire year. Know where you stand. Then you can plan your actions to get maximum tax benefits during the year. *Examples:*

■ If you're buying tax shelters, the earlier in the year you go into them, the better. Many write-offs for tax shelters are dependent on the amount of time spent in the venture.

■ If you have incentive stock options to exercise, you should be aware of the tax consequences of your choices. The earlier in the year you have this information, the easier it will be to make the best choice.

■ If you run a small business, you might consider incorporating and setting up a pension or profit-sharing plan. Taking action early in the year can give you the time you need to get expert advice and professional input.

Don't wait until a few weeks before your return is due to start thinking about tax strategies. Year-end planning is a year-long process.

Source: *New Tax Traps/New Opportunities* by Edward Mendlowitz, CPA, Boardroom Special Report, Springfield, NJ 07081.

Benefits Of Early Calculations

Early projection of your income tax liability is becoming increasingly important. *Reasons:*

Tax Reform drastically changed the rules of the game. You can't plan your year-end tax strategy until you know how you are affected by realities such as the passive-loss rule, new limitations on deductions, new capital gains rules, and the Kiddie tax.

The Alternative Minimum Tax (AMT) is hitting many taxpayers. You must know about it in advance in order to avoid it or minimize its impact.

Penalties for underpaying quarterly estimated taxes are stiffer, rules are tougher, and violations are more easily caught by IRS computers. Tax projections are essential to avoid underpayment penalties.

Computers have made income projections much easier and faster to do. Many accounting firms now perform them for their clients routinely—an expensive and time-consuming task in precomputer days.

Gift-Tax-Exclusion Trap

Unlike charitable contributions and business losses, unutilized gift-tax exclusions cannot be carried over for use in a later year's computations. So if the annual exclusion is not fully utilized in any single year, it is forfeited forever. That places a great premium upon timing. The earlier a person starts an annual gift program, the greater are the potential dollar benefits of the annual exclusion. If a person lacks the cash to make gifts in a particular year, he/she might borrow money for that purpose. And the gift need not be in cash if property with a determinable value is given for immediate enjoyment.

Source: *Encyclopedia of Estate Planning* by Robert S. Holzman, Boardroom Classics, Springfield, NJ 07081.

Early-Filing Trap

The IRS encourages taxpayers to file early—so they'll get their refund sooner, it says. But my experience has been that taxpayers who file before April 15 seem to be more prone to an audit than taxpayers who file later. Although no scientific evidence can be produced to support my observation, you lose nothing by obtaining an automatic four-month filing extension from the IRS and waiting until the last possible date to file.

Source: Ms. X, Esq., a former IRS agent who is still well connected.

Before you file your return...

How To Avoid IRS Trouble

Don't mail your return until you've double-checked everything. *Don't forget to:*

■ Include your name, address, and Social Security number on the first page of your return. If you use the IRS preaddressed label, correct any wrong information.

■ Write your name and Social Security number on every page you send to the IRS.

■ Attach copy *B* of your W-2 Form.

■ Sign and date the return. (Both spouses must sign a joint return.)

■ Staple your check or money order to the return. Don't forget to sign the check and write on it your Social Security number, the form number, and the tax year.

■ Copy the return for your own records.

■ Include every form and related schedule.

■ Recheck arithmetic.

■ Address the return to the Internal Revenue Service Center in your state. Some tax professionals believe that the preaddressed envelope that comes with your return contains computer codes that mark the return for an audit. However, other experts say that using the IRS envelope will speed up your refund check.

■ Mail the return on or before April 15. Use stamps—not an office postage meter, because the IRS won't accept this as proof if there is any doubt as to when your return was actually filed.

Tax Return Choices

You have until the time you file your return to make decisions that could cut your tax bill...

Should you and your spouse file a joint return or separate returns? Most married couples are better off filing a joint return. But some couples, particularly those who have substantial individual incomes, will pay less tax if they file separate returns. The new tax rates, the repeal of the $3,000 two-earner married-couple deduction, and the new limits on miscellaneous deductions and medical expenses can, in the right circumstances, make it beneficial to file separate returns. *What to do:* Figure your tax bill both ways before you decide whether to file a joint return or separate returns.

Do you qualify for tax-favored head-of-household filing status? You may qualify if you're single, widowed, separated or divorced and maintained a household that is the principal residence of a child or dependent relative for more than one-half of the year. Head-of-household tax rates are lower than individual tax rates.

Should you "expense" rather than depreciate the cost of business equipment you bought last year? You can write off in the year of purchase (rather than depreciate over a number of years) up to $17,500 of business equipment or property. If you expense, you can get the deduction now; if you depreciate, the deduction will be spread over a period of years. You needn't have used the property for the full year to expense it. For example, if you bought business equipment at the end of December and used it exclusively for business for only a few days, you can still take the full $17,500 expensing deduction.

Should you take depreciation deductions under accelerated methods (big deductions in early years, smaller deductions later on) or under the straight-line method (same amount each year)? *Important consideration:* Accelerated depreciation may be subject to the Alternative Minimum Tax. See your tax adviser.

Do you qualify for income averaging on lump-sum pension payouts? Taxpayers born before 1936 can choose between 10-year averaging at old (1986) tax rates or 5-year averaging at new tax rates. *Another option:* You can defer taxes by rolling over all or part of the payout into an IRA or other qualified retirement plan. Each choice has its benefits and drawbacks. *Best:* Work through the various pros and cons with a tax adviser.

Source: Howard J. Sample, partner, and C. Randolph Holladay, senior tax manager, Price Waterhouse, 1251 Ave. of the Americas, New York 10020.

What The IRS Knows About You

The IRS gets information from third parties and matches this information to you through its computers. Stay one step ahead by being extra careful to report on your tax return what the IRS already knows about you. (You should receive from the third parties copies of all the information they send to the IRS.) *What the IRS knows and how:*

Your income. The IRS knows, of course, if you have been paid over $600. The payer must report this payment to the IRS on Form 1099-MISC, *Statement for Recipients of Miscellaneous Income.* Included in this category:

- Free-lance income.
- Rent or royalty payments.
- Prizes and awards that are not for services.
- Payments made by medical and health-care insurers to a doctor or other supplier of medical services under an insurance program.
- Attorney's and accountant's fees for professional services.
- Witness or expert fees paid by a lawyer during a legal proceeding.
- Payments made to entertainers for their services.

Your wages. The IRS knows from your W-2 Form exactly how much you earned in regular income, bonuses, vacation allowances, severance pay, moving-expense payments, and travel allowances. Your W-2 must be attached to your return.

Interest income. The IRS knows if you've been paid any interest. Banks and financial institutions must report these payments to the IRS on Form 1099-INT, *Statement for Recipients of Interest Income.* Trap: Some interest income is reported to the IRS even though you haven't received it yet. It must be reported as part of your income.

Dividend income. The IRS knows if you received over $10 in money, stock, capital-gain distributions, or property from a corporation. The corporation must report these payments to the IRS on Form 1099-DIV, *Statement for Recipients of Dividends and Distributions.* Important: Make sure the report agrees with your records.

Tax-refund income. The IRS knows about tax refunds you receive. State and local governments must report such payments of over $10 on Form 1099-G, *Statement for Recipients of Certain Government Payments.* Important exception: If you didn't claim the state and local taxes that you paid as itemized deductions on your federal return, you don't have to report these refunds as income. If you receive a Form 1099-G, analyze it carefully to see whether you must include it in income or if you qualify under this exception.

Gambling winnings. The IRS knows about money you won from horse racing, dog racing, jai alai, lotteries, raffles, drawings, Bingo, slot machines, and Keno. It's all reported to the IRS on Form W-2G, *Statement for Recipients of Certain Gambling Winnings.* The general rule: Payments of $600 or more must be reported by the payer. *Exceptions:* Bingo payments of $1,200 or more and Keno payments of $1,500 or more will be reported.

Other income the IRS knows about:

- Original-issue discounts.
- Mortgage interest received from individuals in the course of a trade or business.
- Money received from broker and barter exchanges.
- Distributions from pension and profit-sharing plans, IRAs, etc.
- Cash payments of over $10,000 received in a trade or business.
- Cash deposits of over $10,000 made to your bank account.
- Fringe benefits received from your company.
- Social Security benefits.
- Tax-shelter participation.
- Unemployment income.

Source: John L. Withers, special consultant for IRS regulations and procedures, Deloitte & Touche, Washington Service Center, 1900 M St. NW, Washington, DC 20036.

Top 10 Filing Mistakes To Avoid

1. Incorrect amount of tax entered from the tax table. Find your correct filing status at the top of the tax table and copy the correct amount from that column onto your return.

2. Error in computing the credit for child- and dependent-care expenses. Carefully work through Form 2441 and the accompanying worksheet contained in the instructions. The child-care credit could be limited if you are subject to the Alternative Minimum Tax. The worksheet will help you figure out if the limit applies.

3. Not claiming the earned income credit. Low-income taxpayers may be entitled to a credit. To see if you qualify, use the earned income-credit worksheet contained in the instructions for filing your tax return.

4. Income tax withholding and estimated tax payments entered on the wrong line. Federal income tax withheld is reported on one line. Estimated tax payments go on the next line.

5. Wrong Social Security number. If you use the IRS peel-off mailing label, check to make sure your number is correct. And...double-check your Social Security number on your W-2.

6. Indicating overpayment to be credited to estimated tax...when you actually want a refund. Be sure to mark the correct line.

7. Adding income, deductions, or credits incorrectly. Double-check the arithmetic for all these amounts before filing your return.

8. Entering Social Security tax withheld instead of federal withholding tax. Copy the amount of federal tax withheld from Box 9 of your W-2.

9. Incorrect computation of refund or balance due.

10. Computation error when figuring medical and dental expenses. You must figure your Adjusted Gross Income *before* you can calculate the deduction for medical and dental expenses. Read the instructions carefully for the rules on how to do this.

What To Do *Now* About Next Year's Return

There are certain things you can do now to make the job of preparing next year's return easier:

■ Get Social Security numbers for dependent children who will be one year old, or older, by the end of the year. The numbers must be listed on Form 1040. (Call your nearest Social Security office and ask them to send you Form SS-5, *Application for Social Security Number Card.*)

■ Keep track of all tax-exempt interest income you receive. You've got to report it on Form 1040, even though it's not taxable.

■ Get Form 8615 from the IRS if you have children under age 14 with more than $1,300 of unearned income. *Note:* If the child's gross income was less than $5,000, you may elect to report it on your own tax return. Use Form 8814.

■ Sort out your records of interest payments. Tax Reform made big changes in this area. Make sure you have the right forms.

■ Set up a separate bank account for any money you borrow to make investments (e.g., stocks, bonds, real estate, etc.). *Reason:* To substantiate any deduction for investment-interest expense, you must be ready to prove that the money you borrowed was actually spent on investments rather than for personal use.

■ Pay close attention to miscellaneous expenses, such as job-hunting expenses, professional dues, etc. Some miscellaneous expenses are fully deductible, and others are deductible only to the extent that they total more than 2% of your Adjusted Gross Income. (Fully deductible miscellaneous expenses, such as moving expenses, must be listed on the return separately by type and amount.)

■ Segregate T&E records into travel and lodging expenses (fully deductible) and meals and entertainment expenses (only 50% deductible). Meal and entertainment expenses must be listed on the tax forms separately.

■ Segregate your records of "active" and "passive" income and loss from partnerships and S corporations. They're listed separately on Schedule E, and the tax rules for the deduction of losses are entirely different.

■ Keep accurate records of income and expenses of your rental real estate. Keep separate records of units that you yourself actively manage and those that you don't manage. The tax rules on deducting losses are different. (For vacation homes that you rent out for part of the year, keep a diary showing when you used it personally and when it was rented out.)

When To Audit-Proof Your Return

The threat of being audited faces all taxpayers, whether they stick their necks out or not. However, there are some ways to effectively reduce your chances of being audited. (Certain factors often trigger audits—for example, very large medical, charitable, interest, or miscellaneous deductions, and large state tax payments for a previous year.)

If you have unusual or questionable deductions in a year or just feel that you have deductions that might cause an audit, attach copies of proof of your claims to your return. If the return is flagged for audit by the computer, an IRS agent (a live human being) might review it before it is sentenced to audit. This agent, seeing your substantiation, might approve your return. Though the IRS discourages taxpayers from attaching such proof to their returns, it's a proven escape hatch for an audit.

Source: *New Tax Traps/New Opportunities* by Edward Mendlowitz, CPA, Boardroom Special Report, Springfield, NJ 07081.

Tactics for itemizers and nonitemizers

Why Not To Deduct All Your State Taxes

You may be entitled to deduct all your state withholding taxes and estimated payments as an itemized deduction on your federal return. Suppose you overpay your state taxes. If you include the overpayment when you claim your state-tax deduction, you'll have to pay income tax on the refund in the year you receive it. (If you don't include the overpayment in your deduction, you won't have to pay taxes on the refund.) If tax rates are steady or declining, and you'll remain in your current tax bracket, it's a good idea to deduct as much as possible.

However, if tax rates are increasing or you'll be in a higher tax bracket when the refund is received, deduct only the amount owed, not the overpayment. For instance, let's say you're in the 15% bracket when you take the deduction, but when you receive the refund, you're in the 28% bracket. The tax benefit of the deduction (15% of the overpayment) is worth less than the tax you pay on the refund (28%).

Another area to consider is the Alternative Minimum Tax. If you become subject to the AMT, you don't get any benefit of state-tax deductions. *Advice:* Again, don't claim all of your state taxes as a deduction on your federal return if you think you're a candidate for the AMT. Limit your deduction to the amount that isn't going to be refunded. In this way, when you receive the refund, it won't be taxed as income.

Source: *New Tax Traps/New Opportunities* by Edward Mendlowitz, CPA, Boardroom Special Report, Springfield, NJ 07081.

Itemizers' Loophole

The standard deduction for joint filers is $6,550 in 1995 (indexed for inflation). If your total itemized deductions for that year are below this amount, you must take the standard deduction; you can't itemize. *Strategy:* Beat the limit by bunching two years' worth of deductions into one. If your deductions average $5,000 a year, arrange to pay $3,000 in one year and $7,000 the following year. You would then get the $6,550 standard deduction in year one and $7,000 of itemized deductions in year two. *Deductions susceptible to bunching:* Charity, medical expenses, miscellaneous business expenses, real estate taxes, state income taxes.

Source: Edward Mendlowitz, partner, Mendlowitz Weitsen, CPAs, 2 Pennsylvania Plaza, New York 10001.

Sales Tax Can Add Up To Savings

Sales taxes no longer qualify as itemized deductions. They are absolutely out—but not always (because we are talking about taxes, after all).

If you buy a big-ticket item, you will not be able to claim an itemized deduction for the state or local levy on the new purchase. But don't throw away the receipt—add the sales tax to your cost basis.

For property used in your trade or business, you will be able to increase your depreciation deductions. For other assets, adding the sales tax to your cost will reduce any eventual gain you might have to report on a subsequent sale.

For example, suppose you buy a delivery truck to be used exclusively in your business. The purchase price is $25,000 plus an additional $1,500 in state sales taxes. The whole $26,500 is depreciable. Suppose, further, that you buy a painting for $25,000 plus $1,500 for the sales levy. When, after the artist has passed on, you sell the work for $30,000, your taxable gain will not be $5,000, but only $3,500. Keep records. They'll save you money.

Source: *New Tax Loopholes for Investors* by Robert A. Garber, Boardroom Special Report, Springfield, NJ 07081.

Tax Breaks For Nonitemizers, Too

Even if you don't itemize deductions, you can still subtract certain expenses from your Gross Income to arrive at Adjusted Gross Income. And you may be eligible for certain tax credits.

Important: The real opportunities are on the *long* Form 1040. Few of these tax breaks are on the *short* Form 1040A, and there are none on the shorter Form 1040EZ.

Adjustments

- *Alimony payments.*
- *IRA contributions* if you qualify for deductions and *Keogh plan contributions.*
- *Self-employed health-insurance deduction*—up to 25% of the amount paid for health insurance on behalf of yourself, your spouse, and dependents.
- *Penalty on early withdrawal of savings.*

Credits

Credits are especially valuable because they can be subtracted directly from your tax bill. *The most common:*

- *Child- and dependent-care credit,* if you incurred costs for care of children under 15 or disabled dependents while you work. Attach Form 2441 to your return.
- *Credit for the elderly* or for the permanently and totally disabled (attach Schedule R).
- *Foreign tax credit.* Attach Form 1116.
- *Other credits,* including the general business credit.

Angles on a very, very special tax

It's Not Too Late to Avoid the Alternative Minimum Tax

The AMT applies to more taxpayers than ever. Ask your tax adviser if you're in any danger of being hit with the Alternative Minimum Tax this year. If you are, there may still be time to avoid the tax by eliminating or reducing your tax preferences. *Here are some planning suggestions:*

■ *Income from "private-activity" municipal bonds**—normally tax-exempt—counts as income for AMT purposes. *Tax-saving strategy:* When buying tax-exempt municipals, check whether they're private-activity bonds. *Note:* If you're in no danger from the AMT, you may want to buy private-activity bonds, as many of them pay higher interest than other municipals.

■ *Incentive stock options you exercise*—to the extent that the option price is less than market value. *Tax-saving strategy:* Defer exercising the option. Or exercise *some,* but not enough to subject you to the AMT.

Deductions not allowed for AMT purposes:

Medical deductions. Under the AMT, medical deductions that exceed 10% of your AGI are deductible, compared with 7½% under regular income tax rules.

Other disallowed deductions: State and local taxes, miscellaneous deductions (including employee business expenses), accelerated depreciation in excess of straight-line depreciation, tax-shelter and other "passive" losses...and certain deductions normally allowed to oil, gas and geothermal investors.

If you can't avoid the AMT this year, try to defer these deductions whenever possible to a later year when they'll be allowable. *Note:* These are quite complicated strategies that require consultation with your tax adviser as soon as possible.

*The term "private-activity" bond means, generally, any industrial development bond or student loan bond issued after August 7, 1986, the interest on which is exempt from tax under Code Section 103(a).

Source: Laurence I. Foster, tax partner, middle market practice, KPMG Peat Marwick, 345 Park Ave., New York 10154.

Alternative Minimum Tax Can Work For You

The Alternative Minimum Tax is basically a tax that disallows most deductions and charges a flat rate on all income. The tax is 26% on the first $175,000 of AMT income and 28% on income over that. The biggest problem with the Alternative Minimum Tax is that most people don't realize they're subject to it until after they file their return. (*Those who are most vulnerable to the AMT:* Taxpayers who claim large miscellaneous deductions or large deductions for state and local income taxes, real estate taxes, and personal property taxes. Also vulnerable are those who exercise incentive stock options, donate appreciated assets to charity, and have tax-preference items.)

Solution: Early in the year, do a financial projection so that you know where you stand relative to the Alternative Minimum Tax. If you find you're a candidate for the AMT, you can plan to make it work for you.

The key is to maneuver in the exact opposite direction of the way you would go to save regular taxes. That is, accelerate the receipt of income and defer deductions on the payment of expenses. In this way, you'll pay only the AMT rate rather than your personal rate, which is likely to be higher. Also, you'll save deductions for a year in which they'll benefit you.

Source: *New Tax Traps/New Opportunities* by Edward Mendlowitz, CPA, Boardroom Special Report, Springfield, NJ 07081.

AMT-Avoidance Loopholes

Strategies that can keep you out of the AMT:

■ Find investments that produce passive-income to offset your passive-tax-shelter losses. Reducing your net deductible losses may keep you out of the AMT. Consider income-producing limited partnerships and rental properties, such as office buildings, parking lots, etc., which throw off passive income.

■ Exercise incentive stock options with care. Exercise only enough options to bring your AMT up to a point just short of your regular tax.

■ Avoid prepaying state and local income tax if paying it early throws you into the AMT.

■ Unload "private activity" municipal bonds if the interest income makes you liable for the AMT. See your broker.

All about estimated taxes

Smart Way To Handle Estimated Taxes

The law on making estimated tax payments is stiffer these days. It is more important than ever not to overlook opportunities to cut payments to the legal minimum.

Basic rule: Pick the payment rule that results in the lowest required payment. Underpayment penalties will not be applied when taxpayers make estimated payments at an appropriate rate through the year that equal:

■ 90% of the actual tax liability for the year.

■ The amount of actual tax liability in the prior year if your income that year is $150,000 or less. If it's above, you must pay 110% of last year's liability to avoid penalties.

Estimated taxes are to be paid through four *equal* quarterly payments. If you have a large gain late in the year, and make a correspondingly large estimated payment in the last quarter, you may incur a penalty for not having made estimated payments at an even rate during the year.

Safer: Avoid penalty by *annualizing* estimated payments, an option overlooked by many taxpayers. Under this method, you are required to make estimated payments only as income is earned during the year. Thus, if most income accrues late in the year, estimated payments can be deferred until late in the year.

How to do it: Fill out the annualized installment worksheet on IRS Form 2210 and file it with your return.

Cash-saving strategies for companies:

■ Keep funds for corporate estimated payments in a bank that is an authorized depository. Put the cash in a high-interest time-deposit account that matures on the day an estimated payment is due. Then simply transfer funds on that day.

■ Reduce estimated payments now if the company intends to make a purchase later this year that will give it a large investment credit.

■ Reduce payments as soon as it appears that an unexpected business or casualty loss will reduce income.

■ File for a quick refund of overpaid corporate estimated taxes. File Form 4466 before filing the tax return for the year.

Underpayment cautions:

Individual taxpayers sometimes intentionally underpay the first payments for the year, then make up the difference with a large final payment. *Danger:* The penalty applies from the date of each underpayment. The IRS may not detect the ploy. But if it does, the penalty must be imposed.

Legitimate variation. Salaried taxpayers may find at the end of the year that income taxes have been underwithheld. *Possible reasons:* Both spouses work (the withholding tables sometimes give this result). Or investment income was higher than anticipated. *What to do:* Have the employer withhold a large amount of the year's last paychecks. The withholding is treated as though it occurred at an appropriate rate over the course of the year. *Result:* Penalties are avoided.

Paying the Least Possible Estimated Tax

Many people, especially those who get large windfalls during the year, become concerned about paying sufficient estimated tax. Such people are unaware that there's an ironclad exemption from paying full estimated taxes on the windfall if the amount of withholding tax or regular quarterly estimated tax payments is equal to or greater than the previous year's total federal income tax, including self-employment tax. *Caution:* This exception can't be used by all taxpayers. It applies if your income last year was $150,000 or less. If your income was above that you must pay 110% of last year's tax to avoid penalties.

If you find that you've underestimated your quarterly payments or underwithheld your taxes, give your employer a check to cover the underpayment before the end of the year. This amount will be added by your employer to your withholding and will appear on your W-2. In this way, you'll avoid the IRS's penalty for underpayment of taxes.

Source: *New Tax Traps/New Opportunities* by Edward Mendlowitz, CPA, Boardroom Special Report, Springfield, NJ 07081.

You've Done Something Wrong: Big Tax Refund

If you got a fat tax refund this year, don't feel too happy about it. It means you overpaid your estimated taxes or had too much withheld from your salary. In effect, you made an interest-free loan to the government when you could have been using the money for yourself—in an interest-paying bank account.

Trap: The IRS can withhold all or part of your refund to offset a tax liability, a debt to a government agency (for instance, a student loan), or unpaid child support.

What to do: File a new Form W-4 or W-4A to reduce the amount withheld from your salary. If you pay estimated tax, reduce your quarterly payments.

Caution: Don't overdo it. You can be hit with *underpayment* penalties, unless withholding taxes plus estimated tax payments amount to at least 90% of your total tax bill (or 100% of the previous year's tax bill in certain cases).

Advice: If you do have a refund coming, take it in cash. Don't apply it toward next year's tax. *Reason:* If you made a mistake on your return and your taxes turn out to be more than you expected, you can't tell the IRS to take it out of your refund—that money has already been applied to next year's tax bill. You'll have to come up with cash.

Advantages of overseas banking

Swiss Bank Accounts

It's best to open a Swiss bank account, especially a large one, in person. However, you can easily open an account by mail. Just write to the bank, asking for forms and information. (Type your letter. Swiss bankers complain of illegible mail from the United States.)

You must have your signature verified at a Swiss consulate or bank or by a notary public. The bank will provide forms.

You should execute a power of attorney over the account (unless it's a joint account). Under Swiss law, the power of attorney remains in force even after the depositor's death. If you have qualms about a power of attorney, you don't have to deliver it to the person. Leave it with your attorney, to be delivered only in case of your death or disability.

Swiss banks offer current accounts (checking), deposit accounts (saving), and custodial accounts (the bank will hold your stock certificates, gold, or other property for a fee).

As in the United States, there are demand deposits and time deposits. Some accounts require notice to withdraw more than a specified amount. Interest varies with the type of account. The rates are not high, however, compared with those of US banks. The appeal of Swiss banks lies in safety and the soundness of the currency.

Accounts may be in Swiss francs, US dollars, or another stable currency (depending on economic conditions when the account is opened).

Taxes and Regulations

Although there are no US restrictions on Swiss bank accounts, your income tax form asks if you have any foreign bank accounts. If you answer "yes," you must fill out Form 90–22.1 and file it by June 30.

Interest on foreign accounts is taxable like any other income. You can take a credit for foreign taxes paid.

If you have an account in Swiss francs, and the franc increases in value relative to the dollar, you may be liable for a capital gains tax when you withdraw money and reconvert it to dollars. Losses arising from decreases in value may not be deductible in regard to personal accounts.

Switzerland imposes a withholding tax on interest, but Americans can get refunded by showing they are not Swiss residents. Your bank will send you the forms. (*Note:* The bank sends in the tax without disclosing depositors' names. To claim the refund, however, you must, of course, disclose your identity.)

At one time, the Swiss imposed severe restrictions on foreign accounts. Only the first 50,000 francs of an account could draw interest, and accounts above 100,000 francs were charged "negative interest" of 40%—nearly a confiscatory rate. These restrictions, and others, could conceivably be reinstated if economic conditions change.

Even when the restrictions were in force, however, they were not retroactive. They did not apply to existing accounts—only to deposits made after the rules were adopted (another reason you might want to act now).

Source: Stanley C. Ruchelman, tax partner, Deloitte & Touche, 1633 Broadway, New York 10019.

Foreign-Bank-Account Loopholes

If you have more than $400 of dividend and interest income, you *must* answer the question about whether or not you have an account in a foreign bank. The question is on Schedule B (Interest and Dividend Income). *Loopholes:* Even if you do have foreign accounts, you can answer "no" if their combined value was $10,000 or less during the year...or if your accounts were with a US military banking facility.

Source: *Instructions to Schedule B, Form 1040.*

Recordkeeping hotline

Recordkeeping Alert

As a result of Tax Reform, recordkeeping is now necessary in some areas that never required records before. *Crucial:* Keep flawless records.

IRA contributions. For most people, the new rules have cut out deductible Individual Retirement Account contributions. If you *or* your spouse has a company pension plan and your Adjusted Gross Income is greater than $50,000 ($35,000 for single taxpayers), your IRA contributions aren't deductible. However, *nondeductible* contributions to IRAs are still allowed (generally up to $2,000).

Recordkeeping alert: Taxpayers who have both deductible and nondeductible IRAs must now begin keeping special, detailed records of all their contributions for tax purposes. *Reason:* When you withdraw money from your IRA, the IRS aggregates all your IRA accounts together and treats the withdrawal as if it were both from your deductible and your nondeductible contributions, even if they were in separate IRAs. *Result:* Part of every withdrawal is going to be taxed, and part of every withdrawal is going to be tax-free.

Since the deferred earnings on IRAs are taxed at withdrawal, every withdrawal must be broken down into three parts to figure out the tax:

- Earnings on the IRA. (100% is taxed at withdrawal whether the earnings are from deductible or nondeductible contributions.)

- Return of a deductible contribution (i.e., contributions made before 1987, while you were still allowed to deduct the contribution on your tax return). It's taxed at withdrawal because it *wasn't* taxed in the year you made the contribution.

- Return of a nondeductible contribution (i.e., contributions made in 1987 or after that will not be deductible on your tax return). It's not taxed at withdrawal because it *was* taxed in the year you made the contribution.

Income shifting. Gifts to children under age 14 that generate investment (unearned) income over $1,300/year will be taxed at the parents' tax rates.

Recordkeeping alert: Avoid mixing this type of unearned income with the child's earned income (which is always taxed at the child's own rates no matter how much he/she earns). Put the unearned income into an account that is separate from the earned income so there will be no question as to how to treat the income for tax purposes.

Meal and entertainment expenses that you incur in the course of your business are only 50% deductible. This limit applies whether you are eating out alone or entertaining clients in order to get new business. *Included in this limit:* Food, beverages, cover charges, gratuities, taxes, theater tickets, etc.

Exception: An employee who is reimbursed for these expenses by his employer doesn't have to worry about this rule once he has properly accounted for them to his employer. The employer, rather than the employee, takes the 50% deduction.

Recordkeeping alert: Don't lose or misplace a single receipt for meal and entertainment expenses. Keep a diary to record the details, especially if you entertained others. Carry this diary around with you at all times.

Source: Stuart R. Josephs, Western regional tax partner, BDO Seidman, 7777 Alvarado Road, La Mesa, CA 92041.

Interest Recordkeeping Requirements

The IRS requires that you document fully the flow of funds for all loans you take in order to determine the deductibility of the interest.

Personal mortgage interest on two residences is fully deductible up to certain limits. The deductibility of other interest depends on how the funds are used.

For example, funds you borrow for the purpose of making investments are deductible to the extent of your investment income. Personal interest isn't deductible. Interest that you pay on funds used to purchase a passive activity or real estate is lumped with the gains or losses from that activity. To the extent that there's a net loss, the interest may not be deductible because of the limitations inherent in those transactions.

The recordkeeping requirements are very stringent. In the past, if you borrowed money on a margin account, the IRS presumed that the interest was for investment purposes. Now the burden is on you, the taxpayer, to show proof of the flow of funds.

Advice: If you borrow money and want to get a tax deduction for the interest, keep careful records to indicate the uses and applications of the monies borrowed. Also, keep records proving you repaid the principal. Obviously, if you have a choice of which loan to repay first, you should repay the loan that gives you the least deductibility of interest.

Source: Edward Mendlowitz, partner, Mendlowitz Weitsen, CPAs, 2 Pennsylvania Plaza, New York 10001.

Retaining Records

Most records have to be held for only three years after the due date of your tax return. That's when the statute of limitations expires for tax audits by the IRS and refund claims by the taxpayer. But some records should be kept *indefinitely,* especially those relating to the acquisition of property, whether by purchase, gift, or inheritance. *Reason:* If you ever sell the property, you can't determine profit or loss without proof of its original cost or other tax basis.

Lost Records

John and Louise Kranc deposited all their records with their accountant in order to prepare their tax return. The accountant lost the records. The Krancs then argued that the substantiation requirements for their deductions should be waived because it wasn't their fault that the records had been lost. *Tax Court:* The Krancs were out of luck. They should have kept copies of the records they gave to the accountant.

Source: *John M. Kranc,* TC Memo 1987-343.

The magic of amended returns

Finding Hidden Treasures In Old Returns

Most taxpayers are afraid that they'll trigger an audit if they file an amended return. This fear, which is common and understandable, prevents them from getting refunds they're entitled to. *The truth about amended returns:*

- They are *not* an automatic invitation to an audit. (Very few, in fact, are ever audited.)
- Many types of amendments are processed routinely.
- Some amendments are safer than others.
- The audit rate for amended returns, while higher than for regular returns, is still quite low.
- You can minimize the risk of an audit by sending back-up documents with your Form 1040X (the form used for making amendments).
- Since the IRS may check your original return beyond the item you're amending it for, play it safe. If there are deductions on your original return that you'd have trouble substantiating, you might not want to run the risk for a small refund.

Audit Avoidance

The fact that the IRS will scrutinize an amended return shouldn't prevent you from claiming a legitimate deduction. Just be prepared to prove it.

To minimize the risk of an audit, be sure to attach copies of receipts or other proof. *Caution:* Claim refunds only for items that you *can* prove. For instance, if you're filing an amendment to claim a large noncash charitable contribution, attach an appraisal supporting your valuation. Don't file amendments for items such as out-of-pocket expenses for charity work for which you don't have receipts.

State amendments: If you file an amended federal income tax return, remember to also file an amended return claiming a refund for overpaid state and local taxes.

Safest Amendments

The safest amendments involve methods of figuring the tax. The IRS will check the math, scan the return for obvious errors, and, if none are found, mail a refund check. *Amendment opportunities:*

Lump-sum pension payments. Check to see if 10-year averaging applies to you. This special rule can sharply reduce tax on lump-sum distributions.

Social Security tax overpayments. If you worked for more than one employer in a single year, you may have paid too much Social Security tax.

Tax credits. Did you neglect to take tax credits while they were available?

Joint returns. If you and your spouse filed separate returns, you can amend to file jointly. For most couples, joint returns produce a lower tax bite. But if you've already filed jointly and now feel you would have done better with separate returns, it's too late. The cutoff date for switching from a joint return to separate returns is the original due date of the return.

Not-So-Safe Amendments

Any item that would have raised eyebrows on your original return will be checked on an amended return. *The IRS looks most closely at:*

- Travel and entertainment expenses.
- Tax-shelter losses.
- Unreimbursed business expenses.
- Big charitable donations of property.
- Casualty losses.
- Transactions involving relatives or companies in which you have an interest.

Source: Edward Mendlowitz, partner, Mendlowitz Weitsen, CPAs, 2 Pennsylvania Plaza, New York 10001.

How To File An Amended Return

When: Amended returns must be filed within three years after the date your original return was due or two years after you actually paid the tax, whichever is later. A tax return that you filed early is treated as if it were filed on the due date of the return. If you filed your tax return late, you must file your amended return within three years from the date you actually filed. *Exception:* You have *seven* years in which to amend your return to claim bad debts or worthless securities.

What to file: File your amended return on Form 1040X. This form has space to write your income, deductions, and credits as you reported them on your original return, and the changes you want to make for those amounts. *Important:* Include explanations for the changes you are making and the year you are amending on Page 2 of the amended return. You must calculate the new tax on the corrected amount, just as you would on your regular return.

Where to send it: Mail the amended return to the IRS Service Center where you now live. If you moved during the year, mail it to the service center at your new address. Be sure to complete the information on the front of the 1040X about where your *original* return was processed in order to expedite your return.

Caution: When you amend your federal tax return, your state tax liability from that year may be affected, too.

Defenses, loopholes, and gimmicks

New Tax Attacks/New Defenses

The Revenue Act of 1987 (not to be confused with the Tax Reform Act of 1986) is designed to raise more money for the government, coming mainly from corporate or business taxes. But some of the provisions of the new Revenue Act affect *individual* taxpayers directly, and in some cases favorably.

No underpayment penalty—if your estimated and withheld taxes equal at least 90% of your final tax bill.

Partnerships, S corporations, and personal-service corporations can elect to keep the fiscal year they used in the past rather than switching to a calendar year as required by the Tax Reform Act of 1986. *Important:* In order to make this election, certain tax payments must be made by partnerships and S corporations.

New problems to deal with:

■ Home mortgage interest—on your principal residence and one second residence. *Old law:* Interest fully deductible on mortgages up to the cost of the home and improvements, plus any additional amounts borrowed to cover medical and educational expenses. No specific dollar limits. *New law:* Interest deductible on mortgages up to $1 million spent to acquire or improve a home, plus up to $100,000 of home-equity loans (borrowed for any purpose). For married couples filing separately, the figures are $500,000 and $50,000. Loans made before October 14, 1987, are not subject to these new limits.

■ Family employment. Employment of one spouse by the other, or employment by a parent of a child 18 years of age or older (rather than 21) is now subject to Social Security tax.

■ No child-care credit can be claimed for the expense of sending a child to overnight camp.

■ Phone service tax (3%), scheduled to expire on December 31, 1987, was extended through 1990 and has now been made permanent.

■ IRS fees will be charged for IRS letter rulings, determination letters, and opinion letters.

■ Top estate- and gift-tax rate stays at 55%. Also, the lifetime estate- and gift-tax credit and the benefit of graduated rates are phased out for transfers totaling more than $10 million, adding, in effect, a 5% surtax and making the top tax rate 60% for large estates.

■ Publicly traded partnerships such as Master Limited Partnerships (MLPs) will generally be treated as corporations, or their income will be treated as portfolio income, not passive income, and cannot be offset by losses and credits from passive activities (tax shelters).

The New Penalities...
And How To Avoid Them

Penalty for failure to pay tax. This penalty remains at ½ of 1% of the tax due per month, but it could increase to 1%. If you have been sent several notices to pay overdue tax and you still have not paid, the IRS may decide to collect it against your assets. At that time, the penalty increases to 1% of the tax due per month. Avoid the excess penalty by responding to the IRS's correspondence and paying the overdue taxes before the IRS gets this far.

Penalty for substantial understatement of tax liability. Taxpayers who understate the amount of tax due on their returns by the greater of 10% or $5,000 will be subject to a 20% (increased from 10%) penalty on the amount of the understatement.

You can avoid this penalty if you have substantial authority for the understatement. Or, you can disclose all the relevant facts with respect to that amount on your return by attaching a statement with an explanation showing reasons for the way you treated the item on your return.

Penalty for failure to obtain a taxpayer identification number (TIN). You must list the Social Security, or tax identification number (TIN), for each dependent age one and older claimed as an exemption. There is a $5 penalty for each failure to include a dependent's TIN on the return.

Negligence penalty. The amount of the negligence penalty has not been increased by Tax Reform from 5% of the entire underpayment. However, the negligence penalty can be applied in more circumstances since Tax Reform, such as...

- A failure to make a reasonable attempt to comply with IRS provisions.
- Any careless, reckless, or intentional disregard of the rules or regulations.
- Any behavior considered negligent by the courts.

Fraud penalty. The amount of the fraud penalty has been increased from 50% to 75% of the part of the underpayment that is attributed to the fraud. However, once the fraud is found on *any* portion of your tax return, the entire underpayment will be tied to the fraud unless you can prove otherwise.

Penalty for failure to register a tax shelter. All tax shelter organizers must register with the IRS and obtain a tax-shelter identification number. The penalty for failure to do so is 1% of the entire amount invested in the tax shelter. *Minimum penalty:* $500. The $10,000 maximum on this penalty was eliminated by Tax Reform.

Knowing The Internal Workings Of The IRS

The secret of success in dealing with the IRS is *knowledge.*

Taxpayers who turn out to be winners know how to avoid the pitfalls in the system. They know the limits of the IRS's power.

And they know how to arm themselves in advance, like tax professionals, with thorough knowledge of IRS practices and procedures.

Avoiding Traps

The three biggest traps to avoid in your dealings with the IRS...

Trap: Ignoring IRS notices. IRS personnel are almost gleeful when they come across a taxpayer who repeatedly ignores notices. The Service responds incrementally to a taxpayer's nonresponse. Each instance is documented for eventual use of the IRS's awesome collection powers.

Even at the earliest stages of a tax dispute, it's dangerous to ignore IRS letters and notices. A taxpayer who fails to respond to a notice damages his/her credibility with the auditor, and credibility is the key to success at an audit. Suppose you don't have all the written proof you need to support a deduction. An auditor can accept your word for some of the items you don't have proof for...if he believes that you are truthful.

Self-defense: Respond promptly to every IRS notice and letter. Respond in writing *and* by telephone, where appropriate.

Trap: Playing "hardball" with an agent when your proof is weak. Taxpayers who are audited often try to browbeat the agent by threatening to appeal his/her decision. This tactic almost always backfires. The agent typically reacts by doing everything he can to make sure the taxpayer gets the appeal in the weakest possible position. His case against the taxpayer will be fully documented and backed up by meticulous workpapers.

Better strategy: Turn the audit into a game of damage control. Emphasize the reasonableness of the items you've claimed. Accept the agent's assessment when you're really wrong and can't prove an audit item.

Trap: Making provocative remarks to a revenue agent. Resist the temptation to say things like, "That was allowed last year" or, "Nobody ever questioned that before." Comments like these are very dangerous. If the agent reacts badly, he can obtain approval to reopen for examination on that issue all your past returns that are still open to audit under the statute of limitations.

Safe audit strategy: Respond to the agent's questions and don't argue your case until *after* he has finished the exam and proposed adjustments.

IRS Limits

A great many misconceptions have developed over the years about the power and workings of the IRS. Taxpayers who know the real limits of the IRS's power have an advantage. *Common fallacies:*

Myth: The IRS knows everything there is to know about your finances. This is just not so. The IRS gets W2s and 1099 reports from people who pay you taxable income...and these are matched by computer with your tax return. Other than that, the only thing the IRS keeps on file is information directly relating to your taxes—tax payments, credits against payments, balance due, record of filings, audit results, history of collection of back taxes, and related items.

The IRS maintains no information about your lifestyle, travel habits, family affairs, etc.

Strategy: Taxpayers' time is better spent working on their own financial records than worrying about what IRS computers might have on them.

Myth: Filing an amended return greatly increases your audit risk. Not so. Although amended returns are compared with original returns by an experienced IRS returns classifier, the chance that the amended return will be audited is remote and the risk only slightly greater than the risk that an original return will be audited.

Strategy: File your amended return a day or two before the statute of limitations expires. You want the statute to have expired when the IRS looks at your return.

Loophole: Once the statute has expired, the IRS can only assess tax that offsets the refund you've claimed. They can't assess additional tax.

Myth: Auditors don't have the power to negotiate the settlement of cases. They do. Official IRS policy says that only appeals officers have the authority to settle cases. But auditors have *de facto* power to negotiate settlements—and they do so on a regular basis. They're under constant pressure from their managers to limit the number of cases that are closed without agreement.

Strategy: Press the auditor to the hilt to accept your credible oral testimony in support of your deductions. Know that he can, if he chooses, accept such evidence to settle the case.

Arm Yourself Like a Pro

Tax practitioners have an edge in dealing with the IRS. They've learned from experience the practices, procedures, and policies the Service operates under. *Example:*

Policy Statement P8-47, approved in 1987, says that the appeals office of the IRS is responsible for resolving disputes to the maximum extent *without* litigation. Tax practitioners know that the IRS does not want to go to court over routine cases. This gives practitioners leverage in negotiating settlements with the appeals division.

Now, at last, these internal workings of the IRS are available to taxpayers under the Freedom of Information Act. You don't have to tell the IRS why you want the material. The fees to get them are reasonable, and a request for the information doesn't trigger any other action by the IRS.

To get a copy of the *examination policy statements* currently in effect, write to:

Internal Revenue Service
1111 Constitution Ave.
Washington, DC 20002
Attention: Reading Room Disclosure Officer

Include the following paragraph in your letter:

"If you deny this request, please cite the specific exemption you claim and notify me of the appeals procedure, including time limitations. Should you have any questions and/or you cannot fill this request within the time frames prescribed by law, I can be reached at (give your address and phone number)."

Other useful IRS documents you can request under the Freedom of Information Act:

■ *Revenue Agent's Handbook.* This is the guidebook agents use in audits. It tells them how to proceed with examinations by occupation, industry, and type of return.

■ *Collection Manual.* This gives guidelines for collection employees. It tells them what assets to go after first and how to get them. Procedures on how and when to use levies, liens, and seizure are described.

Note: To obtain a copy of the Freedom of Information Act, write or call your local Federal Information Center, listed in your local phone book under US Government.

Source: George S. Alberts, former director of the Albany and Brooklyn IRS district offices.

Buying Life Insurance As A Tax Gimmick

Universal life insurance is really a disguised savings account with income that accumulates on a tax-free basis because of special life insurance laws. The tax-free accumulation is often at interest rates that are higher than those given by municipal bonds. *Added bonus:* You're provided with adequate or necessary life insurance.

Caution: Be very careful about selecting a universal life insurance policy. Each company has a different proposition to make. Find out what the cost will be if you don't keep the policy until the contracted date of maturity. Also, compare the advantages of universal life insurance with those of other investment opportunities.

Source: *New Tax Traps/New Opportunities* by Edward Mendlowitz, CPA, Boardroom Special Report, Springfield, NJ 07081.

Tax-Free-Income Loopholes

One of the shortest sections of the federal Tax Code is Section 61. It defines gross income as "all income from whatever source derived." But don't take this literally. There are many kinds of income that are not taxable. *Types of income that you don't pay federal income tax on:*

Gain on the sale of your home.

■ If you buy a new home within two years before or after you sell the old one, no tax is generally owed on the gain, if the new home costs at least as much as the amount you got for the old one.

■ If you (or your spouse) are at least 55 years old, any gain up to $125,000 is tax-free. (You must have owned and lived in the home for at least three years out of the past five.)

Gifts you receive. Any gift tax is payable by the person who makes the gift. The recipient gets the gift free and clear of tax.

Money you borrow. Normally, borrowing is *not* a taxable transaction. But you'll be taxed if you borrow from your IRA, if you borrow more than $50,000 (or half your account) from your company pension fund, or, in some cases, if you get an interest-free loan from your company or a family member.

IRA rollovers. No tax is payable on a lump-sum distribution that is received from a company pension plan if you put it into an IRA within 60 days. (Tax will be withheld, however, if you don't transfer the money directly from the company plan to the IRA trustee.) You can also take money tax-free from your IRA if you roll it over within 60 days into another IRA.

Inheritances. Beneficiaries don't pay federal estate tax on anything they inherit—the estate pays any tax that's owed. Moreover, if you inherit property that's increased in value, you receive it at its "stepped-up" estate value. You would then use this value, rather than the original cost, to calculate your taxable gain if you sell the property.

Life insurance proceeds. The beneficiary gets the full amount tax-free. But the estate may be liable for estate tax on the proceeds.

Property settlements between spouses in divorce or separation proceedings. The recipient owes no tax at the time property is transferred. (There may be a tax later if property is sold at a gain.)

Child-support payments. They are tax-free to the recipient. Alimony payments to a spouse or ex-spouse, however, are taxable to the recipient.

Money recovered in lawsuits for personal injuries or defamation of character. But money recovered to compensate you for lost wages or other income *is* taxable.

Workers compensation payments.

Disability payments from accident and health-insurance plans. The payments are tax-free if *you* paid for the insurance, but taxable if your employer paid the premiums.

Federal income tax refunds. (But any interest the IRS pays you on a late refund *is* taxable.)

State income tax refunds...provided you didn't itemize deductions on your federal return for that year.

Municipal bond interest. Generally, it's exempt from federal income tax and sometimes from state and local taxes, as well. However, interest from some "private purpose" municipal bonds is subject to the Alternative Minimum Tax. And, municipal bond interest is taken into account in figuring your income level to determine whether any of your Social Security benefits are taxable.

"Like-kind" property exchanges—swaps of tangible property or real estate are tax-free if the properties are of similar nature.

Vacation home rental. If you rent your vacation place out for 14 days or less, the income is not taxed.

Kids' wages. Dependent children can earn up to $3,700 of salary tax-free.

Kids' investment income. Dependent children can receive up to $600 of unearned income tax-free (dividends, interest, etc.).

Scholarships and fellowships granted on or before August 16, 1986, to candidates for degrees, are tax-free. But, if granted after that date, they are tax-free only to the extent they are used to cover tuition, fees, books, and course equipment. Grants for room and board, etc., are taxable.

Fringe benefits from your employer. *Examples:* Health insurance, pension contributions, up to $50,000 of life insurance coverage, up to $5,000 of death benefits, education expenses (up to $5,250 a year), certain child- and dependent-care, legal services under group plans, and supper money.

Meals and lodging, if furnished by your employer for the employer's convenience—for example, to enable the employee to remain at the workplace.

Source: Edward Mendlowitz, partner, Mendlowitz Weitsen, CPAs, New York 10001.

Hide Assets From The IRS—Legally

Many people keep assets in a safe-deposit box thinking that no one will ever find out about it. But the name of the renter of a safe-deposit box isn't kept secret. It doesn't help to rent a box in your own name; there's an organization that, for less than $100, will run a search of every bank in the country to see if you are a safe-deposit box customer. And the IRS, if it's looking for assets of yours, will do a bank search for safe-deposit boxes held in your name. (It's especially easy for the IRS to track down boxes that you pay for with a personal check...it simply goes through your canceled checks.)

To conceal the existence of a safe-deposit box:

■ Ask your lawyer to set up a nominee corporation—a corporation that has no other function but to stand in your place for the purposes you designate, such as to rent a safe-deposit box.

■ Rent a box in the name of the corporation and pay for it in cash. Your name and signature will be on the bank signature card, but the *corporation*, not you, will be listed as the box's owner on the bank's records. And because you paid cash, there will be nothing in your records to connect the box with you.

■ You can, if you wish, name another person as signatory in addition to yourself. Then, if something happens to you, that person will be able to get into the box.

Additional protection: Having a safe-deposit box in a corporation's name permits the box to be opened by your survivors without the state or the bank being notified of your death and having the box sealed. Otherwise, the survivor must get to the box before the funeral to look for a will and to find whatever else may be there.

Source: Edward Mendlowitz, partner, Mendlowitz Weitsen, CPAs, New York 10001.

2

TAX LOOPHOLES

EVERYTHING THE LAW ALLOWS

Tax Angles
For Investors

Investment self-defense

The Right Way To Report Investment Income

Distributions from money-market funds. Report the distributions as dividends, on Schedule B of your return, and not as interest. It's a common mistake (and the source of many IRS computer notices) to report amounts paid by the XYZ Fund as interest income rather than as dividend income. The funds' 1099s report the income to the IRS as dividend income, and that's the way you should report it on your tax return.

Stock held by your broker. The right way to report dividends received from stock held in street name by your broker is as dividends received from the *broker* as nominee—and not from the company (General Motors, for example). Report the dividends, as shown on the 1099, as received from your broker as nominee.

If you're in a partnership, or are a stockholder in an S corporation, or the beneficiary of a trust or an estate, you should get a Form K-1. It shows the amount of income and expense attributable to you from that entity. Be sure to report income and expenses as shown on the K-1 (which is issued under your Social Security number).

Investors, Beware

Ordinarily dividend and interest income is not subject to tax withholding. But failure to report that income will subject taxpayers to an *automatic* 20% withholding. The IRS recently sent notices to 150,000 taxpayers who had not reported their dividend and interest income on past years' returns.

A Trap To Avoid When You Borrow And Invest

If I borrow against my life insurance policy at a low rate and place my borrowings in high-yielding investments, can't I avoid the consumer-interest deduction bar imposed by Tax Reform by deducting what I pay on my life insurance loan as investment interest?

Yes, but under IRS rules, it is not enough to show that you borrowed a certain amount and then made an investment of a like amount. You must show that you made an investment with the *actual money* that you borrowed.

For example, you might be required to show that you deposited the check received from the insurance company *directly* into your brokerage account or into an account that you use *exclusively* for investing. If you commingle the borrowed funds with your personal funds for a significant period of time, a deduction may be hard to get.

Get Proof Of Investment Interest

If you plan to take a deduction for investment interest, be prepared to prove that money you borrowed was actually used for investment purposes, not for personal expenses or business. Even if you borrow from investment accounts, such as stock margin accounts or cash management accounts, you're still going to have to prove that you used the borrowed money for investment purposes.

Source: *Proposed IRS Regulations.*

Strategies to know

How Not To Lose Big Stock Profits And Other Capital Gains

Devise strategies that enable you to pay the lowest taxes on capital gains after Tax Reform. *Key to success:* Understanding the changes affected by Tax Reform and adopting strategies that work best for you.

Game Strategies

Long-term gains. Look carefully over market conditions and your whole capital gains picture. If you are expecting to realize large net capital gains in the near future, compare your tax brackets for this year and next. If you will be in a higher bracket next year, don't wait until then to recognize your gain. Accelerate gains by selling stock this year and having it taxed at this year's lower rate.

Utilize losses. Capital losses can be used to offset capital gains. So if you have unrealized losses sitting in your portfolio, you might consider realizing them to minimize your capital gain.

Caution: If you sell stock for the purpose of creating a loss, don't purchase identical stock for 30 days before and 30 days after the date of the sale. The "wash sale" rule disallows the recognition of your loss if you make an identical stock purchase within this time limit.

Strategic planning. Perhaps you'll decide to defer recognizing your capital gains, either because you'll be in a lower tax bracket or you just want to put off paying taxes even though they may be higher. (The tax bill on gains realized in one year won't be due until you file your tax return in April of the next year.) At the same time, you may be concerned that the stock market will go down and you could lose some of your gains.

Special Strategies

You can lock in your gain and defer taxes to the next year through two different strategic moves.

■ **Short sales against the box.** Instead of selling the stock that you actually have in your possession, you borrow identical stock through your broker and sell that stock this year. Wait until next year and return the loan to your broker with your own stock that you've been holding. The sale isn't considered to be completed until you've given your shares to your broker, so it's not taxed until the next year. At the same time, you've locked in your gain this year.

■ **Buy a put option.** This is the right to sell your stock at a guaranteed price before a specified date in the future. If you buy a put option that doesn't expire until the beginning of next year, you've locked in your gain this year and deferred the tax until next year, too. (Don't forget to consider the cost of the put.)

Advantage over short sales: You can decide not to exercise your option if it turns out that the value of the stock has increased next year. Just let the option expire and sell the stock for the higher value.

Source: Robert A. Garber, vice president, executive financial services, Salomon Brothers, Inc., One New York Plaza, New York 10004.

Tax-Advantaged Investing

Despite Tax Reform, some investments remain that will give you a tax break as well as a worthwhile return. *You might consider these:*

Municipal bonds are exempt from federal tax and, in some cases, from state and local taxes, too. A municipal bond from the state in which you reside generally is not taxable on your state or local return. But if you purchase a municipal bond from another state, you may pay state and local taxes on it.

Special planning: Certain private-purpose municipal bonds are subject to the federal Alternative Minimum Tax (AMT) even though they are free from regular federal, state, or local tax. It's important to figure out whether or not you will be subject to the AMT. If you aren't, these "AMT bonds" are excellent investments. They usually pay a higher interest rate than other municipal bonds to make up for the AMT factor. But if you are not otherwise subject to the AMT, you will escape tax altogether. Your broker should know which bonds are AMT bonds.

Series EE savings bonds are exempt from state and local taxes. The interest earned on these bonds can be taxed in one of four ways. You decide which will enable you to pay less in taxes.

■ You can pay tax on the interest as it's earned every year, even though you haven't received any of it yet.

■ You can defer paying tax on all the interest earned throughout the years until you cash in the bond at maturity.

■ You can wait beyond maturity and pay tax on all the accumulated interest when you cash in the bond.

■ You can convert the EE bond at maturity into a Series HH savings bond. The interest earned on the EE bond remains tax-deferred until you cash in the HH bond. However, HH bonds pay out interest annually to the owner. You must pay tax on this interest each year.

■ Interest may be tax-free if used to pay educational costs—see page 85.

Investor strategy: Purchase savings bonds that will mature after you retire, when you are in a lower tax bracket because your income is lower.

Tax-shelter investments. The rules for deducting tax-shelter losses have become very complicated since Tax Reform. Basically, losses from all passive activities, with the principal exception of real estate, can be used only to offset income from passive activities.

Shelters that are producing losses may be offset with *passive-income-generating shelters (PIGS).* The income from the PIGS will then be effectively tax-free. At least this way you'll get some kind of tax advantage from a losing tax shelter.

Source: Richard J. Shapiro, Grant Thornton, 7 World Trade Center, New York 10048.

Year-End Strategies

While the economic reasons for buying and selling in the stock market are critical, strategies to minimize your tax burden must also be considered. A year-end review of your portfolio is essential. *Possibilities:*

Sell short against the box. This locks in your gain on the date of the transaction while deferring tax on the gain until next year. To make a short sale against the box, you sell borrowed shares now and replace them with your own shares after year-end. The transaction isn't closed for tax purposes until you use your shares to replace the borrowed shares. *Problem:* A short sale against the box doesn't change the holding period of the securities. If they were short-term at the time you initiated the sale, they remain short-term, even though the transaction stays open for a year. *Note:* The holding period of a security is important.

Tax swaps. Look for bonds or other fixed-income securities in your portfolio that are trading for less than their original cost. Sell these securities and reinvest the proceeds in *similar* but not identical ones. The sales will generate capital losses, which can be applied against other capital gains and up to $3,000 of ordinary income. *What's similar:* A similar bond might be one of a *different* company with the same rate of return, maturity date, and credit rating. Or it might be one of the same company with a slightly different return and maturity date. *Trap:* If you buy a substantially *identical* security within a 31-day period of the sale, you create a "wash sale" and the loss will be disallowed for tax purposes.

Wash sales. You may want to create losses that can be used to offset capital gains and shelter up to $3,000 of other taxable income. As long as you're careful to avoid the wash sale rule, you can lock in securities that have dropped in value while substantially retaining your current investment position. You can do this by *doubling up*—that is, buying a matching lot of the same securities you own, holding the new lot for 31 days, then selling the *old* lot at a loss. Or you can lock in losses by *selling and buying back* the same securities after waiting the required 31 days.

Worthless securities are deductible only in the year they become worthless. The IRS keeps a list of companies whose stock has become worthless during the year. If the company isn't on the list, the IRS won't accept your deductions, unless there's a real transaction or you can otherwise prove worthlessness.

Loophole: Sell the stock to a friend or business associate for $1. You will then have a real transaction that proves its worthlessness.

Additional loophole: Wait 31 days after making the $1 sale and buy the stock back from the purchaser. You'll get your deduction and still have the stock, which could rebound.

Loophole: If you learn that a stock became worthless a few years ago, file an amended tax return (Form 1040X) for that year, claiming the loss. You can go back *seven* years to claim deductions for worthless securities on amended returns. This is allowed by Reg. Section 301.6511 (d)-1(a)(1)(ii).

Buy put options. A put is the right to sell a stock at a specified price—the exercise price—before a specified date. A put can lock in an unrealized gain, protect you from a market decline, and defer tax on the gain until next year. *To defer tax,* buy puts that are exercisable next year. *Note:* A put, like a short sale, stops the holding period for the security. It doesn't convert a short-term gain into a long-term gain.

Capital losses. Consider realizing up to $3,000 of capital losses. *Note:* There's no advantage to realizing more than $3,000 of losses, since that's the most you can deduct in any single year.

Important: Stock in small corporations (no more than $1 million of paid-in capital) may qualify as Section 1244 stock. Losses on the sale of Section 1244 stock are not subject to the $3,000 capital-loss deduction limit. You can deduct up to $50,000 ($100,000 for joint returns). Check with your tax adviser to see if the stock qualifies.
Source: Edward Mendlowitz, partner, Mendlowitz Weitsen, CPAs, Two Pennsylvania Plaza, New York 10121.

Deducting Investment Expenses

Deductible investment expenses include property taxes, depreciation, and depletion, and any other expenses directly connected with the production of investment income, such as:
■ Legal and professional fees.
■ Fees for investment advice.
■ Fees for tax preparation or advice.
■ Books, magazines, etc., dealing with investment or taxes.
■ Custodial fees for IRAs and Keoghs.
■ Cost of safe-deposit boxes.
■ Investment-related travel costs.
■ 50% of meals and entertainment (e.g., lunch with your broker to discuss your investments).
Deductible expenses do *not* include:
■ Expenses that are considered part of the purchase price of an investment (e.g., broker's commissions).
■ Costs of attending investment seminars or conventions; the new law specifically bans any deduction.
■ Any expenses in connection with passive investments, such as limited partnerships.
Don't forget the 2% floor. Under Tax Reform, miscellaneous expenses (including most investment expenses) are not fully deductible. First, you must subtract 2% of your Adjusted Gross Income (AGI). For instance, if your AGI is $50,000 and your investment expenses are $1,500, your deductible expenses are only $500. *Calculation:* $1,500 total, minus $1,000 (2% of $50,000).
But suppose your miscellaneous expenses include both investment and noninvestment expenses. The law requires you to apply the 2% floor to the noninvestment expenses first.
Example: Your AGI is $50,000. Your miscellaneous noninvestment expenses total $800. Your investment expenses are $900. The 2% floor is $1,000 (2% of $50,000). It is first applied to the $800 of noninvestment expenses, leaving only $200 to be applied to investment expenses. *Total deductible investment expenses:* $700 ($900 total, less $200 remaining of the 2% floor). This does not affect your total deduction for miscellaneous expenses, but it could affect your net investment income and, therefore, your deduction for investment interest.
Source: Laurence B. Rossbach, Jr., vice president, Smith Barney.

Tax shelters live on

Opportunities After Tax Reform

Despite Tax Reform, many tax-shelter opportunities *still* exist. But some individuals have rushed into them without understanding the limitations or *dangers* involved.

Here's a rundown of today's tax-shelter pitfalls and opportunities.

Oil and Gas

This is the *last* of the old-time tax shelters that *still* lets you deduct large passive losses against ordinary income. Large current deductions are available here as before, but at a price.

Before Tax Reform, a typical investor would buy into an oil-drilling deal by obtaining a limited partnership interest that restricted his/her financial liability to the face amount of his investment.

Now, however, to obtain deductible losses from an oil well, an investor must acquire a *working interest.* And such investors are fully liable personally to the business's creditors. In the event of an underinsured casualty (such as a fire), a lawsuit, or some other unexpected liability, the investor's personal assets (such as a bank account, car, home, etc.) may be attached by creditors.

Bottom line: Tax benefits are still there, but the risk of claiming them is far greater. The professional skill and responsibility of the shelter's management team is more important than ever.

Ginnie Mae Securities

Government National Mortgage Association securities (Ginnie Maes) have become *very* popular in the past couple of years because of the *government-guaranteed* interest they pay, and because many states *exempt* them from state tax.

But Ginnie Maes are seriously misunderstood by many investors and pose dangerous *traps* for the unwary:

■ While the interest paid on a Ginnie Mae is guaranteed by the federal government, the *principal* amount of your investment is *not.* Ginnie Maes represent mortgage commitments, and when interest rates drop, mortgage holders are likely to refinance, paying off their loans at face value. Many investors who thought they were buying securities that were fully US guaranteed have *lost* large amounts of money after investing in a fund that bought Ginnie Maes at a steep premium only to have them redeemed at face value.

■ The US Supreme Court has ruled that Ginnie Maes, while federally guaranteed, are *not* securities issued by the US government. That gives states and local governments the right to tax them. Be sure to check the policy of *your* state.

Tax-Exempt Bonds

Despite the cut in federal tax rates, municipal bonds are still an attractive investment. However, because of the risk of investing in an uncertain market, it's best to invest in *short-term* bonds, those with maturities of three to five years.

Overlooked Shelters

Tax-exempt money-market funds. They offer a tax-free return without the time and money commitment that's required by a bond investment. Check with your broker.

Savings bonds. These are *no longer* just for the small savers. Many smart top-bracket investors now buy $15,000 worth of Series EE bonds each year, the maximum investment allowed by law. *Advantages:*

■ The bonds are *exempt* from state tax.

■ You have a choice as to how they're taxed under federal law. You can *defer* the tax until a future year. Or if you're in a low tax bracket or have offsetting deductions, you can elect in any year to have them taxed immediately.

■ The 4% yield on these bonds is a guaranteed *minimum*. Since the yield will always match 85% of the five-year Treasury-note rate, EE bonds offer protection against inflation and high interest rates unobtainable from most other investments.

■ On maturity, EE bonds can be converted on a *tax-deferred* basis into Series HH bonds, providing *cash* income. The appreciation on the EE bonds will remain untaxed, an ideal retirement tactic.

Source: Steven B. Enright, director of financial planning, Seidman Financial Services, BDO Seidman, 15 Columbus Circle, New York 10023.

Anti-Tax-Shelter Rule Relief

Congress created a number of limited exceptions to the passive-loss rule, which prohibits investors from writing off losses from passive activities (such as tax-shelter investments) against income from nonpassive activities (such as salary). Investors who want a tax shelter can consider the following:

■ *Losses from rental real estate,* such as a house or small apartment building, that you actively manage, can offset up to $25,000 of nonpassive income each year. This deduction is phased out for taxpayers who have an Adjusted Gross Income (AGI) of $100,000 to $150,000 and eliminated for those reporting an AGI of more than $150,000.

■ *A "dealer" in real estate* is not treated as being in rental real estate, which means his losses are not subject to the passive-loss rule. A person who subdivides lots and sells them would probably be considered a real-estate dealer.

■ *Hotels and motels,* in which substantial services are rendered to customers, are not considered to be real-estate rentals and are not automatically considered to be passive activities.

■ *Losses from working interests in oil and gas properties* are generally exempt from the rule. (A working interest is one that bears the cost of developing and operating the property.) *Trap:* Working interests owned by a limited partnership or an S corporation are generally not exempt working interests.

■ *Rehabilitation and low-income housing projects.* Investors can offset up to $25,000 of regular income with tax credits from investments in such properties whether or not they materially participate in the project.

Source: Jerry S. Williford, partner, Grant Thornton, CPAs, 2800 Citicorp Center, Houston, TX 77002.

Insurance—a great investment vehicle

The Darlings Of Tax Reform

Since Tax Reform policies went into effect, the insurance industry's deferred annuities have become one of the most attractive investment products around.

Deferred annuities can serve as an alternative for individuals whose incentive to continue to make IRA contributions was greatly weakened by Tax Reform. Although contributions to a deferred annuity are not tax deductible, earnings do accumulate tax deferred. *Advantage over an IRA:* There is no limit to the amount of money you can invest in an annuity.

The new variable annuity can serve as the ideal replacement for investments that used to receive the benefit of favorable long-term capital gains treatment. Long-term gains from investments in stocks can be sheltered in a variable annuity. That income is not taxed until you withdraw your money.

How Annuities Work

An individual buys an annuity from an insurance company, paying a lump sum or a series of payments over time. In return, the insurance company guarantees that the funds will grow at a certain tax-free rate. Then, beginning on a specified date, the individual receives regular income payments for life.

Payments depend on the amount of money contributed to the account, the length of time the funds are left in it, and the rate of return earned on the funds. Also a factor in determining the size of the payments is whether you include your spouse and other heirs as beneficiaries. Different options enable you to have payments continue to your spouse, or to your children, or for a minimum of, say, 20 years, regardless of who is there to receive them after you die.

Deferred annuities, therefore, can be considered part insurance and part investment. If you are willing to part with at least $5,000 (the minimum amount can differ from company to company) for five years or longer, you can be guaranteed a competitive, tax-free return on your funds. Because the earned income is not taxed until you begin withdrawing the money (presumably at a lower tax rate), your funds accumulate much faster than they would if they were taxed. The insurance component, of course, is guaranteed regular monthly income payments for the rest of your life—taking the worry and risk out of budgeting for your retirement income. Also, should you die before you begin receiving payments, your heirs are guaranteed to receive the full amount of your original principal.

Fixed Rate Versus Variable

There are two basic types of deferred annuity—fixed and variable.

Fixed annuity: The insurance company guarantees that your funds will grow at a specified rate for a specified period of time. Most companies guarantee a specific rate of return for at least the first year. Thereafter, the rate usually fluctuates at least once a year, according to the then-prevailing interest rates. Although the rates of return for fixed annuities may vary, your principal always remains intact.

Variable annuity: The rate of return is determined by the performance of investments you select from a broad range of mutual funds offered by the insurance company. Investing in a variable annuity is almost identical to investing in a family of mutual funds. You have the same exchange privileges and the choice of putting all your money into one fund or a blend of different funds, or even of dividing your money between a fixed annuity and a variable annuity. You can earn a much larger return than you might with a fixed annuity. However, if your investments perform poorly, your original principal may diminish.

The minimum investment for a deferred annuity is generally $5,000, although some single-premium annuities can require a one-time lump-sum investment of as little as $2,500. A flexible premium annuity, paid over time, may have an initial minimum as low as $1,000 and require small monthly payments.

Most companies levy an annual management charge of 0.5%–1.5% of total assets. If you invest in a variable annuity, you will also pay a percentage of your total assets to cover management costs for the mutual fund.

Insurance companies typically charge a declining surrender fee of 5%–6% (which usually falls to zero after five or six years) if you liquidate the principal of your annuity. And if you withdraw your money before age 59½, the IRS will charge you a penalty.

Source: Alexandra Armstrong, Alexandra Armstrong Advisors, Inc., 1140 Connecticut Ave. NW, Washington, DC 20036.

Real estate—a shrewd investment

Using Real-Estate Shelters Profitably Now

Although Tax Reform changed the tax benefits from ownership of real estate, there are still significant tax advantages that continue to make these shelters smart investments.

Invest in income-producing shelters if tax shelters you own from previous years are still generating tax losses. This will balance out shelter losses that you otherwise wouldn't be able to deduct because of the passive-loss rules. The income from the income-producing property will be tax-free because it's offset by the losses.

Example: You own real estate that has been generating tax losses. To offset them, you buy property that yields a 10% return. Since the losses from the one property will balance out the income from the other, you will get the 10% tax-free.

To find the income-producing shelters, look at...

■ *Interest expenses.* A shelter purchased mainly with borrowed funds will have a very high interest expense and, therefore, lower income. Look for a shelter with less debt.

■ *Depreciation schedules.* Real estate placed in service after May 13, 1993, must be depreciated over 39 years if it's nonresidential property

Aggregate your losses from all tax shelters, not just those from real-estate tax shelters. Losses from a real-estate passive activity can offset income from any other type of passive activity and vice versa. Be sure to look at *all* your passive shelters, including equipment-leasing deals, research and development shelters, cattle-feeding shelters, etc.

Invest in real estate for the pure economics of the deal rather than for the tax savings—especially when you believe it's a good bargain. You'll eventually make considerable money when the property appreciates in value. *Bonus:* The appreciation on the property is tax-free until you decide to sell.

Source: Arthur I. Gordon, tax partner, Ernst & Young, 787 Seventh Ave., New York 10019.

Tax Magic In REMICs

REMICs (Real Estate Mortgage Investment Conduits) are mortgage-backed securities that get favorable treatment under the Tax Reform Act of 1986. IRS regulations permit interest-paying REMIC securities to be issued at *floating* interest rates. REMICs can be backed by mortgages on *manufactured* housing or mobile homes that are single-family residences.

Source: *IRS Notice* 87-41.

Secrets of housing investments

Tax Reform's New Tax Shelter

To encourage investment in housing, the Tax Reform Act of 1986 created a brand-new tax credit for low-income housing. The effect is to make this type of investment one of the few remaining tax shelters favored by the tax law.

Ten-Year Credit

The credit amounts to 9% of the qualifying costs of new construction for a period of 10 years. Remember, this is a *direct credit against your tax,* not just a deduction from income. That means a $10,000 investment could get you up to $900 a year in tax savings *for each of the next 10 years.*

A credit of 4% is given for federally aided construction irrespective of subsidies, or for the acquisition of already existing housing.

Another big tax advantage: The credit is *not* subject to the new rules on "passive" credits, which can normally be used only to offset "passive" income. The low-income housing credit can be used to shelter up to $25,000 of income from *any source*—wages, salaries, dividends, or whatever. Moreover, any unused portion of the credit may be carried over to future years.

More Advantages

An investment in low-income housing may also yield the following advantages:

■ Because of leveraging (borrowing the money for construction costs), low-income housing developments may generate passive tax losses, which can serve to offset passive income from other investments.

■ Your investment may produce a positive cash flow. But you should not expect big income. Because rents are controlled, low-income housing isn't a high-yield investment.

Investor Guidance

Know exactly with whom you're investing your money. Low-income housing isn't a field for amateurs. The law sets out a complicated maze of regulations on housing use, income level of occupants, rents to be charged, etc. States share in the administration of low-income housing, so state regulations are also involved. To qualify for the low-income housing credit, a project must comply with all these rules for 15 years.

If it fails to comply at any time during the 15-year period, the credit is subject to recapture—meaning investors may have to give back all or part of their tax savings.

To date, most low-income housing investments have been privately placed with big investors, although there have been some large public offerings by developers in California and Massachusetts. But Congress is under heavy pressure to simplify the law and get rid of unnecessary restrictions. Consult your tax or investment adviser for developments.

Rehabilitated Housing

If you rehabilitate a certified historic structure (listed in the national register) or a building put into service before 1936, you can claim a percentage of the annual rehabilitation expense as a credit against your tax bill. The credit equals 20% of expenses for certified historic structures and 10% for structures put into service before 1936. It applies only to the cost of the structure and its rehabilitation—not to the cost of the land.

Source: William Brennan, editor and publisher of *The Brennan Reports,* a newsletter on sophisticated tax and investment strategies, Brennan's Financial Advisory Corporation, Box 882, Valley Forge, PA 19482.

Big, big benefits in bonds

Buy Zero-Coupon Bonds Better

Zero-coupon bonds are a powerful, but often misunderstood, investment tool. *How they work:* The bond pays no cash interest to its owner. Rather, it's bought at a price far below its face value and is held for appreciation. For example, a 12% 20-year bond that will be worth $100,000 on maturity might be bought for only $10,000 today.

The big benefit derived from these bonds is the compound-interest factor. In effect, your return on the bond is automatically reinvested in it at the same interest rate.

Example: The 20-year bond mentioned above provides about $90,000 of appreciation earned at a rate of 12% annually. By contrast, a conventional $10,000 bond earning 12% will pay only $24,000 in cash interest over the same 20 years. It's up to you to find a way to reinvest this cash. If you can't do so at a rate of at least 12%, you'll lose out.

But there are drawbacks to zero-coupon bonds as well:

■ The bond's annual appreciation is taxable income to its owner, even though the bond generates no cash with which to pay the tax. *Advice:* Avoid this tax trap by buying bonds through your IRA or Keogh account, which is tax-exempt. Or place a bond in trust for a child who's in a low (or zero) tax bracket.

■ The compound-interest factor can work against you if interest rates go up after you purchase the bond. When higher interest rates are available from other investments, the market value of your bond might well go down.

■ Because of this interest-rate risk, zero-coupon bonds are not good liquid investments. You should plan on holding the bond until it matures.

Zero-coupon bonds can be bought with maturities ranging from six months to 30 years. Bonds may be backed by both federal and local governments, as well as by corporations and banks. Ask your broker for details.

Source: Glen Miller, director of tax, Ernst & Young, 1 IBM Plaza, Chicago 60611.

A Shelter For You And Your Kids

US savings bonds can be a very effective tax shelter. In some instances, they pay higher interest rates than longer-term Treasury bonds. The tax on the interest is deferred until the bonds are cashed in. This gives you a higher current return and pushes the tax off until a period when you may be in a lower tax bracket.

Follow the exact opposite strategy when dealing with your children's US savings bonds. If the interest on the bonds is deferred until the bonds are cashed in, it's likely your child will be in a higher tax bracket (since all the income is accumulated). Therefore, have the child file a return electing not to defer tax on the interest. This way, the interest is reported each year, when it can be sheltered by the child's $600 exclusion. When the bond is cashed in, there's no tax due on the interest except possibly for the final year's portion.

Source: Edward Mendlowitz, partner, Mendlowitz Weitsen, CPAs, 2 Pennsylvania Plaza, New York 10001.

Alert for business investors

Tax Break For Investors In Small Corporations

Investors who suffer losses on the sale of stock in small corporations may be entitled to special tax treatment—if the stock qualifies as "Section 1244" stock. Normally you can deduct only $3,000 of your net capital losses in any one year. But this limitation doesn't apply to Section 1244 stock. You can deduct up to $50,000 of losses a year ($100,000 on joint returns).

Stock can qualify for Section 1244 status if it meets these three tests:

■ The corporation's total paid-in capital (including the Section 1244 stock) doesn't exceed $1,000,000.

■ For the five years preceding the loss, the corporation derived most of its income from its business operations.

■ The Section 1244 stock is issued in exchange for cash or property, not stock in another company, or securities.

Small-Business-Investment Trap

Holley Homes Co., an S corporation that was being examined by the IRS, agreed to extend the statute of limitations concerning a possible tax liability. When the IRS finally sent an increased tax bill to Holley's investors, they said that *they* hadn't signed the extension, so they shouldn't be liable for the tax. *Tax Court:* The income of an S corporation is taxed directly to its investors and reported on their personal returns. Thus, an extension that's agreed to by the company applies *automatically* to its investors. They owed the tax.

Source: *Daniel M. Kelley,* TC Memo 1986-405.

Investments In Bankrupt Companies

I own stock in a company that's gone bankrupt. I'm told I can't deduct my loss yet because it won't be "final" until the bankruptcy proceedings are finished, but I don't want to wait years. Can I speed up my deduction?

Yes. Sell your shares in the company to a third party for any small sum you can get. Use the sale price to compute your loss on the shares. You can then claim the loss as a deductible capital loss on your tax return or use it to offset other capital gains you might have.

Escape hatches for investors

Escaping IRS Limits On Losses

At the heart of the Tax Reform Act of 1986 is the anti-tax-shelter provision called the passive-loss rule. Although the purpose of the rule is to curtail tax-shelter abuses, it reaches far beyond those investments that are usually thought of as tax shelters. *Trap:* Investors who don't fully understand the rule are almost certain to be caught in its net.

The Passive-Loss Rule

The law requires you to separate your income and investment losses into two categories: One for "passive activities" and one for "nonpassive activities." It then prohibits you from offsetting income from nonpassive activities, such as salary, with losses from passive activities, such as tax-shelter investments. Passive activity losses may offset only passive activity income.

Passive activities:

■ Limited partnership interests of all kinds (i.e., tax shelters).

■ All rental activities.

■ Business activities in which the taxpayer does not materially participate, including sole proprietorships, S corporations, and general partnerships. "Materially" means being involved year-round on a regular, continuous, and substantial basis.

Nonpassive activities:

■ Work that pays wages, salary, or commissions.

■ Investment that yields "portfolio income," such as dividends, capital gains, interest, or royalties.

■ Business activities in which there is material participation by the taxpayer.

Who's affected: The passive-loss rule applies to individuals, trusts and estates, personal-service corporations (self-incorporated doctors, dentists, lawyers, etc.) and S corporations. It does not apply to regular "C" corporations. Closely held C corporations are subject to the rule in a modified form (see below). *At greatest risk:* High-income taxpayers who have invested heavily in tax shelters.

Carryovers

Unused passive losses may be carried indefinitely into future years when they may be used to offset future passive income. The accumulated unused losses on a property may generally be used to offset the gain when the property is sold. And if the unused losses are more than the gain, the excess may be written off against nonpassive income. *Trap:* This break does not apply to property that is sold to a family member or to a business that you control.

Troubleshooting

Individuals who are locked into investments that throw off large passive losses must use new strategies to deal with their losses. *Recommended:*

Find investments that produce passive income, which will absorb the passive losses. *Trap:* Income from a mutual fund is not considered passive. Only investments that fit the new law's definition of a passive activity will generate passive income—for example, income-producing limited partnerships and rental properties.

Income-producing limited partnerships. Unfortunately, in many parts of the country, there are very few passive income deals available. Demand is great, so expect to pay a premium.

Rental properties such as occupied apartments, office buildings, parking lots, and shopping centers. You don't have to be a limited partner in these deals to get passive income, because all rental activity is considered passive under the new law, whether it's in the form of a limited partnership or not.

Convert nonpassive income into passive income. You might do this by converting a corporation that is not subject to the passive-loss rules into a corporation that is subject to the rules.

Example: Convert a regular corporation that is throwing off a great deal of taxable nonpassive income into an S corporation, then hire a manager to run the S corporation. Income from an S corporation in which the owner does not materially participate (that is, in which he is not involved year-round on a regular, continuous, and substantial basis) is passive income.

Restructure leasing arrangements with your business. Suppose you are currently leasing a building that you own to a manufacturing company that you own. You've been renting the building to the company at a rate of only $100,000 a year. Your depreciation deductions on the building give you a tax loss, which you needed and could use under the old law. But under the new law, you can't use the loss. What you need now is passive income.

What to do: Increase the rent to $300,000 a year, which is the building's fair market rent today. This will give you net income (above the depreciation deductions), and it will be passive income, because it comes from rental activity.

Break for Closely Held Corporations

Closely held corporations that are not personal-service corporations are subject to the passive-loss rule in a modified form.

Losses from a closely held corporation's passive activities may be used to offset the business income of the corporation. For example, a small manufacturing firm could offset net income from its operations with losses from tax-shelter investments. While the owner of a closely held corporation, as an individual taxpayer, will probably not wish to continue to invest in tax shelters, his corporation might very well want to.

Added incentive: Corporate rates are higher than individual rates. That makes tax-shelter losses more valuable to a corporation than to individual owners (assuming they could use the losses). *Restriction:* The corporation may not use passive losses to offset portfolio income (dividends, investment interest, etc.).

Source: Jerry Williford, partner, Grant Thornton, CPAs, 2800 Citicorp Center, Houston, TX 77002.

...And more investment advice

Limited Partnerships

Sooner or later, your broker will probably suggest putting some money into limited partnerships as a way in which you, as an individual, can join together with other investors who are interested in diversification beyond stocks and bonds to buy real estate, oil and gas properties, or other hard assets.

Typically, you need $2,000 or more to invest in a public limited partnership—these are partnerships that are regulated by the SEC. Private partnerships are really for high-net-worth individuals who have at least $30,000 to invest. Though Tax Reform removed the fast tax write-offs that partnerships used to offer, they still provide a way to invest in hard assets without double taxation of dividends, as with stocks.

But limited partnerships can be extremely tricky for the unwary investor, warns the president of one of the few firms that make a secondary market in limited partnerships—Ronald T. Baker of Partnership Securities Exchange, Inc. This secondary market can be more treacherous than penny stocks since there isn't much supply, and it's usually difficult to analyze what a partnership is truly worth.

A basic problem is that limited partnerships, which can be either private (averaging $25,000 per investment) or public (averaging $8,000 per investment) are run by a general partner, who presumably has the expertise to choose good properties and manage them efficiently.

That's not always true, of course. Too many investors have learned that, much to their sorrow. In fact, there's an inside joke in the industry that in the beginning, the general partner has the experience and the limited partners have the money. But in the end it's the general partner who has the money and the limited partners who have the experience.

Public partnerships, of which about $100 billion have been sold in the past 15 years—far more than the number of initial public capital raised—have to file with the Securities and Exchange Commission before sending out an offering. But there is effectively no supervision after that. Because they don't trade actively, security analysts don't follow partnerships either.

Result: Partnership general managers are the least accountable money managers in the US. And they face so many conflicts of interest that it's not surprising that many of these managers eventually take advantage of their situations.

Under these circumstances, investors take a real chance in investing in limited partnerships formed as so-called *blind pools*, in which you put in money *before* properties are acquired. These are usually sold by brokerage firms.

Better: An *old* limited partnership, so that it can be analyzed to see if it's profitable. Once you've located a partnership that fits your profile, stick with it.

Before buying any limited partnership, ask a lot of questions. Try to establish how much the shares are really worth. If a partnership initially went for $1,000 a unit, and now can be had for $500, maybe it's really worth only $200.

Source: Ronald T. Baker has been involved in the secondary market for limited partnerships since 1982.

Mutual-Fund Guidelines

The most obvious way to plan long-term wealth building in mutual funds is to purchase them in a tax-deferred vehicle such as an individual retirement account. Then the miracle of compounding goes on for a very long time (depending on the number of years until you reach retirement) without any withdrawals for tax payments. However, there are other tax considerations that may affect your portfolio.

Keep all your monthly fund statements. If you have the statements, your reinvestment basis is your cost basis. Lose the statements, and your original investment price is the basis of all reinvested distributions.

Investors pay tax on their share of the fund income before management costs are deducted. Now more than ever you should be in low-management fee funds that charge .75% or less. A fund that charges a 2% management fee had better perform really well for you to own it.

Take your loss on poorly performing funds, since all losses and gains are merged to figure out your taxable income. Even if you have a net loss, it's deductible against other income, up to $3,000 per year.

Try not to buy a fund right before a dividend payment because the dividend will be income, and the price of the shares usually falls. These large distributions are often a known yearly event.

Whenever you can, open separate accounts in the same name for successive investments. This gives you a sales receipt that is proof of a separate tax basis for each investment purchase.

Source: Steven James Lee, president, Steven Lee Consulting Co., Dedham, MA 02026.

Eliminate Or Defer Tax On Investment Income

In general, income you receive on investments is taxed immediately. However, there are certain exceptions:

■ *Municipal bonds.* The IRS considers the interest on most such bonds to be tax-exempt. If the bond is issued by your state, the interest is also exempt from state tax.

■ *Series EE bonds.* Tax on the interest is deferred until you receive the proceeds, usually when you cash in the bonds. You can also roll over the proceeds by converting the EE bonds into HH bonds.

■ *US Treasury bills.* If you purchase a T-bill that comes due in the next taxable year, you don't have to report any portion of the interest until you cash in the bond. In many cases, the payment of tax on the income can be deferred for as long as one year (the maximum period for which Treasury bills are sold).

■ *Stocks.* If you invest in stocks and they increase in value, you aren't taxed on this profit until you sell the stock. However, any dividends you receive are currently taxed. If you buy the stocks on margin and pay margin interest, you can deduct the interest to the extent that you have portfolio income. If you pay margin interest equivalent to the amount of the dividends received, the investment will be carrying itself.

Exception to the exceptions: Interest on zero-coupon bonds is taxed on an annual basis, even though the interest isn't available to you until maturity.

Source: Edward Mendlowitz, partner, Mendlowitz Weitsen, CPAs, 2 Pennsylvania Plaza, New York 10001.

Traps to avoid in stocks

Stock-Investment Pitfall

I invested my IRA account aggressively in the stock market and took a big loss in the recent crash. Will I be able to deduct it?

No. Losses that are incurred in an IRA account are *not* deductible. That's one reason why, from a purely *tax* point of view, many experts think that IRAs should be invested in interest-bearing securities such as bonds and certificates of deposit (so that the principal is safe and interest earned is tax deferred) while appreciating assets, such as stocks and mutual-fund shares, should be held *outside* of an IRA (so that capital losses can be deducted if they occur).

Of course, your *overall* goal should be to choose investments that will maximize your gain over time *after* taxes.

Investment Failure

When Equity Funding failed, Donald Crowell suffered a $55,000 loss on his investment in its stock. When its management was charged with 105 counts of securities fraud and mail fraud, Crowell tried to deduct his loss as a *theft* loss rather than as a less valuable capital loss. *Court:* A theft-loss deduction is available only when a wrongdoer takes property from you *directly.* Since Crowell had bought his stock on the open market, he had never had any direct contact with the company—thus, he wasn't entitled to the deduction.

Source: *Donald W. Crowell,* TC Memo 1986-314.

3

TAX LOOPHOLES

EVERYTHING THE LAW ALLOWS

Retirement Tax Traps And Opportunities

Get the most for your retirement

Retirement Tax Loopholes

The tax laws are peppered with loopholes designed to help us live comfortably in retirement.

Tax-free home sales. If either you or your spouse is 55 or older when you sell your house, and you have owned and lived in it for three of the past five years, the first $125,000 of profit is completely tax-free…if you wish it to be. This tax break is optional, not mandatory. It can be taken only once, and if one spouse has taken it previously, it can't be taken again by a married couple, even though the other spouse never used it.

It's important that you not waste the exclusion, since you lose it once you use it. Do not elect the exclusion if:

■ You plan to buy another house. In this situation you qualify for another tax break—tax deferral. Homesellers can defer tax on their profits by investing them in another house within two years of the sale. Using tax deferral preserves your right to take the $125,000 exclusion on a future sale.

■ The profit on the sale of your home is relatively small. If you use the exclusion for a $15,000 gain, neither you nor your spouse may use it again, ever. You may be better off paying the tax on a small gain and saving the exclusion.

Loophole for soon-to-remarry couples: If one spouse-to-be has used the exclusion and the other hasn't, the spouse who hasn't used it should sell his or her house prior to the marriage and take the exclusion. It will not be available if the sale occurs after the marriage.

Gifts to grandchildren. Think twice before selling appreciated assets, such as securities, to provide cash gifts for your children and grandchildren. It may be better to give the assets directly to the kids and let them sell them. A gift of the property will save tax (and create a bigger gift) if the recipient is in a lower tax bracket than you. The recipient will pay less tax on the gain than you would at your high tax bracket.

The giving strategy changes if the recipient intends to retain the property. In this case, it's better to give cash now and let the intended recipient inherit the appreciated property. *Reason:* The recipient will inherit the property at a stepped-up basis—that is, its value at the date of your death. He or she won't have to pay capital gains tax on the property's increase in value.

Rent a condominium from your children. One way to get Uncle Sam to subsidize the cost of supporting an elderly parent is for the children to buy the parent's retirement condominium and rent it to the parent. At the very least, the children will get tax deductions for mortgage interest and property taxes. These deductions will produce a greater tax benefit to high-income children than they would to a low-bracket retired parent. And if the children charge the parent fair market rent, they will also be able to take depreciation deductions on the condo. The Tax Reform Act of 1986 allows you to deduct up to $25,000 of rental losses if your Adjusted Gross Income is less than $100,000. This loss allowance is phased out between $100,000 and $150,000 of Adjusted Gross Income.

Plan in advance for nursing-home care. Before the government will pay your nursing-home bills, you have to use up the money that's in your name. *Strategy:* Put your money into a trust that pays you income but doesn't allow you to touch the principal. Then only the income will be lost to nursing-home care—you won't lose the principal. *Caution:* In most states, a trust that is set up within three years of a person's entering a nursing home won't be effective. Check with an attorney about your state's laws.

IRS vs. remarriage. A married couple, both age 65 or older, will pay more tax on a joint return than the combined tax they would pay if they were single. *Another consideration:* If income (including tax-exempt income), plus one-half Social Security benefits exceeds certain levels, half the Social Security benefits are taxable. *The levels are:* $25,000 for a single person, or $32,000 for a married couple. Combining incomes on a joint return may force taxation of Social Security benefits that would completely have escaped taxation if the couple hadn't married. *Note:* 85% of benefits are taxable if your income is above $34,000 if you're unmarried, and $44,000 if you're married.

Retirement-plan distributions. You must start taking money out of your Individual Retirement Account by April 1 following the year in which you reach age 70½. *Loophole:* You may be able to slow the distribution down (take less in the early years) by using actuarial tables. Check with the IRA trustee to see if a slower distribution schedule can be used for your payouts.

Power of attorney. Many elderly people fail to plan for the possibility that they might become unable to handle money. *Suggestion:* Give a power of attorney over one bank account to a relative or other trusted person. If you become incapacitated, that money will be available for your care.

Life insurance. Consider setting up a trust to take out life insurance to pay the estate taxes that will eventually go to the government. Premiums for people in their early sixties are lower than you might think. This can be a low-cost way of paying estate taxes.

Source: Edward Mendlowitz, partner, Mendlowitz Weitsen, CPAs, Two Pennsylvania Plaza, New York 10121.

Protect Your Social Security Benefits

Your Social Security benefits are taxable if your total income for the year exceeds these dollar limits:

- $25,000, if you are single.
- $32,000, if you are married and file a joint return.
- $25,000, if you are married, do not file a joint return, and do not live with your spouse.
- Zero if you are married, do not file a joint return, and did live with your spouse at any time during the year.

Trap: Total income includes tax-exempt income, such as interest received from municipal bonds, which is free of income tax. If you are likely to exceed the income limits, consider these following strategies:

- Invest in assets that appreciate in value without producing current income—essentially Series EE savings bonds or growth stocks. Such investments can help keep you under the income limit.
- Time that income (IRA withdrawals, etc.) so that you receive it advantageously, such as when you have offsetting deductible expenses.
- Divorce. While a married couple filing jointly will have a $32,000 income limit, two single people can take $25,000 each, or $50,000 together.

For now and the future

You Have More Time To Set Up A SEP

A Simplified Employee Pension (SEP) is a retirement plan through which employers make contributions to a retirement account on behalf of their employees. The employer may claim a deduction on these contributions, while the employees aren't required to declare the contributions as income.

Good news: If you wish to open a SEP for your employees, you have until the due date for filing your tax return for the current year (usually April 15 of the following year) to do so. You don't have to rush to set it up by December 31 of the current year, as is necessary when opening a Keogh plan.

Source: *New Tax Traps/New Opportunities* by Edward Mendlowitz, CPA, Boardroom Special Report, Springfield, NJ 07081.

Funding Your Keogh Plan

If you're self-employed, you can set up a tax-deferred retirement plan called a Keogh plan. You're not taxed on your contributions or their accumulated interest until you collect the benefits, usually when you retire.

One of the tax requirements of a Keogh plan is that the account must be opened before the end of the year in which you're claiming a deduction. However, it doesn't have to be fully funded until you file your tax return (including extensions). *Advice:* Open the account before December 31 with a nominal amount or an amount as low as the lending institution will accept. Before your return is prepared, consult your tax adviser to determine how much money to contribute to your Keogh plan.

Source: *New Tax Traps/New Opportunities* by Edward Mendlowitz, CPA, Boardroom Special Report, Springfield, NJ 07081.

Simple Form For Keogh Plans

Form 5500EZ is a simplified form for reporting on Keogh plans that cover only *one* person or an individual and his/her spouse who wholly own a business. The form can also be used for a partnership plan that covers only partners and spouses if the plan meets the law's coverage tests and isn't combined with any other plan. The form may *not* be used by any business that leases employees or is part of a group under common control.

Borrow From Your Pension Plan

Did you know that you can usually borrow from your pension plan? You must have a good reason for the borrowing and definite repayment arrangements. Also, you must pay interest on the loan at the going rate.

There are limitations on the maximum amounts that can be borrowed as follows:

Vested Portion in Pension Plan	Maximum Amount of Borrowing
Up to $100,000	50% of amount of plan
Over $100,000	$50,000 maximum amount

Source: *New Tax Traps/New Opportunities* by Edward Mendlowitz, CPA, Boardroom Special Report, Springfield, NJ 07081.

The Magic of 401(k) Plans

Benefits Of A 401(k) Plan

You can volunteer to have your employer deduct from your salary an amount that will be put into your employer's qualified deferred-compensation plan. This is called a 401(k) plan. The amounts, which are set aside for you, earn interest on a tax-deferred basis.

Though similar to IRAs, 401(k) plans are better because if you have reached age 59½ when you withdraw the lump sum of your 401(k), you may be able to use five-year averaging to calculate the tax you owe. *What this means:* You calculate the amount of the withdrawal as if you had received it evenly over five years. Take one-fifth of the lump-sum amount and figure out the tax on that portion. Multiply the answer by five to compute the tax due. The amount will be less than the tax you'll owe on the full amount if you declare it as income for one year, which you must do with an IRA. (*Note:* If you were born before 1936, you may be eligible for 10-year averaging, which is usually even more favorable.)

If your employer has a 401(k) plan available, by all means participate in it. You'll save a substantial amount of tax dollars.

Source: *New Tax Traps/New Opportunities* by Edward Mendlowitz, CPA, Boardroom Special Report, Springfield, NJ 07081.

New 401(k) Plan Trap

Under old law, many companies set up 401(k) salary deferral programs that let executives place a percentage of salary, up to $30,000 total, into a *tax-deferred* retirement savings account.

Trap: Tax Reform *reduced* the maximum amount of salary that may be saved through a 401(k) account. The maximum for 1995 is $9,240. Executives who inadvertently put more than $9,240 into their plan account will owe an excess contribution *penalty tax.* This penalty can hit persons who earned as little as $60,000 during the year, since 401(k) plans often allow executives to save up to 15% of salary.

What to do: Review total plan contributions for the past year *now.* If you contributed more than is allowed, *avoid* the penalty tax by withdrawing the excess before April 15. Then set this year's contribution percentage to save as close to the limit as possible.

401(k) Plans Made Simpler

Banks and other financial institutions can now get approval for master and proto-type 401(k) plans. This will make it easier for companies to establish plans. In the past, each employer had to get *individual* IRS approval.

Source: *Rev. Proc.* 87-18.

Social Security savvy

Social-Security-Tax Loopholes

Social Security tax rates have gone up, but there are still many kinds of payments that are *exempt* from Social Security taxes. *Examples:*

■ Wages paid to your children under age 18—if the business is a sole proprietorship. Wages paid by a corporation, however, are subject to tax.

■ Wages paid to a parent by a son or daughter for services *not* connected with the employer's trade or business. *Example:* Wages for domestic services, such as baby-sitting or housekeeping.

■ Any payments that are not compensation for services—e.g., dividends, interest, rent, gifts, inheritances.

■ Loans from the company by an employee or stockholder. But be sure the loan is fully documented to prove its legitimacy. If the IRS concludes that the loan will not be paid back, it will impose tax.

■ Company fringe benefits, such as payments for accident and health insurance, educational benefits under a qualified plan, and many others. *Exception:* Life insurance policies paid for by your company for insurance in excess of $50,000.

■ The cash value of meals and lodging furnished to an employee by the employer for the employer's convenience aren't included in the employee's wages for purposes of FICA tax.

Social Security Checkup

It's important to check periodically to see that your earnings have been properly credited to your Social Security account. *Reason:* Corrections to your lifetime earnings record must be made within 39½ months after the year in which the mistake was made. *To get a statement of your Social Security earnings:* Pick up a copy of Form SSA 7004 at your local Social Security Administration office and mail it in. Don't expect an up-to-date total, though—the SSA is behind in posting its records.

Social Security Goof-Ups

Mistakes on Social Security records can cause you to lose benefits you've earned. A recent survey showed that almost 10 million Americans were not credited with their full earnings for the years 1978–84.

Those at high risk: People who are self-employed, change jobs frequently, or work for a small company (fewer than 15 employees), and pensioners who return to work.

To get a grand total of your Social Security earnings to date, file a *Request for Statement of Earnings* (Form SSA-7004), available from your local Social Security office. The grand total should match the total of the amounts in the *Social Security Wages* line on your old IRS W-2 forms.*

To verify year-by-year records, file a *Request for Detailed Social Security Earnings Information* (Form SSA-7050), also available from your local Social Security office. If you find a discrepancy between an annual amount and an old W-2 form, alert your Social Security office immediately.

*Problem: You will need copies of your old W-2 forms to prove that an error has been made. And neither the IRS nor your former employers are obliged to keep copies on file past four years.

What to know about IRAs

How To Win With An IRA

Even if you aren't eligible to deduct an Individual Retirement Account, you can still make a nondeductible IRA contribution that will earn interest on a tax-deferred basis. However, before setting up an IRA, determine whether the benefits would outweigh those of other alternatives. Sometimes an IRA isn't the great tax-saving device you think it is.

For example, if you put $2,000 a year into an IRA as a voluntary contribution for a 10-year period, you'll have a total of $20,000. If the money is earning 8% interest, you'll have accumulated $28,973 after 10 years. When you withdraw that money from the IRA, it will become completely taxable. Assuming at that point that you're in the 28% bracket, you'll pay a tax of $2,512, leaving a net to you of the $20,000 that you invested plus $6,461 after taxes.

If, on the other hand, you invest the money in a savings account earning 8% interest a year, you'll have to pay taxes on the interest and, therefore, earn only about 5.76% a year. Over 10 years the saving amounts to $26,054. So you come out about the same as you would with an IRA. However, by not choosing an IRA, you'll have the full use of your funds over those 10 years.

There can be a big advantage in investing in an IRA if you're in a low tax bracket when your IRA comes due. Let's assume all the facts in the scenario above. However, after 10 years you'll be in the 15% bracket instead of the 28% bracket. After taxes you'd net $27,627, a much bigger saving than you'd reap from a savings account.

Source: *New Tax Traps/New Opportunities* by Edward Mendlowitz, CPA, Boardroom Special Report, Springfield, NJ 07081.

Penalty-Free Withdrawals

Although the Tax Reform Act of 1986 clobbered the deduction for Individual Retirement Accounts for many taxpayers, it created a penalty-free way to withdraw money from the account *before* you reach age 59½. *Old law:* You had to pay an additional 10% penalty tax on distributions from IRA accounts before age 59½. *New law:* You won't pay the extra 10% penalty tax if you convert the account to an annuity and receive the money in a scheduled series of substantially equal payments over your life or your life expectancy.

Source: George S. Alberts, former head of the Albany and Brooklyn IRS district offices.

Borrowing From Your IRA

Borrow from an IRA legally by making a short-term loan. Generally, IRA borrowings are prohibited. But it is possible to move funds from one IRA to another as long as the transfer is completed within a 60-day period. *Benefit:* You have use of the funds for 59 days. *Warning:* The exact amount you take out of the first IRA must be placed in the second one within the 60 days. And you can use this device only once in a 12-month period.

IRA Commissions

The IRS has held that commissions paid directly to an insurance agent or broker in connection with an IRA investment are *not* deductible investment expenses. Rather, they are contributions *to* the IRA and count toward the $2,000 deduction limit.
Source: IRS Letter Ruling 8747072.

IRA Trap

To monitor forbidden IRA deductions, employers are required to report on end-of-the-year W-2 forms whether an individual was an "active participant" in the company's retirement plan. With this information the IRS can easily check the validity of a taxpayer's IRA deduction.

IRA Explanation

A *free* IRS publication explains the new rules governing required payouts from IRAs. Call toll-free: 1-800-829-3676. Ask for Publication 930, *Required Distributions from Individual Retirement Arrangements.*

If You Forget IRA Contribution And Claim Deduction

On last year's joint return, my husband and I claimed a $4,000 IRA contribution deduction, as we do each year. However, I just discovered that my husband forgot to make the contribution. What do we do now?

You should file an amended tax return, Form 1040X, for last year, correcting the mistake by omitting the deduction and paying the tax due on the $4,000.

You should do this right away, not only to cut off the *interest* that's running on the underpayment but, also, to minimize the risk of incurring tax *penalties*. If you report the mistake yourself, you will be more likely to avoid penalties for negligence (or fraud) than you will be if the IRS discovers the error on its own. And it probably *will* discover the mistake eventually, since IRA contributions are reported to the IRS via computer tape by the institutions that receive them.

Limits On IRA Deductions

Rules on the deductibility of IRA contributions:

■ *No deduction* if either you or your spouse is covered by a company retirement plan *and* your Adjusted Gross Income (AGI) is more than $50,000 on a joint return ($35,000 if you're single).

■ *Partial deductions* for joint filers who are covered by company retirement plans and whose AGI is between $40,000 and $50,000. Partial deductions for single filers covered by company plans with an AGI of between $25,000 and $35,000.

■ *Full deduction,* as under the old rules, if neither you nor your spouse is covered by a company plan, or if you are covered, but your Adjusted Gross Income is less than $40,000 (joint) or $25,000 (single).

Note: Spouses who live apart for the entire year and file separate returns are subject to the same rules as *single* filers.

4

TAX LOOPHOLES

EVERYTHING THE LAW ALLOWS

Family Tax Strategies

Risks and relief in joint returns

Joint Vs. Separate Returns

Married couples can file a joint return or separate returns. Usually a joint return works out better, especially if one spouse has appreciably higher income than the other.

Nevertheless, filing separately can be advantageous in some situations:

■ Deductions for casualty losses must be reduced by 10% of Adjusted Gross Income (AGI). On a joint return, combined AGI is reduced, even if only one spouse suffered the loss. If separate returns are filed, the loss is reduced by only 10% of that spouse's income.

Example: A husband has an AGI of $70,000; his wife, $20,000. The wife's jewelry, worth $25,000, is stolen. On a joint return, the loss must be reduced by $9,000 (10% of combined income); on a separate return, by only $2,000 (10% of the wife's income).

■ The same considerations apply if one spouse, but not the other, has heavy medical expenses, since you can deduct only expenses in excess of 7½% of AGI— or heavy miscellaneous deductions, which can be deducted only to the extent they exceed 2% of AGI.

Other options: If married persons live apart for the entire year, either spouse may file as head-of-household (with reduced rates) if he or she has an unmarried child or dependent living with him or her for the entire year. The other spouse would then have to file separately (higher rates), unless that spouse also had a child or dependent in his or her household. *Or,* they could file jointly if that works out better.

Caution: The only way to tell for sure whether it's better to file jointly or separately is to take pencil and paper and figure the tax both ways.

Source: Herbert M. Paul, a tax attorney with the firm of Herbert Paul, P.C., 805 Third Ave., New York 10022.

Surviving Spouse Bonus

A widow or widower with dependent children living at home can qualify as a *surviving spouse* and file tax returns using lower joint-return tax rates for *two* taxable years after the year in which the spouse died. Check filing status box 5 on Form 1040.

Married? You May Want To File Separately

Most married taxpayers will pay less tax as a result of filing a joint return. But there are some couples who will pay less by filing *separate* returns because of the changes made by the Tax Reform Act of 1986. You and your spouse should figure your final tax bill both ways before making the decision. *Items that may affect your filing status:*

■ The new tax rates. The change in rate structure may make separate filing better for some couples who previously found joint filing more advantageous. *Caution:* Couples who are planning to benefit from the $25,000 rental-property loss deduction should carefully analyze which way they will pay lower taxes. The spouse who owns the rental property and receives income from it will be allowed to deduct only $12,500 on a separate return, half the amount available on a joint return.

■ The 2% floor on miscellaneous deductions. Tax reform only allows miscellaneous deductions to the extent that they exceed 2% of Adjusted Gross Income (AGI). If one spouse has all the miscellaneous deductions, he/she might individually reach the 2% limit based on his/her own AGI, especially if it's the lower-earning spouse. On a joint return the couple's *combined* income is used to determine the 2% limit, and it could be lost.

■ Repeal of the two-earner, married-couple deduction. Joint filers who both work used to get a tax break of up to $3,000 on a joint return. Couples who filed jointly to get the benefit of this deduction in the past should keep in mind that it's no longer available when deciding whether to file a joint or separate return.

Innocent-Spouse Provision

Filing a joint tax return creates "joint and several liability." This simply means that each spouse is liable for the entire amount of tax, interest, and penalties ever assessed by the IRS on that return. When the IRS discovers that one spouse has understated income, it may be possible for the other spouse to avoid liability for the extra assessment by claiming protection under the "innocent-spouse" provision of Tax Code Section 6013(e). To qualify for this relief, the innocent spouse must generally prove that he/she didn't know of the understatement and had no reason to know of it under the circumstances. *Strategy in negotiating a settlement with an IRS agent:* Convince him/her to include the innocent-spouse relief in the settlement. Then, if it later proves impossible for you to pay the tax and penalties, one spouse will have been able to accumulate assets that are immune from IRS collection methods.

Source: Ms. X, Esq., a former IRS agent who is still well connected.

You can't hide behind a joint account

Perils Of A Joint Account

Raphael and Victoria Burns owed back taxes, so the IRS ordered their bank to pay over a number of CDs that were payable to them. But several of the CDs were jointly payable to other family members. They sued the bank for converting *their* interests in the CDs, and the bank in turn sued the IRS. *Court:* Both the bank and the IRS were free from liability. When an asset is held jointly, it can be seized to settle a debt of any of the owners. Thus, the IRS had a valid claim to the CDs, and the family was out of luck.

Source: *Richard Assen Burns,* D.C., ND, No. A3-86-4.

Individual Liability On Joint Return

John Francis agreed in writing to a tax deficiency, but on the condition that his former wife had to pay half. Mr. and Mrs. Francis had filed a joint return for that year, and she had received half of the refund. *Tax Court:* Mr. Francis had to pay the whole deficiency himself. Couples who file jointly are each *individually* and jointly responsible for paying the tax.

Source: *John R. Francis,* Tax Ct. Dkt. No. 7549-86-S.

Unreported-Interest Trap

A man and his sister shared a joint bank account. All the interest income the account earned was divided equally between them, but he never reported his share of the interest on his tax return. *Tax Court:* The man had to pay a tax on the unreported interest income—and a negligence penalty.

Source: *Estate of Henry Grumet,* TC Memo 1987-583.

Once You Know...

Mrs. Price had to pay tax penalties because she knew that Mr. Price hadn't reported all of his income. She didn't think it was taxable because it was from illegal sources. *Tax Court:* Once Mrs. Price knew about the income, she could no longer claim that she was an innocent spouse.

Source: *Bernadette P. Price,* TC Memo 1987-360.

Children and taxes ...and you

Loopholes In The New Kiddie Tax

Tax Reform discourages income shifting between parents and children under the age of 14 by taxing the children's income from investments at the parents' tax rate. This is the Kiddie tax, and it's a tough one—but it's not airtight. *Key points:*

■ The Kiddie tax is imposed only on investment income over $1,300 for 1995.

■ It doesn't apply to wages or other "earned" income.

■ It doesn't apply to children age 14 and older. Their income is taxed at their own rate, not at their parents' rate.

■ Income shifting is still possible. *Aim:* To deflect income from the parents' high rate to a child's lower tax bracket so that the child will pay a smaller tax on the income than you would pay.

Income-Shifting Strategies

Loophole: Give your children investments that will produce up to $1,300 of income annually. The first $650 of investment income of children under age 14 is completely tax-free. The next $650 is taxed at the child's rate—15%—rather than at the parents' rate. The family's total tax will be somewhat reduced.

Loophole: Buy a 52-week Treasury bill for a child who will turn 14 next year. The income will be taxed at the child's rate rather than at yours, since the child will be 14 and free of the Kiddie tax when the T-bill matures next year. (Whether or not the child is under 14 for the tax year depends on his/her age on December 31.)

Loophole: Hire your children. This is another way to shift income. Instead of giving the children allowances, find them work to do in your business. Pay them reasonable salaries, and deduct the salaries as a business expense. *Savings:*

■ If your business is unincorporated, you don't pay Social Security tax on wages paid to a child who is under 18.

■ A child can earn up to $3,900 totally tax-free. (The tax-free limit on investment income is $650.)

Income-Shifting Investments

The shrewdest investments for children under 14 are tax-exempt, or those on which tax can be deferred until the child is 14 or older and free of the Kiddie tax. *Best:* US savings bonds. With these, you have the option of deferring federal taxes until the bonds mature or electing to report the interest income each year.

Loophole: Take advantage of the annual $650 tax-free amount of investment income that a child can have. If your child's total annual unearned income is less than $1,300, elect to report savings-bond interest year by year. *Benefit:* The first $650 will be tax-free each year, and the next $650 will be taxed at the child's rate. *By contrast:* If you don't make the election, the full accumulation of interest will be taxed when the bond matures. This interest income might push your child into a higher tax bracket. And by not making the election to report interest annually, you will pass up the $650 tax-free amount.

Loophole: Avoid filing tax returns for the child. If the child's total annual unearned income is under $650, make the election to report savings-bond interest annually on the first year's return. You don't have to file another return until the year when the child's investment income exceeds $650. If it doesn't exceed $650 a year, you won't have to file returns—and the whole of the bond's interest will have escaped taxation.

Other Investments for Kids

■ Municipal bonds. There's no Kiddie tax problem with these investments because municipal bonds are free from federal income tax.

■ Growth stock. Buy stock that pays low dividends over the years but is expected to appreciate in value. Sell the stock at a profit after the child reaches 14.

■ Real estate. Buy rental property for your child. It will be considered a passive activity (since the child won't be actively managing it), and any losses will be suspended. The losses can be used in the future when the property is sold.

■ Business interests. Give your child a partnership interest or an interest in an S corporation for a business that's just starting up. In the early years, while the child is subject to the Kiddie tax, there will be little taxable gain. If the business makes a profit after the child reaches age 14, the income will be taxed at the child's rate. Moreover, if there are losses in the early years, they can be carried forward and deducted in later years when the business becomes profitable.

Source: Edward Mendlowitz, partner, Mendlowitz Weitsen, CPAs, 2 Pennsylvania Plaza, New York 10121.

Paying Your Child A Tax-Deductible Allowance

A favorite tax-planning tactic is to have a minor child work for the family-owned business. Income earned by the child is taxed at the child's tax rate, which is likely to be much lower than the parents' rate. In addition, the company gets a deduction for the child's salary. A dramatic taxpayer victory* shows just how effective this tactic can be.

The facts: The taxpayers owned a mobile-home park and hired their three children, aged 7, 11, and 12 to work there. The children cleaned the grounds, did landscaping work, maintained the swimming pool, answered phones, and did minor repair work. The taxpayers deducted over $17,000 that they paid to the children during a three-year period. But the IRS objected, and the case went to trial. *Court's decision:* Over $15,000 of deductions were approved. Most of the deductions that were disallowed were attributable to the seven-year-old. But even $1,200 of his earnings were approved by the court.

Key: The children actually performed the work for which they were paid. And the work was necessary for the business. The taxpayers demonstrated that if their children had not done the work, they would have had to hire someone else to do it.

Walter E. Eller, 77 TC 934.

Source: Irving Blackman, partner, Blackman Kallick Bartelstein, 300 S. Riverside Plaza, Chicago 60606.

Education Savings Bonds

Interest on US savings bonds that are cashed in to pay for educational expenses will be tax-free income for certain taxpayers. *Effective:* Starting in 1990. Applies only to interest earned on US savings bonds issued after December 31, 1989. *Restrictions:*

■ Applies only to people who buy the bonds after reaching age 24.

■ Interest is fully tax-free only for joint filers whose Adjusted Gross Income (AGI) is less than $60,000 ($40,000 for single filers). These figures are indexed for inflation.

■ It is partially tax-free for joint filers with an AGI of $60,000–$90,000 ($40,000–$55,000 for singles).

■ The break does *not* apply to joint filers whose AGI is over $90,000—nor to singles with an AGI in excess of $55,000.

■ To qualify for the tax break, the bonds must be kept in the parent's name and must be redeemed by the parent.

■ Interest is fully tax-free only if the amount of bonds redeemed plus interest during the year is *less* than the amount of educational expenses. Interest is only partly tax-free if the amount redeemed exceeds the amount of educational expenses.

Child's Compensation Taxed

A seven-year-old child received a $30,000 court award for personal injuries. The award will be invested on the child's behalf. How will it be taxed?

A court's award of damages as compensation for personal injuries is *tax-free* when received. However, when the award is invested, the income it produces is taxed under normal rules.

In the case of a child under age 14, investment income exceeding $1,300 may be taxed at the top-bracket rate of the child's parents. To avoid tax, the award may, of course, be placed in an investment that is *tax-exempt* (such as municipal bonds) or in one that will *defer* taxes (such as growth stocks or Series EE savings bonds).

Kiddie Tax Affects Savings

Earnings on your child's savings account, no matter where the money in the account came from, are subject to the Kiddie tax, which taxes all investment income over $1,300 of a child under 14 at the parents' rate. Even if the child earned the money him/herself (for example, from an afterschool job), the interest earned on that money must be included in the Kiddie tax calculations.

Summer Jobs

Children's summer jobs may not be subject to income-tax withholding. A child employed for the summer with no other income, who owed no tax last year and expects to earn less than the standard deduction this year, can avoid having income tax withheld. *How:* By checking boxes 6a and 6b on the W-4 withholding form that your child must file when he/she starts working with the employer...and by writing the word "Exempt" on line 6b.

Dependent-Care-Credit Trap

When you pay wages of $50 or more per quarter to a baby-sitter or housekeeper, you are responsible for withholding and paying a percentage of those wages for Social Security taxes. When you fill out Form 2441 for the credit, the IRS will know that you should have paid this tax and will check to see if you did.

If you have dependents...

Exemptions For Dependents

To get an exemption, you must contribute over 50% of the dependent's support. That includes food, clothing, shelter (including the fair rental value of a home), and other ordinary living expenses. It also includes medical and educational expenses. *To help you get all the exemptions you're entitled to:*

■ *Allocation of support.* Suppose you contribute $10,000 a year to your parents. Each of them contributes $6,000 individually. Normally your $10,000 is allocated equally ($5,000 to each parent), so you don't contribute 50% of support. But if you designate your contribution to *one parent only,* you would provide over 50% of that parent's support and could claim one exemption. (Make a notation on your support checks or prepare a written statement when you start payments.)

■ *Full-time students.* Scholarship grants need not be counted toward support if your dependent is a full-time student for at least five months of the year. *Example:* You contribute $6,000 toward the support of your son in college. He contributes $3,000 of his own and has a $4,000 scholarship. Total support is $9,000. It's not $13,000...the scholarship doesn't count. You provide $6,000 of the $9,000, which is more than 50%, so you get the exemption. *Warning:* Your son cannot claim his own personal exemption, since he is supported by you.

■ *Children of divorced or separated parents* are normally claimed by the parent who has custody, unless he/she signs a waiver (Form 8332) allowing the other parent to claim the exemption.

Is the dependent related to you? The dependent must be a relative, or if not a relative, must be a member of your household for the entire year. Relatives include children and grandchildren, parents and grandparents, brothers and sisters, and uncles, aunts, nieces, and nephews by blood. More distant relatives don't count.

■ *Children* means natural children, adopted children, and stepchildren. Foster children may be claimed only if they lived with you for the *entire* year.

■ *In-laws* (fathers- and mothers-in-law, sons- and daughters-in-law, and brothers- and sisters-in-law) are considered relatives. If you support them, you can claim them as dependents, and you can continue to claim them even after divorce or the death of your spouse.

■ *Stepchildren* are relatives; their spouses and children aren't. But they can be claimed on a joint return, since they are your spouse's relatives.

Other Important Rules

■ You can't claim an exemption for a married dependent who files a joint return with his/her spouse. *Exception:* You get the exemption if the couple owed no tax and filed a joint return just to get a refund of taxes withheld from their pay.

■ The dependent generally must be a citizen, national, or resident of the US, or a resident of Canada or Mexico.

■ If a dependent dies during the year, you get a full exemption for the year. Exemptions are not prorated.

Dependency Loopholes

You can claim a dependency exemption for unrelated individuals. But these dependents must live with you for the entire year, and your relationship can't violate local morality laws. You must provide more than half of the person's support, and he/she must earn less gross taxable income than the personal exemption ($2,500 in 1995).

A parent who provides over half of a child's support can claim a dependency exemption if the child is under 19 or a full-time student. The cost of a child's wedding is considered support. So even if the child lives with a spouse after marriage, the wedding may push the parent's support cost over the 50% mark and entitle the parent to the exemption. *Drawbacks:* The child cannot file a joint return for the year. And the child cannot claim a personal exemption on his/her own tax return.

Dependent Dilemma

A father wanted to claim his daughter as a dependent after she had a nervous breakdown and had to be hospitalized. *IRS ruling:* No exemption. Dependency exemptions are allowed only when the person earns less than the exemption amount. She earned more. Exemptions are also allowed when a dependent child over 19 is a student for five months of the year. She left school after four months. It didn't matter that she left school because of the breakdown.

Source: *IRS Letter Ruling 8623050.*

TINs For Tots

Claiming a dependent who is one year of age or older requires some paperwork. You must list the Social Security, or tax identification number (TIN), for each dependent age one and older claimed as an exemption. There is a $5 penalty for each failure to include a dependent's TIN on the return.

How to get a number: Fill out a Form SS-5, *Application for Social Security Number*, at your local Social Security Administration office.

Uncle Sam and education

How The IRS Helps With Tuition Bills

Some expenses for sending your children to school are deductible. Other ordinarily nondeductible expenses may be turned into tax deductions or credits with the right planning.

Nursery-school and day-care expenses. Married couples can take the child-care credit if the children go to nursery school, day care, or are cared for at home by household help and both spouses work. The credit can be taken when only one spouse works in the following situations:

- When the other spouse is a full-time student for five months out of the year, or
- Where the other spouse is physically or mentally unable to care for him/herself.

Amount of the credit: The calculations are based on your qualifying child-care expenses and your Adjusted Gross Income (AGI). Generally, the higher your AGI, the lower the credit will be.

Special institutions. The cost of sending your child to a special school because he/she is mentally or physically handicapped can be deductible as a medical expense if the school has the resources to relieve the handicap. In addition to tuition, you can deduct related expenses such as transportation to and from the school, meals, and lodging if the child lives there.

Combined child-care credit plus special-school expenses. The expenses for special schooling may sometimes qualify for both a medical expense and the child-care credit. The same expense can't be used to take both, but if you use only part of your expenses to get the maximum child-care credit, you can apply the unused expenses for the medical deduction. Or, you may apply the whole expense toward your medical deduction. In most cases, if you have low medical expenses, applying the expenses to your child-care credit first will give you the lowest tax bill. Otherwise, figure out your taxes both ways to see what is most beneficial for you.

Tax-free dependent care. If your employer has a qualified dependent-care assistance program, you may be able to exclude from income up to $5,000 of dependent-care expenses paid by your employer on your behalf.

Education loans. Deductions for interest on personal loans were completely phased out by 1991. *Strategy:* You can convert this ordinarily nondeductible interest expense into a tax deduction by borrowing against your home and using the proceeds to pay for education. Interest is fully deductible on up to $100,000 in home-equity loans, second mortgages, etc.

Purchase an off-campus house or apartment for your child to live in. There are two ways of handling this:

Treating the house as your second home. The tax law allows you to fully deduct the interest on mortgages to acquire your principal home plus one second home. If you don't already own a second home, this purchase will provide your child with a free place in which to live and provide you with mortgage and property tax deductions. When your child finishes school, the house will most likely have appreciated in value and you will have a profit.

Treating the house as rental property. The rules are more complex and you should consider this strategy only after discussing it with your tax adviser.

■ You must charge your child and any roommates a fair market rent.

■ If you don't actively manage the house, you can't use any losses to offset your salary, dividend, interest, or capital-gain income. You can use losses only to offset other "passive-activity" income, such as income from tax shelters.

■ If you do actively manage the house, you are allowed to deduct maintenance, utilities, depreciation, property taxes, etc., from the rental income, and if you end up with a net loss, you can use it to offset your salary and other income. But you are allowed to deduct only up to $25,000 of loss if your AGI is $100,000 or less. The $25,000 maximum deduction is phased out if your AGI is between $100,001 and $150,000.

Source: Pamela J. Pecarich, partner, and tax managers Jeffrey S. Hillier and Steven M. Woolf, Coopers & Lybrand National Tax Services, 1800 M St. NW, Washington, DC 20036.

Special-School Benefit

Lawrence Fay had two children with language-learning disabilities. He deducted the extra cost of a language-development program at a special school, even though it had *no* psychologists or psychiatrists on staff and the special schooling had *not* been recommended by a doctor. *Tax Court:* The disabilities were real, and the school's teachers had been trained to deal with them. The benefit to the children was so obvious that a doctor's recommendation was not necessary.

Source: *Lawrence F. Fay,* 76 TC 408.

Special-School Risk

If you send your child to a special school for psychological reasons, be sure to choose the *right* school. Otherwise your medical deduction could be disallowed. *Recent case:* A psychiatrist recommended that a child attend a boarding school. The IRS refused to allow the parent to take a medical deduction because the school was not a "special" school, and the curriculum didn't deal with the child's problem in any way.

Source: *Jose F. Pazos,* TC Memo 1987-131.

Tax Trap For Scholarship Winners

Students who are attending school with scholarship aid may be hit with an unexpected tax bill.

New law: Under Tax Reform, scholarships are tax-free only to the extent that they're used for tuition, fees, books, course materials, supplies, and other items that are directly connected to education. Any amounts given for room, board, and personal expenses are taxable. For students who aren't candidates for college degrees, the news is worse. All scholarships and fellowships are fully taxable.

Recordkeeping: Students should keep records *and* receipts for all money spent on tuition, university fees, books, school supplies, and the like. It is up to the student to prove how much of the scholarship went for these purposes and how much, if any, went for personal living expenses.

Another trap: If the student is required to perform any services (teaching, for instance) as a condition of receiving the scholarship, some or all of the grant will be regarded as taxable compensation.

Financing Your Child's Education—Painlessly

If you're supporting a child in college and need to liquidate securities to do so, consider making a gift of the securities to the child and then having the child sell the securities. The profit on those securities is taxed to the child at the child's rate, not yours, which is probably higher.

For example, let's say you're in the 28% bracket and your child needs $30,000 to pay college expenses. You give him/her a gift of securities that had cost you $20,000, and he/she sells them for $30,000. The child would pay tax at 15% on the $10,000 profit instead of your paying tax at 28%. This results in a saving of $1,300 (13% x $10,000).

Caution: Gift tax may be due on gifts worth more than $10,000 ($20,000, if given by a married couple).

Source: *New Tax Traps/New Opportunities,* by Edward Mendlowitz, CPA, Boardroom Special Report, Springfield, NJ 07081.

Defer College Loans

Students who have taken out a Graduate Student Loan (GSL) or Perkins Loan (previously called the National Direct Student Loan) after July 1, 1987, can defer loan payments for six months when they have, or adopt, a child.

For limitations and requirements, consult your loan agreement.

Source: Margaret Henry, policy and program-development division, the Department of Education.

Divorce, separation, and domestic disputes

Most Important Tax Considerations

There are usually four groups of people involved in a divorce—the husband, the wife, the children, and the IRS. It's very important to reduce the participation of the IRS. Extreme care must be taken when drafting separation and divorce agreements. *Points to consider:*

■ Alimony. By definition, payments can't be called alimony unless specified in a written agreement or court decree. In order for alimony to qualify as tax-deductible income to the person paying and taxable income to the recipient, it must consist of regular periodic payments of approximately equal amounts over a period of at least three years.

■ Child support. This is neither a tax-deductible expense for the payor nor taxable income for the payee.

■ Divisions of property. A division of property pursuant to a divorce settlement isn't subject to any tax. (But a later sale of the property may be taxable.)

■ Dependency exemption. Generally, the person who has custody of the children claims the dependency exemption. However, the divorce agreement can change this. Many divorcing couples are concerned not only with the amount of the exemption but also with the filing status of the parent claiming the exemption.

■ Separation before divorce. In certain instances, even though a divorce hasn't been completed, the parent with custody can file as an unmarried head of household.

■ Medical expenses. Sometimes the parent paying the medical expenses is not the custodial parent and doesn't claim the child as a dependent but *is* paying through a company medical reimbursement plan. That parent may still qualify for a reimbursement for the child's expenses if this is allowed by the plan.

Timing a divorce is crucial in tax planning. Let's say a couple separates and one spouse continues to pay the household expenses. If they divorce before the end of the year, they must file separate returns. In this case, the supporting spouse ends up with nondeductible costs, and the other spouse may have nontaxable income. *Advice:* Wait until the beginning of a new tax year to finalize a divorce.

Source: *New Tax Traps/New Opportunities,* by Edward Mendlowitz, CPA, Boardroom Special Report, Springfield, NJ 07081.

Easier Alimony Rules

A property settlement made after a divorce is not tax-deductible, but alimony payments are fully deductible. Tax Reform has made it easier to have your payments categorized as tax-deductible alimony. *Here's how:*

■ *The length of time* that alimony payments must continue has been shortened to three years after separation rather than six years after separation under the old law.

■ *The recapture rules,* which under old law penalized those who paid much larger amounts in the first year or years and smaller amounts in the last years, have been liberalized. The first-year payment can exceed the average of the second- and third-year payments by up to $15,000 under Tax Reform before the recapture rules come into play. The second-year payment can exceed the third-year payment by $15,000.

Domestic Dispute Turned Nightmare

When Biltmore Blackman was transferred to another state, his wife refused to go with him. Blackman had to go but came back on a holiday only to find that another man had moved in with his wife, and they were hosting an all-night party. When Blackman tried to break it up, he was thrown out of the house. The next day, Blackman waited until the house was empty, entered, put his wife's clothes on the stove, and burned them. But the fire got out of control and the house burned down. The insurance company refused to pay, so Blackman claimed a casualty-loss deduction. *Tax Court:* No deduction. You can't claim a casualty loss for burning your own house. *Said the judge:* "We refuse to encourage couples to settle their disputes with fire." *Adding insult to injury:* The court penalized Blackman for filing his return late.
Source: *Biltmore Blackman,* 88 TC No. 38.

Property-Settlement Trap

As part of a property settlement, a husband transferred US savings bonds to his ex-wife. The husband hadn't elected to report the bonds' interest annually, so tax was automatically deferred. (Owners of US savings bonds have the choice of reporting and paying tax on interest each year or waiting until the bond is cashed in.) *IRS ruling:* The husband has to pay tax on all interest that accrued from the time he purchased the bonds to the date he gave them to his ex-wife, even though he hadn't received any of the money.
Source: Revenue Ruling 87-112.

Filing As Head Of Household—Even When You're Not

Head-of-household rates are much lower than "married filing separately" rates. If you're married and have children, but lived apart from your spouse for the last six months of the taxable year, you may file as "head of household" if:

■ Your home was the principal abode for your dependent children for more than half of the year (the full year if the children are foster children).

■ You provided more than half the cost of supporting the household.

■ You or your spouse can claim your children as dependents.

If each spouse maintained a household for one or more dependent children, both would be eligible for head-of-household status. If only one qualifies, the other must file as "married filing separately." There's no rule for determining whether this would result in lower taxes than a joint return; that has to be calculated for each individual case.

Another consideration: You may file as "head of household" if you maintain a home for your dependent parent, even if the parent doesn't live with you.

Deductible Legal Fees

An ex-wife sued to upset what she felt was an unfair divorce decree and agreed to pay her lawyer 35% of what he recovered. Eventually she collected a $500,000 cash settlement and paid her lawyer about $200,000, which she deducted. *IRS objections:* The lawyer's fees were excessive—and in addition, legal fees related to a divorce are a nondeductible personal expense. *Tax Court:* The suit was brought to preserve the wife's right to a *taxable income* from investment properties held by her husband, so the legal expenses were deductible. Moreover, the legal fee was reasonable in that the case took three years of work, and the lawyer would have received nothing if he had lost.

Source: *Beth Van Sickle,* TC Memo 1986-538.

Ex-Wife's Pension

A retired serviceman and his wife divorced while living in a community-property state. The wife received a property interest in the serviceman's pension, and he was ordered to pay her $400 a month from it. *IRS ruling:* The serviceman does *not* have to include the $400 in his own income just because it is initially paid to him. Rather, the $400 is taxable to his ex-wife.

Source: IRS Letter Ruling 8734023.

Unpaid Loans And Divorce

Unpaid loans made by a wife to her husband were deductible as bad debts when he declared bankruptcy—after the couple were divorced. The loans were genuine loans, not gifts. The husband used the money in an unsuccessful business venture and had signed promissory notes for repayment.

Source: *June M. Rodgers,* TC Memo 1985-220.

Delinquent Parents, Beware

A state agency may now intercept tax refund checks owed to parents who are delinquent in child-support obligations. The state social service agency that requests the interception gets the check. When a delinquent father sued to get his refund, the District Court ruled that the refund-intercept program is proper and has been expressly authorized by Congress.

Source: *Richard Edward Larsen,* CD Utah, No. C86-90G.

Benefits of helping parents

Parents Supported By More Than One Child: Who Takes Deduction?

When brothers and sisters support a parent, plan things so that one of them can deduct the parent's medical expenses. *Here's how:*

File a multiple-support declaration (Form 2120). Where several people contribute, this form designates the one who can take the exemption. If they pay at least 10% each, but nobody gives as much as half, any *one* of them can take the exemption if the others agree. Each year a different member of the group can claim the exemption by changing the agreement.

Deduct Your Parents' Medical Costs

You may be supporting your parents by giving them money regularly to pay their bills, including medical expenses.

Suppose you're paying medical expenses for them and also providing half their support, but you can't claim them as dependents because their gross income exceeds IRS limits. You may be able to deduct your parents' medical expenses. The key is for you to pay these expenses directly. Of course, the amount you can deduct is subject to the limitations on your own medical-expense deductions.

Source: *New Tax Traps/New Opportunities,* by Edward Mendlowitz, CPA, Boardroom Special Report, Springfield, NJ 07081.

Family-Medical-Bill Loophole

John Ruch was able to deduct his mother's medical bills, even though he paid them with money that *she* had given him. *Court:* Ruch had received the money through a legal and binding gift from his mother. Since the money was legally his when he paid, he was entitled to the deduction.

Source: *John M. Ruch,* 718 F2d 719.

Shifting Capital Gains

Give appreciated securities to your parents instead of cash if you are supporting them. They can cash in the securities and pay tax on the appreciation in their low tax bracket. You'll avoid paying tax in your high tax bracket.

Caution: A large gain could push your parents into a higher bracket. Of course, if you and your parents are in the same tax bracket, this ploy won't help you (nor will it hurt).

Relatives, in-laws, and the IRS

Buying Relatives' Investment Losses

If you are a high-bracket taxpayer and have a relative with little or no taxable income, consider taking advantage of a tax-law provision that allows you, in effect, to acquire your immediate relatives' deductible losses.

How it works: If a member of your immediate family sells property to you at a loss, that loss can't be deducted. But when you turn around and sell that property, you don't have to pay tax on any gain unless the gain is more than your family member's loss. Even then, only the portion of the gain that exceeds the previous loss is taxable.

Example: John White's mother is very ill. She has some income from dividends and a modest pension. But her deductible medical expenses are so high that her taxable income is zero. Her portfolio includes 100 shares of Consolidated Conglomerate that she bought at $35 a share. The current price is $11. If Mrs. White sells on the open market, she'll have a $2,400 loss that won't save her a penny in taxes. If John buys the stock, he can hold on to it until the price recovers. And although he bought the shares at $11, he won't have a taxable gain until the stock hits $35 again.

Added twist: John can give his mother a note for the purchase price of the stock with a reasonable interest rate. The money can help defray Mrs. White's medical costs.

Who can do it: This special rule applies to any transaction between you and your parents, grandparents, children, grandchildren, brother, sister, or any corporation in which you own more than 50% (by value) of the shares.

Your In-Laws Can Cut Your Tax Bill

If you've suffered a loss on an investment property, you can't deduct it while keeping the property in the family by selling it to a spouse, brother, sister, parent, grandparent, child, or grandchild. It doesn't matter if the sale is perfectly legitimate. The Tax Code prohibits any loss deduction from a sale to one of these relatives.

Loophole: The Tax Code does *not* consider in-laws to be relatives under this rule. So don't sell to your son or daughter—sell instead to your son- or daughter-in-law (or some other in-law). You'll keep the property in the family and get a deduction too.

Nondeductible Support Costs

Melvin Krause's son Peter was an avid golfer who decided to turn pro after graduating from college. Melvin supported Peter financially for five years while Peter tried to establish himself as a golfer, and Melvin deducted the costs he incurred. Peter never paid any money back to his father. *Tax Court decision:* Melvin never had any realistic chance of making a profit from the arrangement. Therefore, he could *not* deduct the support costs as either a business or an investment expense. The payments were simply made to support a family member and were a nondeductible personal expense.

Source: *Melvin L. Krause,* TC Memo 1987-193.

Your spouse and your business

Hiring Your Spouse

Suppose you hire your spouse to work in your unincorporated business. The deduction you claim and the income your spouse reports will offset each other, so you may get no income tax savings from hiring your spouse if you file a joint return. But there are *other* advantages:

■ You can establish benefits programs for your business—such as a Keogh or medical reimbursement plan—and have your spouse receive benefits through them. Of course, benefit-plan costs are deductible.

■ The salary earned by your spouse may entitle him/her to make a deductible IRA contribution of up to $2,000.

Sharing The Business With A Spouse

A dentist started his practice as a professional corporation and, later, formed a service corporation with his wife to hold title to his assets. The IRS said the service corporation had no business purpose and refused to recognize it. *Tax Court:* The IRS had to recognize the service corporation. There was a legitimate business purpose for it because under state law, a wife wasn't allowed to own stock in a professional corporation. The only way he could share the business with her was by forming the service corporation.

Source: *Cecil D. Rhoads,* TC Memo 1987-335.

Spouse's Salary Trap

A wife worked for her husband 30–35 hours a week. The husband gave her a W-2 showing wages, and he listed the amount as a business expense on his tax return. However, he never made any actual payment to his wife. Instead, he deposited the entire business income into their joint bank account. *IRS ruling:* Wages are not wages unless *actually* paid. Depositing funds in a joint account is not payment. Therefore, the wife had no wages and was not entitled to open an IRA.

Source: IRS Letter Ruling 8707004.

Spouse-Employment Trap

A CPA runs his accounting practice as a proprietorship and employs his wife as an office assistant. He deducts her salary as a business expense, but he does not make direct salary payments to her. Instead, he keeps a joint checking account with his wife, treats some of the funds in the account as being hers, and lets her withdraw them to pay personal expenses. He has never issued 1099 or W-2 forms to his wife. *IRS ruling:* The wife's salary is *not* deductible because the CPA has never treated her as an employee by making separate salary payments, keeping formal records of hours worked, or filing W-2s or other employment-related documents.
Source: IRS Letter Ruling 8753003.

IRS suspects gift-givers

Gift-Tax-Avoidance Scheme Backfires

Every taxpayer has the right to take advantage of favorable tax laws and interpretations. The courts have made it clear, though, that taxpayers can't avoid the *substance* of the law by utilizing loopholes in its technical *form*. A recent IRS ruling illustrates this fact.

Two brothers—call them Pat and Mike—wanted to give money to their children. Pat had two, Mike three. Tax law allows married couples to make tax-free gifts of up to $20,000 per person per year to anyone they choose. So Pat and his wife gave $20,000 to each of their two children and each of Mike's three. Mike and his wife did the same. And Mike and his wife also gave $20,000 to Pat and his wife.

Net result: Pat and his wife gave $80,000 ($100,000 to the children, less the $20,000 they received from Mike and his wife). Mike and his wife gave $120,000 ($100,000 to the children, plus $20,000 to Pat and his wife). Each child received $40,000. But no single gift was more than $20,000, so the form of the law was complied with, and the gifts were tax-free. Or so they thought.

The IRS thought differently. *IRS analysis:* The economic result ("substance") of all the transactions was that Pat and his wife made gifts of $80,000, and each of their two children received $40,000. Mike and his wife made gifts of $120,000, and each of their three children received $40,000. The $20,000 gift from Mike and his wife to Pat and his wife was obviously intended to compensate for the extra $20,000 Pat had to lay out because his brother had one more child than he did.

Mistaken Gift

A mother sold land to her sons at what she believed to be the property's fair market value. She didn't realize that she had actually sold it to them for less than half of its fair market value. *Tax Court:* Mother had to pay gift tax *plus* a penalty for failure to file gift-tax returns...*plus* the negligence penalty. Even though she had an attorney, the responsibility to file was hers and she had to pay.

Source: *Katherine Bergeron,* TC Memo 1986-587.

5

TAX LOOPHOLES

EVERYTHING THE LAW ALLOWS

Executive Tax Know-How

All about company cars

Deduction-Limit Traps

When a company provides an automobile for an executive, it must keep very detailed records concerning business use of the vehicle in order to prevent the car's value from being included in the executive's income. Methods used by some companies in the past to address these recordkeeping requirements haven't worked as well since Tax Reform. *Examples:*

■ Giving an executive an *auto allowance* that is included in his/her income. The executive then deducts the business use of the car on his *personal* return.

■ Providing the executive with a company-owned car, but including its *full* value in his/her income. The executive deducts business use of the car on his personal return.

Snag: Tax Reform upset both these alternatives. Under Tax Reform, business expenses cannot be deducted on a personal return, except to the extent that they *exceed* 2% of Adjusted Gross Income (AGI).

Thus, an executive who receives a *car allowance* will have to pay tax on some of it, even if it is used *entirely* to pay business costs...And an executive who reports a *company car* in income will have to pay tax on some of its value, even if it's used only for business.

What to Do

With smart planning, it is possible for executives to avoid the tax cost of the 2%-of-AGI limit, whether the company is subsidizing an executive's use of his own car or providing a car to him outright. *How to do it:*

Convert a car allowance into a reimbursement program. The difference between an allowance and a reimbursement is that a reimbursement is made for *specified* expenses. The executive must give the company an *itemized* report of his/her business driving—including mileage, tolls, parking fees, and the cost of oil and gas—and receive payment either for actual costs or at a rate not exceeding IRS allowance per mile.

Benefit: The payment to the executive is neither included in his income nor deducted on his return, so the 2%-of-AGI limit is avoided. *Danger:* Many companies that say they have reimbursement programs are in fact providing allowances to their executives, because the payments made to them are not based on sufficiently itemized expense reports. Such programs are now subject to IRS scrutiny.

Any company that provides regular payments on a periodic basis *without* checking current expense reports falls into this category. So does any firm that provides a per-day or per-mile travel allowance that lumps together driving costs with estimated amounts for such other expenses as meals and lodging. *Important:* Establish itemized expense reporting and reimbursement procedures now.

Include only part of the value of a company-owned car in the executive's income. The key is for the *company* to make an allocation of auto use for business and personal purposes. Only personal use of the car is included in the executive's income. Since business use of the car is not reported, the executive does not need to take an offsetting deduction, and again the 2%-of-AGI limit is avoided.

Extra benefits: When an executive is provided with a company-owned car, the firm doesn't have to bother making periodic expense reimbursements—so bookkeeping is simplified. And the company can also claim depreciation deductions for the vehicle. But *accurate records* documenting the amount of auto use allocated for business and personal purposes are a *must.*

Two Ways to Keep Records

■ The company can set up its own recordkeeping system for each car—for example, by requiring that an auto diary be kept for each vehicle.

■ The company can require those using company cars to file written statements saying that *they* are keeping records sufficient to document the cars' business use. The company then avoids these recordkeeping duties. However, an executive who signs such a statement but doesn't keep adequate records may be liable to the IRS for negligence penalties.

Source: Pamela Pecarich, partner, and Steven Woolf, Lynn Hogan, and Jeffrey Hillier, managers, Coopers & Lybrand, 1800 M St. NW, Washington, DC 20036.

Sheriff's Car

A deputy sheriff is required to be on call to respond to emergencies 24 hours a day. He is provided with a clearly marked sheriff's vehicle and required to keep it at home so that he can respond to official calls in it. He is prohibited from making personal use of the car, except that he is *required* to commute to his regular place of work in it. *IRS ruling:* An employer-provided car for commuting normally would be a taxable fringe benefit. But here the car is *tax-free,* since the sheriff's personal use of the car has a law-enforcement purpose.

Source: IRS Letter Ruling 8725053.

Drive The Company Car Tax-Free—Almost

Business owners can drive the company car until its cost has been fully depreciated and then switch to keep it for personal use *without* tax liability. The car will not become taxable until it is sold. At that time, there will be a taxable gain to the extent that the sale price exceeds the depreciated basis in the car—that is, the original cost of the car reduced by the depreciation deductions that were claimed.

Business Use Of Your Car

If you use your car less than 50% of the time for business, you can't deduct accelerated (ACRS) depreciation. You can use only the straight-line method of depreciation, writing off the same amount each year.

If you use the car more than 50% for business, you can use accelerated depreciation. However, you are limited in the amount you can deduct for depreciation, as follows, for cars placed in service in 1995: First year, $3,060; second year, $4,900; third year, $2,950; each succeeding year, $1,775. Any depreciation not deducted in one year can be carried forward indefinitely until the entire cost is recovered. Obviously, the deduction pertains only to the business percent of use. For example, if you use your car 80% for business in the first year after buying it, you can deduct $2,448 (80% × $3,060).

You must keep accurate records of the business use of your car. If you don't, expect the IRS to disallow any claims you make. Your records should indicate the mileage of each business trip and all other automobile expenses incurred, including repair bills, tolls, and parking fees. Ensure the accuracy of your records by keeping a diary of all your cash expenses.

Source: *New Tax Traps/New Opportunities* by Edward Mendlowitz, CPA, Boardroom Special Report, Springfield, NJ 07081.

Company-Car Loophole

Everybody seems to have found a way to get around the rules taxing employees for personal use of company-owned automobiles. One way to create a loophole for yourself—a loophole that will be difficult to plug—is to have a second car available for personal use. IRS agents have reported cases of taxpayers buying dinky used cars to substantiate the fact that they have another car available for weekend and after-hours use.

Source: Ms. X, Esq., a former IRS agent who is still well-connected.

Bad News For Executives

More than one out of 10 companies have eliminated company-provided executive cars. Half of the companies that still do provide the cars report it as extra income on employees' W-2 tax forms. *Reasons:* Tax Reform, high insurance costs, and cost-control programs.

Source: *Runzheimer* International Survey.

Cost Cutting

Don't buy company cars for sales and service people. Instead, pay these employees a monthly fee, plus 10¢ a mile, to use their own cars on the job. *Company benefits:* No outlay for extra maintenance and administrative personnel. No losses when used cars are sold. Better employee morale—almost all prefer to use their own cars, and there's no chance that a new employee will get stuck with an overused company auto. To make this system work, ensure that reimbursement for use of a private vehicle covers *all* the costs of operating it.

Source: Stephen Albano, president, Offtech, Inc., Malden, MA, quoted in *Inc.,* 38 Commercial Wharf, Boston, MA 02110.

Perks and fringe benefits

Exercising Incentive Stock Options

Incentive stock options are still attractive employee incentives. The option gives you the right to buy stock at less than the market price. You don't have to pay tax on your capital gain until you sell the stock. *Note:* Capital gain is the difference between the amount you paid for the stock and its fair market value at the time you sell it. The downside is that your *potential* gain, at the time you exercise the option and buy the stock, may be subject to the Alternative Minimum Tax (AMT).

There's a way to decide how much stock to exercise and not subject yourself to the Alternative Minimum Tax. This amount is the point at which the Alternative Minimum Tax would equal the regular tax. *Here's an example:*

Let's say your regular tax is $20,000 and the Alternative Minimum Tax is $9,000. Assume that you have options for 100,000 shares of stocks that were issued at $1 but are now worth $3. You have a potential $200,000 profit. The increment in value is treated as a tax-preference item, and you must determine how much additional tax you would pay on this income. To do this, divide the total of the difference between the regular tax and the Alternative Minimum Tax by the difference in tax rates. In this case, the difference is $20,000 minus $9,000, or $11,000. Divide that by 26% (the AMT flat tax of 26% minus the percent of increase in the regular tax rate, which is 0% since a preference item doesn't increase your regular tax rate). The result is approximately $42,308 in tax-preference income. You can then exercise enough of the options to add up to a tax-preference income of $42,308 and not subject yourself to any additional tax.

If, on the other hand, you exercise all options in one year, you'll have a tax-preference item of $200,000 to be added to your income tax. This will result in an additional tax of $28,000 ($48,000 AMT minus the $20,000 regular tax). In this case, by timing your exercise of stock options, you'd save $28,000 in taxes.

Source: *New Tax Traps/New Opportunities* by Edward Mendlowitz, CPA, Boardroom Special Report, Springfield, NJ 07081.

100% Deductible Business Meals

Company dining rooms, employee cafeterias, and other "eating facilities" operated by an employer for employees are not subject to the 50% limit on business meal deductions if the facility...
- Is located on the business premises of the employer, and
- Brings in revenue that normally equals or exceeds its direct operating costs, and
- Does not discriminate in favor of highly compensated employees.

Source: New IRC Section 274 (n)(2): Amended IRC Section 132(e)(2).

Beat The Limit On Employee Business Expenses

Employee business expenses—including the cost of business meals—are deductible only to the extent that their total, when combined with other miscellaneous deductions, exceeds 2% of Adjusted Gross Income (AGI). This *eliminates* the deduction for many employees. For example, someone with an AGI of $60,000 gets no deduction for the first $1,200 of such costs.

Planning strategy: A deduction for these kinds of items can be preserved by having the company pay for them through an expense account or other reimbursement program. That's because a corporation *can* deduct these kinds of costs as a business expense without reference to the 2%-of-AGI rule. (The company's deduction for business meals and entertainment is, however, limited to 50% of the cost.)

Business meals: Under Tax Reform, no deduction is allowed for the so-called *quiet* business meal—one that furthers good business relations but doesn't involve business directly. To get a 50% deduction for a meal, one must prove not only its cost but also its *specific* business purpose.

Why Reduce Your AGI?

Most unreimbursed employee business expenses are deductible only to the extent that they exceed 2% of your Adjusted Gross Income. However, if your employer pays these expenses, you're not required to report them or pay taxes on them.

One way to take advantage of this benefit is to ask your employer to use a certain amount of your salary to furnish you with a perk or fringe benefit that will include these costs, instead of giving the money directly to you. You've now reduced your taxable income.

Caution: By reducing your gross pay, you risk reducing your pension-plan contributions and Social Security coverage.

Source: *New Tax Traps/New Opportunities* by Edward Mendlowitz, CPA, Boardroom Special Report, Springfield, NJ 07081.

Better Than A Raise

Employee business expenses, along with the cost of investment advice, tax preparation fees, and other miscellaneous items (such as the cost of subscribing to business or investment publications) are deductible, under Tax Reform, only to the extent that their total exceeds 2% of Adjusted Gross Income.

When executives have large unreimbursed business expenses, they may do better to negotiate with their employers for an increase in their reimbursements, instead of a raise. If the executive gets a raise, it will be taxed, while the executive will lose at least part of the deduction for the unreimbursed expenses. However, an increase in reimbursements will be tax-free and completely cover the cost of expenses.

Well-known and hidden deductions

Hidden Deductions In Unreimbursed Business Expenses

If you have any out-of-pocket expenses in connection with your employment, and you don't get reimbursed for them, you may be entitled to deduct them to the extent that they exceed 2% of your Adjusted Gross Income. These expenses include well-known deductible costs, such as those incurred for business entertainment or travel, and business use of your car or home computer. They also include other, not-so-obvious expenses, such as the costs of an attaché case, a special gold or sterling silver pen or pencil set, or pictures to decorate your office. Stationery, office supplies, business cards, and greeting cards to business associates also fall into this category, as do books, subscriptions to professional publications and business newspapers, and dues for professional associations, societies, or unions.

Source: *New Tax Traps/New Opportunities* by Edward Mendlowitz, CPA, Boardroom Special Report, Springfield, NJ 07081.

Business Use Of Your Home Computer

Do you have a personal computer in your home? In order to deduct accelerated (ACRS) depreciation of a home computer, you must use it at least 50% for business. Calculate the amount of your deduction by multiplying the percent of business use by the ACRS depreciation rate. Or you can use the Section 179 write-off, which is $17,500 in the first year, depending on several variables. (Check this out with your tax adviser.)

If you use your personal computer less than 50% for business, you can take only straight-line depreciation. *Caution:* Business use doesn't include use for investment purposes.

If you claim a deduction for your home computer as a requirement of your employment, you must prove that you maintain it at the request of your employer.

Source: *New Tax Traps/New Opportunities* by Edward Mendlowitz, CPA, Boardroom Special Report, Springfield, NJ 07081.

Not To Be Overlooked

■ *Client pass-throughs.* The party that *pays* a meal expense is subject to the 50% deduction limit. Thus, if a company pays for a meal on behalf of a client, and bills the client for the meal, the client may deduct only 50% of its cost. But if the client paid only a general fee for services, it could deduct the whole fee as a business expense, while the company would have to include the whole fee in income and be able to deduct only 50% of the meal costs it incurred. Here the billing of *itemized* meal costs to the client is the key, and this item should be considered when drafting client agreements.

■ *Company parties.* Holiday parties, summer outings, and other traditional company gatherings that take place primarily for the benefit of the company's employees are *not* subject to the 50% limit on meal deductions.

Source: Pamela Pecarich, partner, and Steven Woolf, Lynn Hogan, and Jeffrey Hillier, managers, Coopers & Lybrand, 1800 M St. NW, Washington, DC 20036.

How To Audit-Proof Your Expense Diary

Audit-proofing your business-expense diary is a very simple matter. Just include answers to each of these questions. (An easy way to remember the questions—the four W's and $):

■ Who was with you?
■ Where were you?
■ Why were you there?
■ When were you there?
■ How much money did you spend?

Remember, you need a receipt for all expenses that exceed $25. Otherwise, no deduction will be allowed.

Source: *New Tax Traps/New Opportunities* by Edward Mendlowitz, CPA, Boardroom Special Report, Springfield, NJ 07081.

Salaries, bonuses, and other fees

Reasonable Salary

Two individuals formed a printing corporation and because of their hard work and expertise, it was financially successful. They each paid themselves salaries, bonuses, and pension and profit-sharing payments of more than $400,000 for a two-year period. *IRS:* The payments were unreasonable and were really disguised dividends. *Tax Court:* A study of executive compensation showed that these payments were reasonable and routine in the printing industry.

Source: *Contract Construction Co.,* TC Memo 1987-476.

Delayed Bonus

In January of one year, an executive received a $20,000 bonus for work done the previous year, at the end of which he had retired. *IRS ruling:* The bonus will be treated as compensation to the executive for *this* year. Thus, the executive can use the bonus to make a deductible IRA contribution this year, even though he won't actually perform any work during the year.

Source: IRS Letter Ruling 8707051.

Deductible Profits

A company paid its owner an annual bonus based on net profits. It never paid any dividends, and including bonus, the owner's annual pay totaled as much as $270,000. But the IRS said that the bonuses really *were* dividends and disallowed the company's deduction for them. *Court:* The bonuses were part of a reasonable *salary* arrangement and were *fully* deductible. *Key facts:* The owner had worked up to 16 hours a day in the business over 10 years, personally making it a success. Thus, his salary was well-earned. Moreover, money that could have been used to pay dividends had been reinvested to fund profitable expansion.

Source: *Gerrit Vanderpol,* TC Memo 1987-555.

Owner's Trap

Two equal owners of a very profitable company took large salaries that were equal in size and never had the company pay any dividends. *Court:* The fact that the owners took salaries that were always in direct proportion to their shareholdings indicated that they were taking extra-large salaries, *instead* of dividends. Thus, the company lost its deduction for a portion of the owners' salaries—since dividends are not deductible.

Source: *Owensby & Kritikos, Inc.,* CA-5, No. 86-4073.

Ways To Take Money Out Of The Company

The tax law creates ways for business owners and top executives to be paid by the company in tax-advantageous ways.

■ Interest-free loans can be made from the company to owners and top executives. Loans that have been properly drawn up have repeatedly withstood IRS challenges. *Key:* You must be able to show that the loan is legitimate. So agree to a reasonable repayment schedule and observe all the legal formalities.

■ Pension pay-outs. The new tax law provides that pensions need not be taken right after retirement. The first pension payments can safely be delayed until at least age 70. *Point:* Many executives remain active for some years after they retire. They may continue to do special tasks for the company or act as paid consultants for other businesses. These executives may not need their pension benefits right away. *Advantage of waiting:* The pension plan account continues to accrue earnings tax-free. So you receive greater benefits when you choose to take them. Review the company's pension plan to be sure it allows a delay in drawing benefits.

■ Deferred compensation. The company may not be able to afford a pension plan that covers all employees. But it may still want to provide retirement benefits for top executives. *To do it:* Set up a deferred compensation plan. This takes the form of a contractual commitment to pay top executives a certain amount after retirement. The payments are deductible by the company when made.

■ Stock appreciation rights. Rights may be suitable for some closely-held companies. *How they work:* The executive is treated as if he owned company stock. If the value of the stock goes up by a certain date, the executive receives a payment determined under a prearranged formula. The payment may be deducted by the company. *Advantages:* Managers get an incentive interest in the company that is similar to ownership. But the company avoids increasing the number of its shareholders. *Drawback:* Incentive amounts that accrue under the plan must be charged against corporate earnings, even before they are paid out. So reported earnings are reduced. If the company is sensitive about its reported earnings, this type of plan may be disadvantageous.

Source: Richard Reichler, principal, Ernst & Young, New York.

Business-travel loopholes

Vacation Costs As A Business Expense

Tax Reform has cracked down on many travel-related deductions. But there are still deductions you can take for travel, and you should not miss those that still apply.

Traveling for Business

Travel expenses. You can fully deduct the cost of getting to and from your destination on a trip made primarily for business reasons. This expense remains fully deductible, even if you extend the trip for pleasure or take a side trip for pleasure. In addition, during the business part of your stay, you can deduct the cost of hotel, lodging, local transportation, and 50% of meals and business-related entertainment.

Example: You travel to New York City strictly for business reasons and decide to take a side trip for the weekend, vacationing at a sumptuous Long Island beach resort. The trip between New York City and home remains fully deductible, as long as you can prove you traveled there for business. But the cost of traveling between New York City and the resort is not deductible because that part of the trip is entirely for personal pleasure. Also, the related expenses of meals, lodging, and local transportation while at the beach resort are not a deductible business expense.

Mixing business with pleasure. The cost of traveling to and from your destination on a trip made primarily for vacation or pleasure isn't deductible, even if you conduct some business while on the trip. However, some of the other business-related expenses may be deductible.

Example: You go on a vacation to Florida, but while there you take a customer who lives in Florida out to lunch. Under Tax Reform, 50% of the meal expense is deductible if business was actually discussed during the meal. Be sure to include tax, tips, and parking-lot fees at the restaurant when calculating the 50%. The cost of traveling to the restaurant, if you take a taxi, for example, is 100% deductible.

Ship travel can be an asset on a combined business-vacation trip. *Reason:* Days spent in transit count as business days in the allocations formula. *Example:* A two-day business meeting in Paris is followed by a two-week European vacation. If you fly (one day each way), only 22% is deductible (two business days plus two days of travel out of a total of 18 days away). But if you sail (five days each way), 46% is deductible (two business days plus 10 days of travel out of a total of 26 days away).

Source: Edward Mendlowitz, partner, Mendlowitz Weitsen, CPAs, Two Pennsylvania Plaza, New York 10121.

Acceptable *Per Diem*

Is there an official rate of *per diem* meal expenses that the IRS accepts as reasonable while working away from home?

The IRS recognizes a standard *per diem* meal allowance equal to the greater of $26 to $38 depending on the location, or the rate allowed by the federal government to its employees in the locality where travel occurs.

When reimbursements exceed the *per diem*, an employee must report them in income and claim an offsetting travel-expense deduction, while maintaining all the records necessary to do so. But an employee who receives no more than the *per diem* allowance from his employer need not report it in income.

The *per diem* allowance can be used only by employees receiving reimbursements. Self-employed persons cannot use the allowance to get an automatic deduction for expenses.

Tax advantages in job loss

Tax-Free Severance Pay

In troubled economic times, even top executives sometimes lose their positions. In these circumstances, it is more important than ever that any severance or termination payments receive the most favorable tax treatment possible. *Key:* Severance pay is taxable as ordinary salary. But payments made to compensate the ex-employee for damages are tax-free.

The dismissed employee can bring suit against his former company in court, or before a federal agency (such as the Equal Employment Opportunity Commission), alleging that he suffered damages as a result of his wrongful dismissal. (The dismissal may have harmed his business or personal reputation, caused embarrassment, or resulted in physical or emotional harm.)

The objective: A settlement can be reached with the company that allocates part of the termination payment as compensation for harm. What would have been taxable severance pay is converted into tax-free damages. *Extra benefit:* The company can profit from this sort of agreement as well. Since it is paying its former employee in tax-free dollars, it may be able to negotiate a smaller settlement that gives the employee more in the end.

Severance-Pay Loophole

Under a termination-incentive program, an individual received a payment that was partly in lieu of his contractual right to receive 90 days' notice prior to termination. *IRS ruling:* The portion of the payment received in lieu of 90 days' notice is *not* considered to be a wage payment that is subject to Social Security taxes.
Source: IRS Letter Ruling 8808019.

Entertaining Between Jobs

A salesman who was between jobs could deduct the cost of entertaining customers. He was not in the selling business but was actively seeking another base from which to serve the *same* customers, the Tax Court held. It was important to retain the customers' goodwill.
Source: *Harold Haft,* 40 TC 2.

Deducting The Costs Of Looking For A Job

You can claim job-hunting costs as miscellaneous itemized deductions to the extent that they (and other miscellaneous deductions) exceed 2% of your Adjusted Gross Income. To be eligible for such deductions you must be looking for a job in your present line of work or in a related field. (You can claim these deductions even if you don't get a new job.) These costs include:

■ Expenses for preparing résumés and letters for prospective employers, including typing, printing, envelopes, and postage.

■ Fees to employment agencies, résumé consultants, recruiters, and career consultants.

■ Newspapers and trade magazines you buy for the job ads.

■ Cost of assembling portfolios of your work.

■ Transportation costs, such as cab fares to job interviews.

■ Telephone calls.

■ 50% of meals and entertainment expenses related to your job search.

■ Out-of-town travel expenses to look for a new job, including transportation, lodging, and 50% of meals and entertainment.

■ Fees for legal and accounting services or tax advice relating to employment contracts.

Source: Edward Mendlowitz, partner, Mendlowitz Weitsen, CPAs, Two Pennsylvania Plaza, New York 10121.

Dismissed-Executive Lawsuit

A dismissed executive sued his company over both his employment contract *and* the amount of money he was to be paid for stock held in the company. When the case was settled, he deducted his legal fees. *Claims Court:* The lawsuit involved both business interests and investment interests, so the legal costs had to be split. Only fees relating to the employment contract were deductible as a business expense. Fees related to the stock-valuation issue had to be added to the stock's cost and could be used only to reduce taxable gain when the stock was sold.

Source: *John P. McKeague,* Cl. Ct., No. 90-84T.

Responsibility of corporate officers

Officer Innocence

Jon Carpenter was a vice president and one-third shareholder in a company that failed to pay over-employment taxes starting in 1980. Late in that year, Carpenter was seriously injured in a car crash. The IRS ultimately held all of the shareholders *personally* liable for the unpaid taxes. *Court:* Carpenter was *not* liable for taxes incurred after his injury occurred because, from that point on, he was no longer actively involved in running the business.

Source: *Jon Carpenter,* CD CA, No. 85-1474-HLH-(Tx).

Officer Liability

When the Rock Furniture Company failed to pay taxes withheld from employee wages, the IRS held Nino Madia, an officer of the company, personally liable for them. As a result, Madia was forced into personal bankruptcy. *Court:* Madia still owed the taxes. Personal bankruptcy does not free a corporate officer from liability for a tax bill for unpaid employment taxes.

Source: *Nino Madia,* Bankr. NJ, Adv. No. 85-0084.

Beating The Rap

James Pearson was elected chairman of the board during a year in which the company failed to pay taxes withheld from employee wages. The IRS tried to hold Pearson *personally* liable for the unpaid taxes because he had access to the company's books and records and had the power to sign checks. *Court:* Pearson's authority to write checks did *not* make him responsible for the taxes. The fact was that Pearson was *not* active in the firm's daily management. His major concern was merely to find a replacement for the company's ailing president. Thus, he wasn't liable for the tax.

Source: *James H. Pearson,* ND Ala., No. CV 84-P-2885-W.

New-Owner Liability

New owners of a business can be ordered to pay for mistakes made by previous owners during changeover. A new ruling says that in such cases—where those making operational decisions may have little interest in the future of the operation—new owners are liable, unless customers are told about the ownership change. Even a clause in the sales contract specifically insulating the new owners from liability won't stand up in court.

Source: *Brown v. Galleria Area,* SC Texas, 5/18.

Big, big benefits in early retirement

Start Your Own Business With Accrued Pension

Employee Getum has "had it" working for his present boss. He wants out now. He has $100,000 coming from his employer's qualified plan, and he is entitled to and qualifies for lump-sum treatment. Getum learns that the tax bite on the $100,000, if distributed this year, would be $35,000; he needs $50,000 to finance his new business. What to do?

The steps would be as follows:

1. Getum forms a new corporation, Go-Getum Co.

2. Go-Getum Co. adopts a qualified profit-sharing plan.

3. The distribution—the full $100,000—from Getum's former employer's qualified plan is rolled over to the new Go-Getum plan.

4. The new plan would have a provision to allow loans to be made to participants in an amount not to exceed 50% of the participant's vested interest, or $50,000.

5. The new profit-sharing plan would loan $50,000 to Getum to be repaid over five years at 11% interest per annum.

Obviously, the documentation from the new plan itself, the plan administrator's minutes describing and approving the loan, and the note payable by Getum to the profit-sharing trust must be impeccable in every detail.

Source: Irving L. Blackman, partner, Blackman Kallick Bartelstein, 300 S. Riverside Plaza, Chicago 60606.

Pension Bigger Than Salary

A provision in ERISA (the 1974 pension law) makes it possible for a small, closely-held corporation to provide its older insiders, in a relatively short time, with pension benefits substantially larger than their compensation—and with the cost fully deductible by the corporation.

Example: A Mr. Smith, having elected early retirement from a major corporation, starts up his own consulting corporation. He brings his wife into the business as an assistant and has two part-time employees to help her with various chores. He puts his wife on the books for $6,000 a year, although she's worth more. Even though he considers increasing her pay, he has prudent misgivings, because her earnings will only add to the taxable income on their joint return.

Taking advantage of ERISA, Smith sets up a defined-benefit pension plan (where benefit payout is fixed) for his corporation. Under the so-called de minimis provision of ERISA, he can set his wife's defined benefit upon retirement at $10,000 a year—$4,000 more than her annual salary. She's able to escape the benefit limit of 100% of her annual salary because her salary is under $10,000.

To establish the $10,000 benefit, he must show actuarily what it would cost to provide her with a straight-life annuity of $10,000 a year at age 65. That's easy. All he has to do is ask a life insurance company how much such a policy could cost. *Answer:* $140,000 lump sum. Thus, if you figure an 8% annual interest, compounded, it works out that he must put away $10,000 a year for the 10 years—or a total of $100,000.

What we've done is provide her with a benefit worth $140,000, with $100,000 in tax-deductible dollars.

Another plus: If those dollars had been paid to Mrs. Smith as straight compensation (and assuming that Mr. and Mrs. Smith filed joint returns and were in the 40% tax bracket, including federal, state, and local taxes), she would have paid out $40,000 in taxes over the 10 years of employment by the corporation. And that means she'd end up with only $60,000 after 10 years of working—plus interest.

IRS supports employee education

Education Tax Breaks

When you take courses because they are required by your employer to keep your job or because you want to maintain or improve your present job skills, you can deduct tuition, books, supplies, and fees. Transportation expenses, including parking and tolls, are also deductible.

Tax Reform limit: Educational expenses that you pay are a miscellaneous, itemized deduction. Tax Reform allows you to deduct the portion of your total miscellaneous expenses only to the extent that they exceed 2% of your Adjusted Gross Income.

Tax-free education. When your employer has a qualified educational assistance program and pays your tuition bill for you, of course you can't deduct that amount from your taxes. But don't include that reimbursement in your taxable income either. You are allowed to exclude employer-paid tuition of up to $5,250 from your income under a special provision of the tax law. It's treated the same way as any other tax-free fringe benefit.

Source: Pamela J. Pecarich, partner, and tax managers Jeffrey S. Hillier and Steven M. Woolf, Coopers & Lybrand National Tax Services, 1800 M St. NW, Washington, DC 20036.

Deductible Course Fees

A financial consultant enrolled in an advanced-degree program concentrating in taxes and financial planning. He was not required to take the courses for work. *IRS ruling:* The consultant could deduct the cost of tuition, books, and related items as a job-connected educational expense because the degree program will enhance the skills needed in his current job.

Source: IRS Letter Ruling 8706048.

6

TAX LOOPHOLES

EVERYTHING THE LAW ALLOWS

Business Tax
Savvy

Loopholes in setting up a business

Leasing Assets To Your Own Corporation

The fact that the corporate form is selected as the basic means of conducting a business enterprise does not mean that all of the physical components of the enterprise need be owned by the corporation. Indeed, there may be legal, tax, and personal financial planning reasons for not having the corporation own all the assets to be used in the business.

Whether the corporation is to be the continuation of a sole proprietorship or partnership or a wholly new enterprise, decisions can be made about which assets owned by the predecessor or acquired for use in the corporation are to be owned by the corporation and which assets are to be made available to the corporation through a leasing or other contractual arrangement.

For the assets that go to the corporation, decisions must be made about how they are to be held and on what terms they are to be made available to the corporation.

There are several possible choices. *The assets may be owned by:*
- An individual shareholder or some member of his family;
- A partnership, limited or general, in which family members participate; or
- A trust for the benefit of family members.

A separate corporation is still another possibility, but the risk of being considered a personal holding company and incurring penalties due to passive income (including rent and royalties) may make this impractical.

Normally a leasing arrangement is used in order for the assets to be made available for corporate use. Assuming that the rental is fair, it would be deductible by the corporation and taxable to the lessor. Against the rental income, the lessor would have possible deductions for interest paid on loans financing the acquisition of the asset, depreciation, maintenance and repairs, insurance and administrative costs.

These deductions might produce a tax-free cash flow for the lessor. When depreciation and interest deductions begin to run out, a high-tax-bracket lessor might find that he/she is being taxed at too high a rate on the rental income. At this point, he may transfer the leased property to a lower-tax-bracket family member.

He might also consider a sale of the property to his corporation. This sale would serve to extract earnings and profits from the corporation at favorable tax rates. At the same time, it would give the corporation a higher tax basis for the asset than it had in the hands of the lessor, thus increasing the corporation's depreciation deductions. This, of course, would reduce the corporation's tax liabilities and benefit the shareholders—the lessor included, if he/she is a shareholder.

How To Deduct Start-Up Costs Sooner

Avoid being forced to capitalize and amortize start-up costs over a five-year period. The trick is to get "in business" quickly. You can claim business deductions or losses only when you're "in business." (You're considered to be "in business" when you're trying to get sales.) Any subsequent expenses you incur will be to "expand" an existing business, and you can take full deductions for those items.

For example, let's say you want to open a sales organization. The start-up costs include getting products to sell and interviewing salespeople. If you can get one line, no matter how small, and make a few sales, you're considered to be in business. Then you can spend time looking to expand into other products and to hire a sales force.

Source: *New Tax Traps/New Opportunities* by Edward Mendlowitz, CPA, Boardroom Special Report, Springfield, NJ 07081.

Incorporating A Business Tax-Free

You may have a sole proprietorship or partnership and reach a point in the growth of your business where you want to incorporate. There's a special provision in the Internal Revenue Code (Section 351) that enables a business to incorporate tax-free. The only requirement is that the people who own the business before the incorporation own at least 80% of the business after incorporation.

If you incorporate in this way, the IRS can't recapture depreciation deductions or investment credits (if still applicable). If the assets are subsequently disposed of, the recaptures will take place at the corporate and *not* at the individual level, even though you may have initially received the benefit from the investment credit or depreciation.

Source: *New Tax Traps/New Opportunities* by Edward Mendlowitz, CPA, Boardroom Special Report, Springfield, NJ 07081.

How To Set Up A Hobby As A Business

You can set up a hobby as a business and deduct your losses. However, you must be able to prove that the hobby is a for-profit business. If you realize some profit in at least three out of the most recent five consecutive years, it is presumed that the business is for profit. But even if you don't show a profit, you may be able to prove that the business is *intended* to make a profit.

To prove that you have a profit motive in conducting your business, keep detailed records. Present evidence of your advertising campaigns, attempts to generate new business, and sales analyses. It's not necessary to show that you run a big business, reaping huge profits, but only that you have genuine intentions of running the business in a businesslike way.

Source: *New Tax Traps/New Opportunities* by Edward Mendlowitz, CPA, Boardroom Special Report, Springfield, NJ 07081.

Best Way To Set Up A Family Business

A business can be organized as a corporation, a proprietorship, a partnership, or even a trust. Use combined forms of ownership to cut taxes.

Example:

■ Use a corporation to operate the business.

■ Have an individual, as sole proprietor, or a partnership own the machinery and equipment and rent it to the corporation.

■ Have an individual or partnership hold title to the real estate and rent it to the corporation.

■ Use a trust (for the benefit of the children of the owners) as a partner in the partnership (in either the equipment partnership or the real estate partnership or both).

This arrangement reaps some important tax benefits:

■ Tax losses are passed through to the high-tax-bracket owners. When partnerships begin producing income, transfer title to the low-bracket children for income-splitting purposes.

■ Income from the rental goes to the owners without dilution for corporate taxes.

■ Income to children aged 14 or older benefits from income-splitting.

The possibilities for combining the above are endless. Consider such additional entities as S corporations, multiple corporations, and multiple trusts.

Caution: The "passive-loss" rules, imposed by the Tax Reform Act of 1986, severely restrict the deductibility of many partnership losses, S corporation losses, and losses from rental property. Always check with a tax professional before deciding on the structure of your business.

When To Set Up A Venture Partnership

You may be asked to help friends or relatives start up a small business by providing the capital to finance the deal. Set up the business as a partial shelter for the amounts you invest. Uncle Sam helps you reduce the amount that you're investing by allowing you to deduct a large share of the losses. I call such a deal a venture partnership. *Here's how it works:*

You become the limited partner. As such, you're entitled to deduct a very large share of the losses, up to 99%, since you're putting in all the money. At the point that the business turns around, the percentages drop. You might receive 50% of the profits after getting your money back, and the person you helped also receives 50% of the profits. Now both of you can share in the profits as partners, but at the outset you get the benefit of a larger share of the losses. *Caution:* These write-offs are subject to the passive-activity-loss rules.

Source: *New Tax Traps/New Opportunities* by Edward Mendlowitz, CPA, Boardroom Special Report, Springfield, NJ 07081.

Best Tax Shelter In America

Tax Reform has taken *dead aim* at tax shelters. It's no longer possible to offset your salary or investment income with paper losses generated by passive investments in oil wells, real estate developments, etc. Neither is it possible to cut the family's tax bill greatly by shifting investment income to children who are under age 14.

But even under Tax Reform, the *best* tax shelter *still remains*. With it you can generate large paper losses, claim deductions for personal or hobby-like expenses, and legally shift income to your low-tax-bracket minor children.

The best tax shelter is a sideline business.

Here's how a sideline business can be used to get big tax-shelter-type deductions, along with *winning examples* of taxpayers who have *already done it...*

Income-Shifting

Under Tax Reform, investment income exceeding $1,300 for a child under age 14 is taxed at the rate paid by the child's parents. But this rule does *not* apply to the *earned* income of a child.

Result: When a child works for a parent's sideline business, earnings are taxed at the child's own *low* tax rate. Since the parent *deducts* the salary paid to the child as a business expense, the family's total tax bill is lowered by the difference between the parent's *high* tax rate and the *low* or *zero* rate on the child's salary.

Of course, this income-shifting technique is also available for children *over* age 14 and other family members. And even greater tax benefits can be obtained when family members use the salary you pay to make deductible IRA retirement contributions, or when the business pays for deductible benefits.

The only rule that governs paying salaries to family members is that they must actually *earn* their salaries. *Salary deductions have been allowed when:*

■ A doctor paid his four children, ages 13 to 16, to answer telephone calls, take messages, and prepare insurance forms.
Source: *James Moriarity,* TC Memo 1984-249.

■ The owner of a rental property hired his teenage sons to maintain and clean the building.
Source: *Charles Tschupp,* TC Memo 1963-98.

■ A business owner hired his wife to act as the company's official hostess.
Source: *Clement J. Duffey,* 11 AFTR2d 1317.

What Qualifies

A part-time activity can easily qualify as a business. The only requirement is that you operate your activity with the *objective* of making a profit. You *don't* actually have to make a profit, nor do you have to *expect* to make a profit in the near future. *Examples:*

Home Deductions

A major benefit of running a sideline business out of your home is the possibility of claiming a *home-office deduction*. This entitles you to deduct expenses that were formerly personal in nature, such as rent, utility, insurance, and maintenance costs attributable to the office. *Even better:* You can *depreciate* the part of your home that's used as an office, getting large paper deductions that cost you *nothing* out of pocket.

To qualify for the deduction, you must have a part of your home that's used *exclusively* for business and is the *primary place* where you conduct the sideline business. *Winning examples:*

■ A doctor who owned and managed rental properties to get extra income could deduct one bedroom in his two-bedroom apartment as an office.

Source: *Edwin R. Cruphey,* 73 TC 766.

■ A woman who did economic consulting work out of a home office could deduct it, even though her husband, a famous newspaper editor, used the *same* office for nondeductible activities. The Tax Court did *not* reduce her deduction because her husband shared the office.

Source: *Max Frankel,* 82 TC 318.

Big Dollar Deductions

Tax Reform prohibits taxpayers from offsetting their salary and investment income with losses from businesses in which they participate as *passive* investors (as shareholders or limited partners without management duties).

But if you actively manage *your own* sideline business, it's *still* possible to claim big loss deductions. *Important:* Tax losses do *not* necessarily mean *cash* losses. Items such as depreciation on cars, equipment, and real estate can result in *deductible* tax losses while the business is earning a cash-flow *profit*.

A sideline business is presumed to have a profit objective if it has reported a profit in three out of five years (two out of seven years for horse breeders). But such a business may be deemed to have a profit objective, even after reporting *many* years of continuous losses. *Winning examples:*

■ A real estate operator tried to develop and market an automatic garage door opener. He was entitled to deduct $355,000 over 11 years because he had made a sincere effort to sell the door openers.

Source: *Frederick A. Purdy,* TC Memo 1967-82.

■ A horse farm incurred 20 straight years of losses totaling over $700,000. During the *next* seven years, it lost another $119,000, but in two of those years it had profits totaling $17,000. Since the two-out-of-seven-years test had been met, the farm was ruled to be a profit-motivated business, and *all* of its losses were deductible.

Source: *Hunter Faulconer,* 748 F2d 890.

■ A corporate vice president and management expert ran a breeding farm as a sideline and lost $450,000 over 12 years. The loss was deductible because evidence indicated that it often takes 8 to 12 years to establish an acceptable bloodline for the animals involved.

Source: *Lawrence Appley,* TC Memo 1979-433.

Start-Up Tactic

When starting a *new* sideline business, you can protect your deductions by electing to have the IRS postpone its examination of your business status until after you've been operating for *four* years (six years in the case of a horse farm). You'll be able to treat your sideline as a business during that period, even if it earns *continuous* losses. But if you can't demonstrate a profit objective at the end of that period, you'll owe back taxes. Make the election by filing IRS Form 5213, *Election to Postpone Determination That Activity Is for Profit.*

Winning examples:

■ Eugene Feistman, a probation officer, collected and traded stamps for many years. The Tax Court initially refused to let him deduct his costs, saying his collecting was merely a hobby. So he filed a business registration certificate with the local government, opened an account that allowed him to make sales by charge card, set up an inventory, and started keeping good business records concerning purchases and sales.

New ruling: Now Feistman *could* deduct his costs because he was operating in a businesslike manner. The Tax Court allowed him to deduct $9,000 over two years.
Source: *Eugene Feistman,* TC Memo 1982-306.

■ Gloria Churchman, a housewife, admitted that she painted for pleasure, but she was also able to show that she had made a serious effort to sell her works at shows and galleries. The Tax Court allowed her to deduct her expenses and losses, *including* the cost of a studio in her home.
Source: *Gloria Churchman,* 68 TC 696.

■ Melvin Nickerson, an executive who lived in the city, bought a farm and began renovating it on weekends. He intended to retire to it in the future. Although Nickerson didn't expect to make a profit from the farm for another *10 years,* the Court of Appeals allowed him to deduct his renovation costs right away. It said that his expectation of future profits, combined with the real work he put in, sufficed to justify a deduction now.
Source: *Melvin Nickerson,* 700 F2d 402.

■ Bernard Wagner, an accountant, fancied himself a songwriter and music promoter. He hired a band, rehearsed it, booked it, and copyrighted the songs he wrote. Although his chances of success were slight, he *intended* to succeed, so the Tax Court allowed him to deduct his costs and losses.
Source: *Bernard Wagner,* TC Memo 1983-606.

■ J. V. Keenon bought a house, moved into it, then rented an apartment in the house to his own daughter. The Tax Court agreed that he was now in the real estate rental business, so he could deduct depreciation on the rented apartment, along with utilities, insurance, and related expenses. And this was in spite of the fact that he charged his daughter a *below*-market rent. The Court felt that the rent was *fair* because it's safer to rent to a family member than to a stranger.
Source: *J. V. Keenon,* TC Memo 1982-144.

Special tax breaks in your own business

Big, Big Benefits

Since the drastic changes made by Tax Reform, the best source of tax breaks is your own business. *Business owner's tax advantages:*

Fully deductible business expenses. For the self-employed, business expenses are deductible in full directly from gross income. Employees may deduct their business expenses only if they itemize, and the deduction is reduced by 2% of Adjusted Gross Income (AGI).

Full home-office-expense write-off. If you run a business from your home, you may deduct not only property taxes and mortgage interest but also a percentage of depreciation, utilities, insurance, repairs, and any other costs. You get these deductions, even if they result in a tax loss. *Essential:* To take these deductions, you must reserve a part of your home exclusively for business.

Greater tax-deferred retirement savings. Tax Reform severely limited IRAs and capped 401(k) contributions at $9,240 in 1995 (indexed each year for inflation). But Keogh plans for the self-employed were practically left untouched. Business owners may make annual deductible contributions of up to 20% of business income or $30,000—whichever is less—to a defined-contribution plan and may stash away even more in a defined-benefit plan.

Potential drawback: If you have employees, you must include them in your plan on a nondiscriminatory basis. *Exceptions:* You may exclude employees under 21, those who have worked for you for less than a year, and part-timers with fewer than 1,000 work hours in a 12-month period.

Hiring your kids. Their wages are deductible business expenses, and they can earn up to $3,900 a year (indexed for inflation) tax-free. If they open an IRA, up to $2,000 more is tax-free. If they do make enough to be taxed, it's at minimum rates. And you may still claim them as dependents.

Caution: Kids must perform actual services for reasonable compensation. Phony jobs and inflated wages don't stand up to IRS scrutiny.

Hiring your spouse. *Advantages:*

■ Your spouse may participate in any retirement plans that you have for employees (pension, 401(k), etc.). In some cases, he/she may qualify for deductible IRA contributions.

■ If your spouse accompanies you on a business trip as an assistant or colleague, you may write off travel expenses for both of you.

Timing income. If you use the cash accounting method, you can easily defer income from one year into the next. You just don't send out bills late in the year—you wait until January.

More deductible transportation expenses. Going to work and coming home are *nondeductible* commutation expenses. But if you work out of your home, you're already at your place of business when you get up in the morning. So *all* travel costs are deductible—trips to visit customers, buy supplies, mail correspondence, etc.

Justifying transportation deductions is also easier for business owners. Employees may be asked by IRS auditors why they weren't reimbursed by their company if their travel costs were truly "ordinary and necessary" business expenses.

Fully deductible casualty losses. Business casualty losses (from fire, theft, accident, natural disaster, etc.) may be written off in full against business income. But personal casualty losses are deductible only for itemizers, and the deduction is reduced by 10% of AGI, plus a $100 deductible.

Full write-offs for bad debts. A business's bad debts may be deducted in full in the year in which they become uncollectible. But personal bad debts are treated like capital losses—you may deduct only up to $3,000 a year.

How To Offset Operating Losses

For the past year, I have been running an unincorporated start-up business. So far it's still losing money, and I don't have enough income to offset my losses. Can I carry them into next year? If so, is there any limit on the amount?

Since your business is unincorporated, its losses must first be deducted on your personal return against your income from other sources. If this leaves you with a net operating loss for the year, you can carry it *back three years* (to get a refund of past years' taxes)...or *forward 15 years* (to offset future income). There's no limit on the amount you can carry back or forward.

Figure your carryback or carryforward using IRS Form 3621. If you carry back your losses, you can get an *expedited refund* of previous years' taxes by filing Form 1138.

Great Tax Breaks For Business Owners

The owners of a closely-held company often have to *personally guarantee* the company's debts. Such owners often overlook the fact that they can charge a *fee* for providing this service and that the company can *deduct* this fee as a business expense.

In one case, the Claims Court allowed a deduction for fees paid to owners equal to 3% of a major financing deal. *Key facts:* Each shareholder separately decided how much of the loan he was going to guarantee, so the guarantee fee *wasn't* distributed in proportion to shareholdings. The company was able to show that the loan plus guarantee was cheaper than other methods of financing. And the 3% fee was reasonable when compared with other guarantee fees paid in similar arrangements.

Source: *Tulia Feedlot*, Cl. Ct., 52 AFTR2d 83-5702.

Strengthening the company's cash flow

Ways To Prepare For A Bad-Earnings Year

Lagging sales and high costs mean many businesses are bracing for a poor-earnings year. It is important to devise tax strategies to strengthen the company's cash flow as earnings erode by using the tax code to the company's advantage.

If the company made money in one year but expects to lose money in the next, it can effectively avoid paying any tax that it still owes for earlier, money-making years by filing Form 1138. This extends the time for paying the earlier year's taxes until the date the present return is due. And the loss shown on the return can be carried back to wipe out the earlier year's tax bill.

A company with losses can get a quick refund of previous years' taxes through its loss carryback by filing Form 1139. The IRS must generally respond to this refund request within about 90 days. The company must file its regular tax return before the Form 1139 is filed. So file the previous year's tax return as quickly as possible.

Using an S Corporation

The S form of corporate organization presents an opportunity for company owners when the company faces a loss. Shareholders of an S corporation, who materially participate in running the business, can deduct the firm's operating losses on their personal tax returns. So they can use the company's losses to cut taxes on their income from other sources. (Nonparticipating stockholders are, however, subject to the passive-loss rules.)

A company with 35 or fewer shareholders may consider reorganizing under Subchapter S to take advantage of this break. An S corporation election must be filed in the first two and a half months of the company's tax year. For a calendar-year firm, the deadline is March 15.

There is a limit to the amount of losses that an S corporation shareholder may deduct. The limit equals the adjusted basis of the shareholder's stock (basically its cost), plus the amount of any debts owed by the company to the shareholder. Owners frequently overlook this limit. Losses that exceed this limit may be carried forward by the shareholder to a year when he has additional basis in the corporation.

Estimated Taxes

When it comes to estimated taxes, many firms routinely base one year's payments on the previous year's tax liability. But the resulting tax payments will be too high if this year's income goes down. So be sure the company's accountants base estimated payments on actual earnings as the year progresses. During a stretch when the company is losing money, it need pay no estimated taxes at all.

If business turns good later in the year as the economy picks up, the company may wind up with a large tax liability after all. And the IRS may ask why the company did not make any estimated-tax payments during the course of a profitable year. If this occurs, file Form 2220. This shows that the company was actually losing money for most of the year and did not owe the taxes. Make sure the company's bookkeepers examine Form 2220 at the beginning of the year. It will show them which records must be kept to protect the company from tax penalties.

If the company is locked into making large pension-plan contributions this year and is afraid that it may not be able to afford them, plan now to ask the IRS for a waiver of the contribution requirements.

The company must be able to show that it is suffering from genuine economic hardship in order to qualify for a waiver. And it must show that the waiver is in the best interest of the pension plan's participants. Show that the waiver will help the company regain economic strength and continue in business.

Consolidated Returns

Often businesses are operated through several different corporations. And the swift-changing economic conditions may affect the separate companies differently. Some profit while others lose. Look at the effects of filing a consolidated tax return. The profits of one company may then be offset by the losses of another. And the net tax bill may be reduced. A consolidated return does not have to be decided upon until the normal time for filing the tax return. At that point, with all the good and bad news in, the results of consolidated and separate filings can be compared to see which one produces the best outcome for the company as a whole.

There are two things a company should not do when confronted by financial difficulties. Never ignore an IRS communication about a tax problem. The IRS takes the worst actions when companies are silent. Instead, have the company's tax adviser answer the IRS in a businesslike manner. And never use taxes withheld from employee wages to meet a cash need of the business. That use of withholding is a crime, involving a possible fine and/or jail term.

Source: Henry A. Garris, tax manager, Richard Eisner & Co., New York.

Legal Ways To Hold Back Payroll Tax

It's not necessary to pay the entire amount due of corporate payroll taxes (FICA and federal withholding) on deadline (three banking days after the 3rd, 7th, 11th, 15th, 19th, 22nd, 25th, and last day of the month, depending on paydays). An employer on eight monthly deposits will satisfy the deposits requirement by making timely deposits of at least 95%. Any underpayment for a deposit period during the first or second month of a quarter must be paid with the first deposit required after the 15th day of the next month. *Another possibility:* Consider switching paydays. Employers paying on the 15th of the month must deposit taxes by the 18th, but if payday is on the 16th, taxes are not due until the 22nd.

Raising Capital Through An ESOP

An Employee Stock Ownership Plan (ESOP) could be the best (or even the only) way for a small, closely-held company to raise equity capital. And ESOPs are actively being encouraged by government policy. But consider the disadvantages, too, before starting one.

The pluses:

■ The ESOP can borrow money to buy company stock. The company then makes tax-deductible contributions to the ESOP as a profit-sharing plan for employees. The ESOP uses the cash to repay the loan. In effect, the company gets a tax deduction for additional capital.

■ The ESOP can also buy stock from present stockholders. *Example:* It can buy from the estate of a stockholder who dies. Or an owner who simply needs money can sell some stock without bringing in an outside interest.

The minuses:

■ Government red tape and constantly changing regulations.

■ Potential liquidity problems when employees leave or retire and receive their stock. They'll want the company or the ESOP to buy it back right away. This could be a problem if cash is short.

■ Expense of putting a valuation on the stock (and the company) at least once a year.

■ Stock ownership is extended outside the family. (But shares are usually voted by a management appointee.)

■ There's no assurance of better employee attitudes and improved productivity. If employee relations were poor before, they'll probably stay that way.

■ Employees may have too many eggs in one basket. If the company gets into real trouble, they might not only lose their jobs but see their retirement nest egg wiped out, too.

For information on ESOPs, write: Employee Stock Ownership Council, 11661 San Vicente Blvd., Los Angeles 90049.

Source: Ron Ludwig, Esq., partner, Ludwig & Curtis, 114 Sansome St., San Francisco 94104.

Carryback Or Carryforward?

Filing a claim to carry back a net operating loss is generally done to recover taxes paid within the previous three years. Caution must be exercised before a claim for refund is filed, especially if *either* the year of the loss or one of the carry-back years contains one or more issues that could result in the IRS's making an assessment for additional tax. *Alternative to filing a carryback claim:* Elect to carry the operating loss forward. *Trap:* The election to carry the loss forward is irrevocable. If the business isn't profitable in the future, the carryover will provide no tax savings.

Source: Ms. X, Esq., a former IRS agent who is still well-connected.

Tougher Penalties

Tax Reform *doubles* the penalty imposed on employers who fail to make timely deposits of Social Security taxes, withheld income tax, and federal unemployment tax. The new penalty rate is 10% of the late payment (up from 5% under the old law). This new rate applies to *all* penalties assessed after October 21, 1986, *regardless* of the date on which the payment was due.

Source: *IRS News Release* 86-153.

Know the rules when filing a company's return

Tax-Return Strategies

The company's tax return is due on March 15 for calendar-year firms (or two and a half months after the end of the tax year for companies using a fiscal year).

Start preparing return-filing strategies early. *Two reasons:*

■ Tough deduction rules require *more* in the way of documentation and paperwork on the part of the company.

■ While preparing this year's return, the company can devise strategies for handling the new rules that will cut next year's taxes as well.

One of the most dramatic tax return changes made by Tax Reform is the rule that requires a number of the overhead costs of manufacturers, wholesalers, and retailers to be *capitalized* (added to the cost of goods sold) rather than deducted immediately.

Costs that may now have to be capitalized: Insurance, repairs, maintenance, utilities, rent, taxes on assets, administrative costs, quality control, handling, and packaging. Also, salary and benefits paid to warehouse workers, along with a portion of the compensation paid to *executives* who make decisions concerning production or resale activities.

Bottom line: The company cannot deduct these costs until it *sells* the inventoried items, so a part of its deduction for them is *postponed*. And a firm using last-in, first-out (LIFO) methods, or with generally increasing inventory levels, may have its deduction postponed indefinitely.

Every wholesaler and retailer subject to the new rules must set up capital-costing accounting procedures similar to those that manufacturers use, just to claim the deductions to which they *are* entitled. (Wholesalers and retailers with average annual gross receipts of $10 million or less during the past three years are exempt from the new capitalization rules.)

A company setting up such procedures to comply with the new rules, as well as manufacturers, must file Form 3115 with its tax return, explaining its change in accounting procedures. This filing will not only affect the current year's taxes but will also have a critical impact on future years' tax bills, since the company will be bound to follow the accounting procedures set up now. And any *mistakes* made now could result in *big* back tax bills in a few years' time.

Business Meals

Everyone is aware that business meals and entertainment costs are only 50% deductible. But some companies have missed the fact that they could lose their deductions *entirely* if they do not meet the tougher rules for *documenting* meal and entertainment costs. *Requirements:*

■ Each meal must be accounted for *separately*. Costs cannot be aggregated.

■ The date, time, and place of *each* meal must be recorded, along with the name of the person entertained and the business reason for the occasion.

Trap: A company that claims a large deduction for the year's business meals may be hit with *negligence penalties* if it does not have the records needed to support the deduction under the new law.

Benefits

Tax Reform multiplied the number of technical rules that apply to qualified retirement plans, generally increasing their overhead cost and reducing their flexibility. At the same time, by reducing the top corporate tax rate to 34%, (35% for taxable income over $10 million) Tax Reform increased the after-tax cost to the company of retirement plan contributions, because the deduction for such contributions produces smaller cash savings.

When working through its tax return, the company may do well to examine the real cost of its pension program and consider low-cost alternatives. *Possibilities:*

Nonqualified arrangements. The company can enter into contractual arrangements with key executives to provide retirement benefits on an individual basis.

Advantages: Retirement benefits can be customized for the particular individual and are not subject to most of the rules that apply to qualified plans.

Drawbacks: The company gets no deduction until the benefits are actually paid. And benefits are less secure since they are not funded by a trust but are merely a general obligation of the company.

401(k) programs. Tax Reform eliminated IRA deductions for those persons who are covered by a qualified retirement plan and have an Adjusted Gross Income (AGI) of over $35,000 per year ($50,000 per year on a joint return). But the company can provide its employees with *better* savings benefits through a 401(k) program. Each employee can reduce his/her taxable income by contributing up to $9,240 (indexed for inflation) to a 401(k), as opposed to the $2,000 permitted for an IRA. And since the company is *not* required to make contributions to a 401(k) program, it can serve as a low-cost supplement to (or replacement for) a traditional pension program.

AMT

Tax Reform increased the tax bill paid by *many* corporations and the complexity of filing a return as a result of the tougher Alternative Minimum Tax (AMT). The AMT adds to taxable income one-half of the *difference* between the amount of income reported for financial and tax purposes.

Example: A company has large tax benefits that just offset its operating income for both regular tax and AMT purposes, but on the certified financial statements given to lenders and investors, it is able to report $500,000 of income for the year. Assuming no credits are available, an AMT tax bill of $47,000 results, even though the tax computation done under regular rules shows *zero* tax due.

Since the Alternative Minimum Tax rules are complicated, they should be checked out with an expert. When working out the current year's tax bill, project AMT liability for the next year. Knowledge of the AMT is important not only when trying to cut the overall taxes but also when computing the company's liability for *estimated* tax payments due throughout the year.

S Status

While reviewing its tax return, a corporation should consider whether it might benefit from electing *S corporation status* for the next year.

■ *Lower income tax rates* may result since an S corporation's income is taxed directly to its shareholders on their personal returns.

■ *Larger after-tax gains* may result from sales of company stock. That's because corporate income that's reported on a shareholder's personal return increases the owner's *tax basis* in the shares. And the taxable gain on a stock sale equals the sale price minus the owner's tax basis.

Important: The deadline for making an S election is March 15 for a calendar-year business, or two and a half months after the start of the year for a fiscal year company — the *same* date on which the corporate tax return is due. But you *can't* get an extension of time to make an S election, so have your accountant consider its advisability now.

Source: James Godbout, partner in the national tax office, Ernst and Young, 1225 Connecticut Ave., Washington, DC 20036.

S corporation magic

S Corporation Traps And Loopholes

Tax Reform has greatly enhanced the appeal of the S corporation—a small business that operates under Subchapter S of the Tax Code.

The big tax advantage S corporations have over regular corporations is that income is taxed only once, directly to the shareholders at their personal tax rates. The income of regular corporations is taxed twice, first on the corporation's tax return and then on the shareholder's return when he/she receives dividends.

Factors In Switching

■ If you borrow from your company's pension plan, the loans must be paid back before you can convert to an S corporation, or you'll face a stiff excise tax.

■ To qualify for S status, the business can't have more than 35 shareholders, it must have only one class of stock, and it can't be part of a controlled group—that is, it can't be a subsidiary of another corporation or have subsidiaries.

■ S corporation owners cannot deduct medical insurance expenses.

■ If you're not active in the management of the business, you could be hurt by converting it to an S corporation. Under the passive-loss rules, an S corporation in which the taxpayer does not materially participate is treated as a passive activity. The corporation's losses are deductible on the shareholder's return only against passive income. If you have no passive income, you'll get no deduction for the losses. *Bigger problem:* Say the corporation has an investment income of $50,000 and an operating loss of $50,000. Under the old law, you could write the losses off against the income. But under the new law, you must pay tax on the investment income and cannot write off the losses, unless you have passive income.

Hidden-benefits loophole. Even if S corporation status won't save you much in the way of income tax, it may still pay you to convert from a regular corporation. *Tax advantages to being an S corporation:*

■ Avoid accumulated-earnings tax problems. The IRS can't raise this issue if you are an S corporation.

■ Avoid unreasonable compensation problems. Since all S corporation income passes through to the shareholders, high compensation is never an issue.

■ Avoid double taxation on disallowed deductions, such as personal travel and entertainment expenses. If you're an S corporation, there's only a single tax on any extra income the IRS charges to the corporation.

■ An S corporation can be on the cash basis of accounting rather than the accrual basis. *Benefit:* When you're on the cash basis you have to pay tax only on the income you have actually collected rather than on all the income you have billed.

Passive-income loophole. Tax-shelter investors who also own a piece of an income-producing, closely held business in which they don't actively participate could benefit if the business is converted to an S corporation. Under the passive-loss rules, tax-shelter losses can be written off only against passive income. The income from an S corporation in which you don't materially participate is passive income under the new rules. Use this income to absorb your tax-shelter losses.

Split-election loophole. Some states permit businesses to operate as S corporations for state tax purposes. It may be advisable *not* to elect S status for state purposes, even though you are electing it for federal tax purposes. *A split election saves when:*

■ You live in a state that has a high individual income tax rate, and

■ Your company does only part of its business in that state.

If the company is a regular corporation, for state purposes it need only report on its state return the portion of its income that is earned in that state—if it does 40% of its business in the state, only 40% of its income is allocated to that state and reportable on the state return. *Problem:* An S corporation cannot allocate. So you may be better off *not* structuring an S corporation for state purposes.

Avoiding the new closing-down-the-business trap. Under old law, when a business was sold and the proceeds were distributed to the shareholders, there was only one tax—the shareholders paid the tax.

New law: When a corporation liquidates its assets, it has to pay tax on the gain, *and* the shareholders have to pay tax on the part of the gain that is passed through to them. This double tax can be as high as 52% in total. It may be possible to avoid the double tax by electing S corporation status.

Source: Edward Mendlowitz, partner, Mendlowitz Weitsen, CPAs, Two Pennsylvania Plaza, New York 10121.

Owner-Employee Salaries

Is it possible to cut employment taxes by having S corporation owner-employees take small salaries while receiving the balance of their profits through dividends?

Perhaps, but there are two problems with this strategy:

■ By reducing salaries, the company reduces its deduction for salary expenses. The resulting income-tax liability increase may outweigh employment-tax savings.

■ When salaries get far out of line with industry norms, the IRS has the power to reallocate payments to owner-employees between salary and dividend accounts. Normally the IRS does this when a regular corporation pays salaries that are too high and dividends that are too low. But, on rare occasions, it has also increased unreasonably low amounts attributed to salary by an S corporation.

Employee benefits and rights

Setting Up An Employee Loan Program

Allowing employees to borrow from pension plans or directly from the company is one of the least expensive ways to enhance the company's benefits offerings. And experience shows that the cost is usually offset by improved morale.

Loans Against Stocks and Pensions

Federal law allows employers with qualified tax-deferred pension plans, 401(k) plans, stock options, or profit-sharing plans to let participants in those plans borrow money against their savings or stocks.

Restrictions:

■ The maximum loan to an employee can't exceed one-half the present value of the vested amount in his pension account, or $50,000, whichever is lower. (The $50,000 loan cap is further reduced by an amount equal to the highest loan balance during the previous year, minus the loan balance on the date a new loan is taken out.)

■ The company must require repayment in five years through level payouts in installments that can't be less frequent than quarterly. Employers must charge an interest rate based on current market conditions. *Recommended:* The Applicable Federal Rate, which is based on an average quarterly rate of Treasury securities.

Federal rules permit employers to set a $1,000 minimum limit on borrowing.

To protect the company from default, require repayments to be made by payroll deductions.

To guard against the possibility that employees may leave the company without repaying, warn them that loans not repaid within 60 days of their departure are deducted from their pension accounts and become subject to tax.

Direct Loans from the Company

Many companies provide direct loans to managers who are being relocated and need extra cash to buy a house in the new location until they've sold the house they're moving from. But loans can also be made for other purposes.

Caution: It's illegal to make an interest-free loan to an employee if it's over $10,000. And interest must reflect actual market rates, such as the Applicable Federal Rate.

But the company *can* save its employees a lot in interest payments by following IRS rules that allow the company to return interest charged to a borrower in the form of additional compensation. The employee thereby pays nothing out of pocket except income tax on the additional compensation.

Example: A company lends a manager $50,000 at 10% a year. Instead of actually collecting the $5,000 of interest, it records a $5,000 interest receipt in its books and at the same time adjusts its books to record a $5,000 pay increase for the employee. The company thereby comes out even, with no interest money changing hands.

The borrower, however, pays income tax on the extra $5,000 in "salary."

Though the *interest* deduction has been phased out, the reduced tax on income still makes borrowing from the company much cheaper than borrowing at market rates from a commercial bank.

Source: Israel Press, tax partner, Deloitte & Touche Financial Services Center, One World Trade Center, New York 10048.

Tax-Free Workers Compensation

A woman was collecting workers compensation through a regular paycheck issued by her employer. The employer was then reimbursed by the workers compensation insurance company. Her W-2 form included these payments as taxable income. *IRS ruling:* The payments were *not* taxable income.

Source: *IRS Letter Ruling 8647040.*

Sex-Discrimination Award

A woman won an Equal Pay Act lawsuit for wage discrimination. She was awarded $66,000 for back wages she should have been paid and an equal amount in damages, as provided in the Equal Pay Act. *Tax Court:* The $66,000 back-pay award was taxable wages, but the $66,000 in liquidated damages was tax-free. It was in the nature of a personal-injury award, and sex discrimination is a personal injury.

Source: *Dorothy M. Thompson, 89 TC No. 44.*

A Word To Employers

Employers must send the IRS a copy of Form W-4 if an employee claims *more than 10 allowances*. Previously, the cutoff point was 14. Tax Reform, however, raised the value of each allowance, prompting the new rule.

Source: *New Form W-4 instructions.*

Business meals, travel, and entertainment deductions

Business-Meal Loopholes

The Tax Reform Act of 1986 put tough limits on deductions for business meals and entertainment. Only 50% of these expenses is deductible. The limit applies to food, beverages, taxes, tips, tickets, cover charges, and whatever else you spend for business purposes on eating out and entertainment. All are just 50% deductible.

Even though the value of deducting an extra $1 of business-meal expenses was reduced because of the drop in tax rates, the incentive to get the biggest deduction legally possible still exists.

The Angles

■ *Reimbursement angle.* Employees are not subject to the 50% rule if their company reimburses them for business-meal and entertainment expenses. It's the company that's subject to the rule—the company must limit the amount of the deduction it claims on its tax return to 50% of the amount given to reimburse the employee. *Bottom line:* The tax law has no adverse effect on the expense account of an employee who is reimbursed in full for business-meal and entertainment costs. It may be more desirable to have your employer reimburse you than for you to receive an expense allowance and deduct meal and entertainment expenses on your own return, as they will be limited to 50%.

■ *Lodging loophole.* The 50% rule applies to business meals (including those you eat while traveling away from home on business) and to entertainment expenses. But it does not apply to business travel expenses. Hotel bills are a part of travel expenses and, thus, are not subject to the rule. *Question:* What if your hotel rate is stated only on the European or American plan and includes either two or three meals a day? Is your hotel bill (including meals) fully deductible? The new law does not say. This may be a loophole.

■ *Company-party loophole.* The 50% rule does not apply to certain traditional employer-paid social or recreational activities that are primarily for the benefit of the employees. Holiday parties and annual summer outings will continue to be fully deductible.

Strategy: Include in your travel plans conventions that provide three meals a day and a speaker at each meal as part of the cost.

Source: Randy Bruce Blaustein, former IRS agent, now a partner of Blaustein, Greenberg & Co., 155 E. 31 St., New York 10016.

How To Prove Business Purpose Of Spouse On Company Trip

It's possible to deduct the cost of taking your spouse on a business trip. The key is to prove your spouse's involvement in the business aspects of the trip. *Guidelines:*

■ Explain your job responsibilities to your spouse.

■ Involve your spouse in interacting with people relevant to the trip and with other spouses who are present. They should discuss general aspects of the job being worked on. There's no need for detailed descriptions of the business project.

■ Make sure there are official functions, such as seminars, dinners, and parties, to which spouses are invited. (If you're not self-employed, ask your employer to specify that it's mandatory to take spouses to these events.)

■ Eat all your meals with business associates. Make sure that business is discussed at each of these meals and that your spouse participated in the discussions.

■ Document all of your spouse's ideas on the business by having your spouse write memos to you containing these ideas.

■ If it's the policy of the company not to pay for spouses on business trips but to require the spouses' attendance, request a written memo from your employer stating this policy.

Source: *New Tax Traps/New Opportunities* by Edward Mendlowitz, CPA, Boardroom Special Report, Springfield, NJ 07081.

Business-Gift Loophole

An advertising company employed an independent salesman. As favors to prospective customers, he gave out $40,000 worth of tickets to shows and sporting events. The company paid for the tickets and deducted their full cost. *IRS position:* The company's expense deduction was subject to the limit of $25 per recipient under the tax law. *Court's decision:* The ticket expenses were deductible by the company. The $25 business-gift limitation applied to the independent salesman, not to the company that employed him.

Source: *World Wide Agency, Inc.,* TC Memo 1981-419.

Expense Formula Fails

A company had many representatives traveling on the road. It reimbursed their travel costs for transportation, meals, and lodging on a cents-per-mile basis. *IRS ruling:* The number of miles an employee travels doesn't give an adequate indication of the amount he/she spends on meals or lodging. Thus, the company's reimbursement formula is *not* sufficient to make the reimbursements tax-free.

Source: IRS Letter Ruling 8634029.

Travel And Entertainment Rules

The Tax Reform Act of 1986, as amended, limits deductions for most meals and entertainment to 50% of cost. Moreover, the expenditures qualify as *business* meals or *business* entertainment only if business is actually discussed. Business transportation (air fare, cabs, etc.) remains fully deductible, but travel to *investment* seminars or *investment* conventions is not.

Here's a checklist showing the deductibility of some common travel and entertainment expenses:

Type of expense	Deductible
■ Lunch with customer; business discussed before, during, or after the meal	50%
Cab fare to restaurant	100%
No business discussed	None
■ Air fare to Chicago to call on customer	100%
Lodging in Chicago	100%
Meals in Chicago (alone)	50%
Meals with customer, no business discussed:	
a. Your meal	50%
b. Customer's meal	None
■ Air fare to L.A. for doctor to attend medical convention	100%
Meals in L.A.	50%
■ Air fare to Houston for investment seminar	None
Lodging in Houston	None
■ Tickets to ballgame for taxpayer and customer; business discussed	50%
Cab fare to game	100%
Food and drink at game	50%
■ Complimentary theater tickets for customer; taxpayer *not* present	None
■ Lunch at service organization as member	50%
■ Tickets to charity golf tournament run by volunteers	100%
■ Greens fees, carts, food and beverages consumed while hosting customers; business discussed	50%

Trooper Costs

Minnesota State Troopers were required to take their *on*-duty meals in public restaurants to maintain public visibility. When *off* duty, they were required to make sure their patrol cars were parked *off* the street. Steven Pillsbury and Karl Christey were troopers who claimed business deductions both for their meal costs and the cost of renting garage space for their vehicles. *Court:* The meals were properly deducted because they were clearly a required part of the job. The garage costs were *not* deductible because it was not necessary for the troopers to rent garage space in order to keep the cars off the street.

Source: *Steven Pillsbury,* D. Minn., No. 3-85-1361.

On-The-Job Meals

Robert Walsh worked in a grocery store and was required to be on the premises at all times during his shift, in order to meet emergencies. For meals, he bought food from the store, ate on the premises, and deducted the cost as a business expense. *Tax Court:* To get a deduction a worker must be required to buy meals that are *provided* by the employer. Walsh was *not* entitled to a deduction because he could have brought his lunch from home.

Source: *Robert M. Walsh,* TC Memo 1987-18.

New tax surprises for businesses

Traps And Opportunities In The Revenue Act Of 1987

The Tax Reform Act of 1986 generally required partnerships, S corporations, and personal-service corporations to adopt the same tax years as their individual owners (generally calendar years), unless they could establish a business purpose for operating on a different fiscal year. This would have required many businesses to *change* to a calendar year, thereby accelerating the taxes from the deferral period.

The Revenue Act of 1987 contained *relief* from this provision by allowing partnerships, S corporations, and personal-service corporations to retain their current fiscal years. However, certain partnerships and S corporations may be required to make a partial deposit of taxes that are deferred through use of a fiscal year. Check with your tax adviser for details.

The 1987 Revenue Act also made these changes that affect corporations:

■ *Vacation pay*. Under the old law, an accrual-basis company could elect to deduct a reasonable addition to its vacation-pay reserve for amounts earned during the year and paid up to eight-and-a-half months after year-end. The 1987 Act repeals this election, limiting the deduction to amounts paid within two and a half months after year-end.

■ *Dividends-received deduction*. The Tax Reform Act of 1986 had allowed a corporation to claim a deduction for 80% of the dividends it received from another corporation. The 1987 Act reduced this deduction to 70% when the company receiving the dividend has a less-than-20%-ownership interest in the company paying it.

■ *S election and LIFO*. Under the 1987 Tax Act, when a regular corporation that uses LIFO (last-in, first-out) inventory accounting procedures elects S corporation status at the end of its last regular-corporation tax year, it must make an inventory valuation using the FIFO (first-in, first-out) method. The amount by which the FIFO inventory valuation exceeds the LIFO inventory valuation will be taxable income to the company. Any increase in tax is payable in four yearly installments.

■ *Estimated taxes*. A company that underpays quarterly estimated taxes may be liable for tax penalties. A 1991 law set a new minimum amount that must be paid by a corporation. This amount is generally 100% of the year's final tax bill.

Source: S. Theodore Reiner, director, tax client communications, Ernst & Young, 1225 Connecticut Ave. NW, Washington, DC 20036.

Two Business Traps And How To Avoid Them

Bad-debt deductions. Under the old law, rather than deduct bad debts on an individual basis, companies could use the *reserve* method. This allows a business to use past experience to predict the percentage of total receivables that would go uncollected in the future and claim a deduction for them now. Tax Reform, however, revoked the reserve method. Now the general rule is that *all* bad debts must be deducted on an individual basis.

Trap: To deduct an individual bad debt, a company must show *more* than just that the debt has not been paid. The company's records must show *when* the debt went bad and also indicate evidence of *why* it is uncollectible.

Companies could face the disallowances of large deductions if they fail to set up the necessary accounting systems before undergoing an IRS examination.

Capital gains. Under Tax Reform, capital gains are taxed at the same rate as ordinary income, but businesses must keep records to differentiate between ordinary income and capital gains, and between long-term and short-term gains.

It is essential to continue keeping such records because capital gains and ordinary income remain subject to *different* tax rules. For example, while a corporation's ordinary losses are currently deductible and can be used to generate a tax refund from a loss carryback, capital losses can be used only to offset either current, past, or future capital gains. Capital losses are *not* deductible against ordinary income.

Source: Arthur I. Gordon, partner, Ernst & Young, 787 Seventh Ave., New York 10019.

Depreciation Finesse

Tax Reform changed the rates of depreciation that apply to most kinds of business property, and most companies know it. But it's easy to overlook the smaller changes in the rules that can have a big impact on the final tax bill. *Two examples:*

■ Under the *half-year convention,* a company could claim a half-year's worth of depreciation deductions for equipment that is put in service as late as one day before year-end. So many companies rush to make large equipment purchases just before the tax year closes. *Trap:* Tax Reform created a *mid-quarter* convention. If more than 40% of a company's new depreciable equipment is put in service during the last quarter of the year, the company will get only about *six weeks'* depreciation for it, instead of six months'. Equipment acquisitions should be timed with this 40% limit in mind.

■ Under the old law, improvements to real property leased by the company could be depreciated over the term of the lease. Now such improvements must be depreciated over 39 years, even if this is longer than the term of the lease. The after-tax cost of improvements should be figured with this change in mind, and compensation for improvements may be sought from the lessor.

The company should have its tax experts look through the depreciation rules for other hidden provisions that may apply to the special kinds of property it uses.

Source: Arthur I. Gordon, partner, Ernst & Young, 787 Seventh Ave., New York 10019.

Business winners

Lawsuit Insurance

Jack Feather owned a group of corporations that marketed health and fitness products, including the Mark Eden bust developer and the Cambridge Diet. Over a period of years, the corporations earned millions of dollars but were also subject to a large number of lawsuits alleging consumer fraud. Feather collected only a modest salary and never had his companies pay any dividends. But then the IRS assessed the *accumulated-earnings penalty tax,* alleging that Feather was cutting his personal tax bill by hiding profits in the business. *Tax Court:* The corporations had a *good business reason* for accumulating large cash balances—to meet potential legal liabilities. Thus, the tax was *not* imposed.

Source: *Mark Eden, et al.,* TC Memo 1987-101.

Stretching Deductions

Proving a tax deduction for the business use of a company car can be difficult when your records are less than complete. The best proof is a diary, or log, of the business use of the car. But even without a log you may still get the deduction if you can come up with a reasonable explanation of how the car was used for business. *Real story:* An IRS agent was examining the business use of a company's stretch limo. No log had been kept, but the following explanation was offered. The car was used to transport company executives and out-of-town customers from the airport to hotels, from hotels to business meetings, and to and from restaurants during evening hours. Yes, the owner of the company did have use of the limo, but it was insignificant. *Result:* The deduction was allowed in full.

Source: Ms. X, Esq., a former IRS agent who is still well-connected.

Penalty Escape

One company avoided the accumulated-earnings penalty tax by convincing the court that it was engaged in a very *volatile* business. Since it could never predict its working capital needs with any certainty, it had a good business reason for retaining large cash balances that might be needed in case of an emergency.

Source: *EMI Corp.,* TC Memo 1985-386.

Smart Shareholders

A company needed to expand, so its shareholders *personally* bought 48 acres of land on which a new plant could be built. They leased the land to the company, which deducted its lease payments as a business expense. *IRS attack:* The company could have bought the land itself. The deal was set up this way just to get the company a deduction for money that was being taken out of the business by the shareholders. *Tax Court:* Deduction allowed. *Key facts:* The company had a real business need for the property. It paid a fair market rent. And the arrangement served a business purpose by insulating the real estate from potential creditors.
Source: *Osterlund, Inc.,* TC Memo 1987-40.

Tax-Free Reimbursement

A company's accountant made a mistake on the tax return, and the company had to pay extra taxes. The accountant reimbursed the company for his mistake. *Letter Ruling:* The company does not have to include the receipt of this money in its taxable income because there was no economic gain.
Source: IRS Letter Ruling 8604065.

S Corporation Reprieve

An S corporation sold some of its shares to a resident of the United Kingdom. But S corporations are *prohibited* from having foreign shareholders, so its S election would be automatically terminated. As soon as the firm discovered the error, it revoked the sale and refunded the price of the shares. *IRS ruling:* Since the mistake was inadvertent and rectified as soon as it was discovered, the firm's S election would continue in force.
Source: IRS Letter Ruling 8718047.

Confidential Documents

The IRS wanted a company to hand over documents regarding a tax deficiency. *Tax Court:* The company didn't have to give them to the IRS. *Reason:* The documents were protected from the IRS because they contained information that had been prepared in anticipation of litigation and was intended to be confidential.
Source: *Sundstrand Corporation,* 89 TC 810.

Employment-Tax Relief

The operator of a trucking business treated his drivers as independent contractors. But an IRS auditor ruled that the drivers were really employees and said the operator owed back employment taxes. He appealed the auditor's finding. *Final ruling:* The drivers were in fact employees. But it was standard industry practice to treat such drivers as contractors, and the operator had filed all required tax returns and information returns in a manner that was consistent with their treatment as contractors. Thus, the operator was entitled to relief from the back-tax bill. Employment taxes would be due only in the future.
Source: IRS Letter Ruling 8711004.

A Loan Is A Loan...

Max Schnallinger owned Mimi's, Inc., which ran a very successful restaurant. Schnallinger wanted to expand, so he founded Max's, Inc. to start a second restaurant. Max's, Inc. borrowed $100,000 from Mimi's but went broke before it could repay anything. The IRS said the $100,000 was a *taxable dividend* from Mimi's to Schnallinger, since it was money that he had taken out of the company for his personal benefit. But the Tax Court ruled for Schnallinger. *Key:* The loan was fully documented, bore a reasonable rate of interest, and was approved by the boards of both companies. Since the companies *acted* as if the money was a loan, it was a loan.
Source: *Maximillian Schnallinger,* TC Memo 1987-9.

Interest Claim In Liquidation

When a company liquidated under Chapter 7 of the Bankruptcy Code, the IRS made a claim for back taxes and interest. *Court:* Interest on taxes receives a *lower priority* than other claims in a Chapter 7 liquidation. Because the company did not have enough assets to pay its creditors in full, the IRS could *not* collect.
Source: *National Automatic Sprinkler Co. of Oregon,* Bnkr. D. Or., No. 383-01591-S7.

Company's Late-Filing Excuse

A parent company wanted to file a consolidated return with a subsidiary that it recently acquired. It requested IRS permission, as required. *Problem:* The request was filed late because of an error made by the firm's outside accountant. *IRS ruling:* Since the mistake wasn't the company's fault, the filing deadline would be extended, and the late request would be accepted.
Source: IRS Letter Ruling 8628022.

IRS Forgives Company

An owner of an S corporation gave some of his shares to a trust that he set up to benefit his children. He didn't realize that most trusts are *not permitted* to own stock in an S corporation. The mistake wasn't discovered until the company prepared its tax return for the year. The shares were then promptly transferred to a qualified shareholder. *IRS ruling:* Normally the creation of a nonqualified shareholder will *terminate* a corporation's S election. But since the transfer to the trust was inadvertent and the mistake was corrected as soon as it was discovered, the company would be allowed to *retain* its S status.
Source: IRS Letter Ruling 8701006.

Company Wins And Loses

On examining a company's books, the IRS found that employment taxes were due on benefits that had been provided to workers. The company paid the taxes and also paid the portion that was owed by the workers. *Good news:* Although the company wasn't legally obligated to pay the tax on behalf of the workers, it could still deduct the tax as a business expense. *Bad news:* The amount of tax paid on behalf of the workers was *extra income* to the workers, upon which both the company and the workers would owe *additional* employment taxes.
Source: IRS Letter Ruling 8635004.

Deductible Kickbacks

When Ray Bertolini paid over $160,000 in kickbacks to secure business for his trucking firm, the Court of Appeals ruled that the cost was *deductible* as a business expense. *Key facts:* The payments he made weren't illegal under state or federal law...and there was a genuine relationship between the health of his business and the kickback payments.
Source: *Raymond Bertolini Trucking,* 736 F2d 1120.

Business losers

Self-Insurance Trap

Under a company's medical self-insurance plan, an employee who incurred a medical cost would submit a claim to the company, which would examine and process the claim and ultimately make a reimbursement payment. To account for the delay between the time that medical services were received and the time payment was made, the company set up a reserve account showing its liability for medical care received but not yet paid for. At year-end, the company deducted the amount in this account as an accrued business expense. *Supreme Court:* The company wasn't finally liable on a claim until the paperwork was finished and the claim was *approved*. Thus, the reserve account wasn't a fixed liability, and the company could *not* deduct it.

Source: *General Dynamics,* S. Ct. Docket No. 85-1385.

When A Loan Isn't A Loan

The three equal owners of a private company each borrowed $9,500 from the firm, signing an interest-free demand note in return. The corporate minutes authorized the loan to each shareholder. *IRS ruling:* The three owners never intended to repay the so-called loans, so they were really *taxable dividends,* as evidenced by the fact that each owner had taken an identical amount *and* by the fact that the only payments on the loans by the three were made immediately after the start of an IRS audit.

Source: IRS Letter Ruling 8749002.

No Special Privilege For Family Business

The IRS ordered a family business to produce certain records. The owner refused, citing protection against self-incrimination. *Court:* While an individual can claim the privilege and refuse to produce subpoenaed records, a corporation has *no* right against self-incrimination. Since the family business was incorporated, it had to produce the records.

Source: *M&H Plastics, Inc.,* ED Calif., No. CIV-S-85-1523-RAR.

Levy Trap

Murray's, Inc. agreed to pay Virginia Cutshaw 5% of the price of any business that she brought the company. According to the agreement, Murray's had to pay Cutshaw when it received payment from the customer. Cutshaw made a $500,000 sale, and soon after the IRS issued a levy demanding that Murray's turn over to the IRS the $25,000 owed to Cutshaw. But since Murray's wasn't yet receiving payments from the customer, it felt it didn't owe Cutshaw anything and ignored the levy. *Court:* Murray's owed Cutshaw $25,000 as of the date the sale was completed, even if the agreed-on date for payment hadn't yet arrived. Thus, the IRS *could* demand the $25,000, and Murray's was liable for a *50% penalty* for refusing to comply.
Source: *Ruble Murray,* Ed Tenn., No. CIV-2-85-208.

Stock-Option Trap

One company set up an incentive stock-option program, then discovered that it didn't meet certain technical requirements of the law. The company amended the plan to meet the law's requirements, then asked the IRS to approve its status. *IRS ruling:* The IRS does *not* have the authority to provide retroactive approval to options that were *not* qualified when granted.
Source: IRS Letter Ruling 8616052.

Lying To The IRS

A private company failed to make its tax payments on time, though it filed a tax form saying it *had* made the payments. The company was suffering a cash shortage. When the IRS also penalized the company for willfully filing *false* tax forms, the company protested that it had good cause for its actions. *Court:* A lack of cash is not a good excuse for lying to the IRS. The penalties are upheld.
Source: *C. Bundy, Jr., Inc.,* ED Wis., No. 86-C-604.

Cash-Transaction Alert

IRS agents and IRS tax auditors regularly review *cash transactions* during business examinations. A $100 penalty is routinely being assessed for *each* business transaction involving more than $10,000 of cash for which no Form 8300 Information Return has been filed with the service. Penalties for intentional violations have been raised to as much as $25,000 or the amount of cash involved in the transaction to a maximum penalty of $100,000.

All about contractors

New Rules For Independent Contractors

Tax Reform has created a whole set of rules for technical specialists who secure work through employee leasing firms and were previously treated as independent contractors. Such specialists include computer programmers, systems analysts, engineers, designers, drafters, and other technical workers. An explanation of these rules can be found by calling your local IRS office and asking for *Notice 87-19.*

Government-Contract Trap

A contractor on a federal project was required by law to make sure that project workers were paid the community's standard wage rate. When the Department of Labor found out that a subcontractor was underpaying workers, it held the *contractor* liable and made it pay the difference, which the Department of Labor forwarded to the workers. *IRS ruling:* The contractor was also liable for *Social Security taxes* on the wage underpayments that it had to make up. The subcontractor wasn't liable for the tax on the makeup payment because it was the contractor that actually made the payment.
Source: IRS Letter Ruling 8628003.

Contractors Vs. Employees

A company used drivers to transport recreational vehicles from the manufacturing plant to retailers around the country. The IRS ruled that the drivers were independent contractors, not employees. *Impact:* The company owed no employment taxes on the money paid to them. *Key facts:* Individual drivers were free to accept or reject work assignments as they chose. They received a lump-sum payment for each trip, out of which they had to pay their own expenses. And they were personally liable for the first $500 of damage done to any vehicle in transit.
Source: IRS Letter Ruling 8636005.

Contractor Liable

The contractor on a construction project made payments to subcontractors, including money that was to be used to pay workers' employment taxes. But the subcontractors didn't pay those taxes. *Court:* The general contractor supplied the money needed to pay the subcontractors' payroll...and knew that the employment tax money was being misapplied. Thus, the contractor was liable for the unpaid tax *and* a 25% penalty.

Source: *Burchfield & Thomas, Inc.,* ED Ky, No. 82-239.

Who's liable for company taxes?

Who's Responsible?

Responsible persons are IRS targets. Even if you don't own the company you are employed by, the IRS can come after you for the company's unpaid payroll taxes. The definition of who is a responsible person, and, thus, liable for payroll tax shortfalls, is quite broad. It is not limited to high-level corporate executives. A bookkeeper or an office manager who pays salaries but does not remit payroll taxes to the government can be made personally liable by a revenue officer whose job is to collect the unpaid taxes. If you have the authority to decide which bills are paid first, and you put payroll taxes at the bottom of the list, you become personally liable.

Source: Ms. X, Esq., a former IRS agent who is still well-connected.

Innocent Owner

When a corporation failed to turn payroll taxes over to the government, the IRS went after the owner. It charged him a 100% penalty and took it out of his personal tax refund. The owner protested that he had hired managers to handle all cash, keep bank accounts, and pay creditors. *Court:* The managers, not the owner, were liable for the withheld tax. Neither stock ownership nor holding corporate office made the owner a "responsible person" for withholding tax purposes. *Key:* The owner had no authority to collect money and to pay debts—or to sign corporate checks.

Source: *Joseph G. Brennan,* ND Ohio, No. C-80-713.

Company Liable For Wrong W-2

A company filed a W-2 Form with the IRS, erroneously stating that an employee's disability benefits were taxable income. The company promised to send the IRS a corrected W-2 but didn't get around to it until after the employee was audited. *Court of Appeals:* The company was negligent in not promptly correcting the W-2 after the mistake was brought to its attention. As a result, it was liable to the employee for his out-of-pocket costs in resolving the matter—phone calls, travel expenses, postage, etc.—and for the value of his time devoted to resolving it.

Source: *Clemens v. Revlon, Inc.,* CA-5, No. 87-4259.

Treasurer Beats Rap

When a steel company failed to pay employment taxes, the IRS held *both* the president and Herbert Oliver, the treasurer, *personally* liable for the unpaid tax bill. But when Oliver protested, the court freed him from liability. *Key facts:* Though Oliver was treasurer of the company, this was *not* his primary job. He was not involved in the company's management on a daily basis, nor in deciding which debts should be paid. And while he had personally arranged a $100,000 loan for the company, the bank had assured him that it would take care of the employment taxes.
Source: *Herbert Oliver,* WD Wash., No. C-84-1177M.

Authority Is Key

Mary Green was a bookkeeper for ACS, Inc. When ACS used its limited funds to pay business creditors instead of employment taxes, the IRS tried to hold Green personally liable for the tax because she had check-writing authority for the company. *Court:* While Green could sign company checks, she didn't have the authority to say which creditors would and wouldn't be paid. Since she merely followed instructions when writing out checks, she wasn't liable for the tax. Moreover, the IRS was *unreasonable* in trying to collect the tax from her, so it had to pay her legal bills.
Source: *Garland R. Pomeroy,* SD W. Va., No. 84-2188.

Worthiness of a home office

Office-In-Home Loopholes

Running a business from your home—full-time or just as a sideline—can generate thousands of dollars in tax breaks. Although Tax Reform did tighten the rules on deductibility of home-office expenses, they're still sufficiently lenient to provide wonderful tax write-offs that pass IRS scrutiny. *Suggestions:*

Set up a home-based sideline business that turns a profit. Form a consulting practice or turn an expensive hobby, such as photography, into a money-making venture. *Tax impact:* The expenses of operating the business are deductible in full against the business's income. And since you run the business out of your home, your deductions include the business portion of your mortgage interest, real estate taxes, depreciation or rent, utilities, insurance, and repairs.

Different trades: Your at-home business need not generate your major source of income. The courts have consistently held that taxpayers can be involved in many different trades and businesses at the same time, each separate and distinct from the others.

Demonstrate your intention of making a profit. It's essential to keep accurate records of your income and expenses, even when your sideline business generates a loss. If the sideline is not profitable in at least three out of five consecutive years, IRS auditors will say that it's an activity not engaged in for profit, so your net business losses will not be deductible. You can overcome the auditor's position, but it's difficult.

Take depreciation write-offs. You can depreciate that portion of your home that serves as an office. To determine the percentage of business use, either divide the number of business rooms you use by the number of rooms in your house, or divide the number of square feet in the office by the total square footage of the house.

The depreciation system you use depends on when you started using your home for business.

Problem: If you sell your house while operating a business out of it, you won't be able to defer tax on the gain on that portion of the house that was being used for business purposes. *Loophole:* In the year you sell, make certain you don't qualify for a home-office deduction by purposely using it for personal reasons. By violating the exclusively-for-business-use requirement, you'll be able to defer taxes on all your house-sale profits. (Of course, you must adjust your tax basis in the house by the business depreciation you've claimed over the years.)

Deduct transportation expenses. If you're an employee, you can convert nondeductible, personal commuting expenses into tax-deductible, local business driving by keeping an office in your home. *The tax rule on commuting expenses is this:* Your first trip of the day (from home to office) is nondeductible, as is your last trip of the day (from office to home). All business-related driving in between is tax-deductible, either at your cost or at the IRS standard mileage rate.

The trick is to make your first and last business stops of the day in your at-home office. Suppose you have a den where you study reports, go through business papers, read business mail, etc. If your home office is the first and last business stop of the day, driving to work and back becomes tax-deductible transportation.

Another option: Collect business mail at the closest post office, or make business deposits at a nearby bank. That way, your nondeductible beginning and ending driving trips of the day will be short, and all other driving will be tax-deductible.

Deduct phone calls. Even if you don't use your home office on an exclusive basis, if you have a separate business telephone, the cost is tax-deductible as an unreimbursed employee business expense (subject to the 2% limitation on miscellaneous itemized deductions). Even if you don't have a separate phone line, any long-distance charges you incur for business are deductible.

Shift income to your children. Those who work for themselves as sole proprietors have the opportunity to shift income to family members by hiring their children. The employment must be *bona fide* and the compensation reasonable.

Source: IRS tax-law specialist Paul N. Strassels, Box 195, Burke, VA 22015.

How To Deduct Home Phone Calls

Business calls made from your home phone are deductible if your employer does not reimburse you for them. Keep the page of your phone bill that lists the long-distance calls as documentation for the IRS.

Also deductible: Phone calls that you make to your office when you are working at home or absent from work because you are sick or on vacation.

Smart idea: If you use your home phone very frequently for business calls, it's better to install a separate phone to be used just for business. This way you won't have to worry about apportioning the monthly service charge, etc., between home use and business use.

Note: You cannot deduct any part of the *basic* charge of the first phone line into your home.

Summer Office

An executive could deduct maintenance costs and depreciation on a separate office he built near his vacation home and used exclusively to review the company's long-range plans. The IRS said the office was a nondeductible personal expense. But the court allowed the deduction. The alternate office was appropriate and helpful to the executive in performing his duties.

Source: *Ben W. Heineman,* 82 TC 638.

More About Home Offices

The ratio of time spent working and the precise kind of work performed in a given locale are crucial to all tax determinations on home-office status by the IRS. *Three landmark cases:*

Homework: A home office is normally deductible only if it is your *primary* place of business. The IRS uses this rule to deny deductions to many persons who are required to bring work home but also have business offices. *Case:* The Court of Appeals has ruled that orchestra musicians could claim home-office deductions for their practice studios in spite of the IRS's claim that their primary place of business was the concert hall. *Key:* The musicians spent more time at home practicing than they did performing. *Impact:* Salespersons, professors, writers, and others who, in fact, spend most of their time working at home can use this case to try to justify deductions for themselves.

Source: *Ernest Drucker,* 715 F2d 67.

Proportion: Sally Meiers owned and managed a laundromat. Each day she spent an hour at the laundry and two hours in her home office, where she did necessary administrative work. The Tax Court denied Sally's home-office deduction because the laundromat, not her home, was her principal place of business. Sally appealed. *Court of Appeals:* Sally spent more *time* working at home than anywhere else. Thus, the home office *was* her principal place of business and the deduction was allowed.

Source: *John and Sally Meiers,* CA-7, No. 85–1209.

Kind of work: A college professor spent 80% of the work week doing research and writing in an office at home. The IRS ruled that the home office was not his "principal place of business" (he had an office at the college), nor was it used "for the convenience of the employer." *Court of Appeals:* The home office *was* the professor's principal place of business, as his college office wasn't private enough for the scholarly work required by his job. Moreover, the use of the professor's home was for the employer's convenience, since it relieved the college of the necessity of providing a suitable office. Home-office deductions allowed.

Source: *David J. Weissman,* CA-2, 751 F2d 512.

Commuting-Cost Loophole

A home office can generate *extra* tax savings. Use it to convert nondeductible commuting costs into deductible travel expenses.

Key: While the cost of commuting between home and work is normally *not* deductible, the cost of traveling between different job sites is a deductible travel expense. And a home office can have the effect of converting your home into a job site.

That's what the Tax Court ruled in the case of an insurance salesman who deducted all his auto-travel expenses. The IRS allowed the salesman's deduction for trips from one client to another but disallowed his deduction for daily travel from home to his sales area. The home office saved the day. The Tax Court found that the salesman's home was a place of business, so *all* his travel costs were deductible.

Source: *Carl F. Worden,* TC Memo 1981-366.

Home-Office Requirements: New And Old

For self-employed persons to legitimately take home-office write-offs, the office must be used:

- Exclusively *and* regularly as the principal place of business, or
- To meet with patients, clients, or customers in the normal course of business.

Employees can write off home-office expenses only when they meet the two requirements above, plus an additional one...the use of the residence must be for the convenience of their employer. And to be deductible, an employee's home-office expenses, added to other miscellaneous expenses, must exceed 2% of Adjusted Gross Income.

Tax Reform limitation: Your deductions are limited to the net income generated by the home-office activity that year. (*Exception:* Real estate taxes and mortgage interest are always fully deductible.) Home-office expenses that can't be deducted because of this provision can be carried over and deducted in future years against net home-office income for those years.

Beating The Home-Office Trap

While a home-office deduction can save you money on your tax return, it can also *cost* you two big breaks when you sell your home. *Namely:* Tax-deferred treatment of profits that are reinvested in a replacement residence...and the $125,000 tax exclusion for sale proceeds received by home sellers age 55 or older.

Trap: A home office is treated as *business* property, not as part of your personal residence. So the portion of house sale proceeds attributable to the office does *not* qualify for these residential property-tax breaks.

What to do: The IRS has ruled that a house *does* fully qualify for residential property-tax breaks if the seller isn't entitled to claim a home-office deduction in the *year of sale*, even if the deduction was claimed in previous years. So if you have a home office, *don't* use it exclusively for business or claim a deduction for it in the year in which you want to sell your home.

Work-At-Home Pitfall

C. S. McKay claimed a home-office deduction for part of her home. She said it was not safe to work at her employer's office after hours. *Tax Court:* Ms. McKay *wasn't* entitled to the deduction because her home office wasn't her *principal* place of work, nor was she required to have a home office by her employer. Her decision to work at home was for her own convenience, so the costs involved weren't deductible.
Source: *Carston Simon McKay,* TC Memo 1986-514.

If you're self-employed...

Free-lancer Smarts

Report income and expenses on Schedule C of Form 1040. There's a big advantage in doing this. Business expenses, such as transportation costs, are deductible in *full* on Schedule C. They are not subject to the 2%-of-Adjusted-Gross-Income limitation that applies when the same expenses are taken on Schedule A of the 1040.

If you get a commission, report it on Schedule C, even if you have no business expenses to write off against it. *Reason:* If the income qualifies as self-employment income, you can use some of it to set up a Keogh plan.

Source: Edward Mendlowitz, partner, Mendlowitz Weitsen, CPAs, Two Pennsylvania Plaza, New York 10121.

Special Advice For The Self-Employed And Moonlighters

Those already in business for themselves know that the IRS is a reality—and those just starting their own businesses will soon learn it. The IRS is a partner and overseer—and it cannot be ignored. Mistakes are costly. Even if your accountant makes the mistake on your return, you pay.

To avoid trouble with the IRS:

Be prepared to explain your style of living. The IRS knows that it takes time to build a growing business. The IRS also knows that some people fraudulently underreport their income. If the circumstances of your enterprise dictate that you report low income or even a loss, be prepared to answer the question "What did you live on?" *Trap:* If you are unable to answer to the satisfaction of an IRS examining officer, you may find yourself involved in a costly investigation or be assessed with a heavy tax.

Cost of living for an individual is derived from one or more of the following sources:

- Current income.
- Borrowing.
- Repayment of money lent to others.
- Gifts and inheritances.
- Support from others.
- Accumulated assets (savings accounts, securities, house, car, cash on hand, etc.).

Caution: The source of assets accumulated before you launched your business may also be questioned.

Your accountant will urge you to keep track of business transactions. You should consider equally important the need to keep track of your personal expenses, including the source of funds for payment of living expenses.

Have separate equipment, etc., for business use. If the nature of your business requires that you make and receive business calls at home, install a separate telephone for that purpose. If you drive a significant number of business miles, keep a separate automobile for that purpose. If your business requires that you do substantial work at home, set aside a room or area of your home as an office. Furnish the area exclusively with office furniture, equipment, and business materials, and use it exclusively for business purposes.

Know your tax responsibilities. Even if you leave the matter of taxes largely to your accountant and bookkeeper, you should take the time and trouble to educate yourself on the subject. The penalties for slipping are prohibitively high. Learn your personal responsibility for income tax, self-employment tax, and estimated tax payments. Then be sure to have some understanding of your responsibility in the area of employment taxes. *Helpful:* IRS Publication No. 15, commonly known as Circular E *(Employer's Tax Guide),* available free of charge from the IRS. You should also be aware of state and local tax requirements.

Caution: In the past, some employers used government trust funds (taxes withheld from employees' wages) to tide the company over periods of weak cash flow. Be advised that the IRS has little patience with such methods. It has an ever-increasing policy of cracking down fast and forcefully on employers who don't follow the letter of the law in handling withheld payroll taxes. If you are in a pinch, ask your accountant to locate an alternate source of funds.

Keep good records. Your accountant has primary responsibility to provide you with a system that clearly and properly reflects your business income and transactions. A simple method of recordkeeping that works is one that is organized to reflect tax return items line by line.

Example: If you are a sole proprietorship, set up your accounts according to the line items on Form 8829. Mark your checks, credit-card receipts, and diary entries with the appropriate type of expense or line number.

For more complex and/or active business enterprises, you would be wise to rely on the expertise of a reputable accountant who is familiar with your type of business. Expect your accountant to set up a recordkeeping system, give business advice, and represent you at the IRS if necessary. It will be money well spent.

Source: George S. Alberts, former head of the Albany and Brooklyn (NY) IRS District Offices.

Audit Targets

High-income taxpayers with self-employment income are priority audit targets under the IRS's stepped-up Schedule C initiative. The service estimates that nearly 40% of all unreported personal income is self-employment income left off Schedule C of Form 1040.

Getting a targeted-jobs tax credit

Certification Trap

For a company to get the targeted-jobs tax credit, a new worker must be *certified* by a state jobs agency as being a member of a target group. If the company doesn't make a *written* request for certification by the time the new hire begins work, it *can't* claim the credit, even if the worker *is* a member of a targeted group.
Source: Revenue Ruling 87-94.

No Credit For Old Jobs

When B&R Food Systems won a food-service contract that had previously been held by another company, it hired 30 of the other company's workers and claimed the targeted-jobs tax credit for them. *Court:* B&R was not entitled to the credit because the workers it hired had performed the *same* services for the other company. B&R hadn't created any *new jobs*.
Source: *B&R Food Services,* ND Tex., No. CA6-84-39.

7

TAX LOOPHOLES

EVERYTHING THE LAW ALLOWS

Property And Charity Tax Magic

New angles for homeowners

Homeowners' Tax Breaks

For the alert taxpayer, the family home can be a major source of tax savings. Federal tax law is studded with provisions that encourage and enhance home ownership, as opposed to other forms of investment.

Mortgage points. For borrowers other than homeowners, mortgage points (a prepayment of interest represented by a percentage of the loan) have to be capitalized and deducted over the life of the loan. But points charged on money borrowed to buy or improve a principal residence are fully deductible by homeowners in the year they're paid.

The glories of giving. Homeowners who take advantage of a technique known as deferred giving can get a large, immediate income tax deduction that will produce cash flow now without sacrificing up their right to live in the house. *How it works:* The owners, a husband and wife, say, give what is called remainder interest in their house to charity. This is the right the charity has to take over the house on the owners' death. But the owners reserve the right to live in the house until the survivor of them dies. The owners get a current charitable deduction for the value of the charity's interest. This is computed from IRS tables and depends on how long the charity is expected to wait before taking over the house.

Joint property ownership. The tax law encourages couples to own the family home in the name of the spouse who is most likely to die first. Statistically, that's the husband.

The unlimited marital deduction means that the first spouse to die can leave the house to the surviving spouse without incurring any tax at all on his death. Yet the property will get a stepped-up tax basis (its cost for tax purposes) to the fair market value at the date of death. No estate tax will have to be paid on the house's appreciated value. When the surviving spouse sells, since she inherited the house at the increased value, the gains tax she will have to pay will be reduced. If the house remains in joint ownership, the widow's tax on the sale will be much higher.

Source: Ivan Faggen, a tax partner with Arthur Andersen & Co., in charge of the Tax Division for the South Florida offices, 1 Biscayne Tower, Suite 2100, Miami 33131.

Selling Your House Tax-Wise

Benefits built into the tax code regarding the sale of a residence:
■ If you sell a house and then reinvest the entire proceeds in another residence within two years, there's a complete deferral of tax on any gains.
■ If you are age 55 or older when you sell your house, you can claim a tax exclusion of the first $125,000 of gain.

To calculate the gain on the sale of your house, subtract the total of your costs (original cost, cost of capital improvements made to the house during your ownership, and your selling expenses, including fixing-up costs) from the selling price. *Estate planning point:* If you die while still owning your house, the IRS will forgive any gain on appreciation as of the date of your death.

Source: Edward Mendlowitz, partner, Mendlowitz Weitsen, CPAs, Two Pennsylvania Plaza, New York 10121.

Repairs Vs. Remodeling

Lorraine Foster owned NTC, Inc., which conducted tax seminars. Foster bought a new home, and NTC spent more than $5,000 to convert the basement into an office, which it used until it went bankrupt. NTC deducted the $5,000 as repairs. *Tax Court:* While the cost of repairing a building may qualify as a deductible business expense, the cost of *remodeling and improving* a property doesn't—it's a capital expenditure. NTC had improved the basement, so the $5,000 was *not* deductible.

Source: *National Tax Consultants, Inc.,* TC Memo 1987-58.

The IRS Is Watching

For several years now, taxpayers 55 or older have been able to sell their home and exclude up to $125,000 of profit from taxation. But this is a once-in-a-lifetime tax break. You (or your spouse) can't buy and sell another home later and claim the exclusion again. To make sure nobody does, IRS computers maintain a list of those who have already used this tax break and check the list against any tax returns claiming the exclusion. Duplicate or questionable claims are referred for investigation.

The New Home-Equity Credit Game

Tapping the accumulated equity in your home can be both a good and a bad way to borrow money. It depends on how much you pay for the privilege and what you're borrowing for:

The upside: Banks and other financial service outlets are making lots of money available for home-equity loans, and there's intense competition to make these loans. That means better interest rates for borrowers. But there's a reason for that. Home-equity lines of credit must give the lender security—an enforceable lien against your home. Whatever they may be called in the ads, they are essentially second mortgages.

The downside: If you can't meet the monthly payments, you may lose your home. Consumer credit counselors worry that people will assume more debt than they will be able to handle, especially if the economy goes into a recession or they lose their jobs.

Comparison Shop

Because home-equity credit loans are offered by so many different kinds of institutions and under so many guises, it's necessary to comparison shop to find the best deal. Don't just focus on the interest rate. *Also compare:* Points or origination fees, which can vary from zero to several percentage points of the principal amount, application fees, appraisal, and credit-checking fees.

Some banks, for example, impose only a $25 or $50 fee to have a new appraisal made. Others charge a full range of fees as if they were processing a first mortgage. Since they're not, those fees may be inappropriate.

Watch out for "teaser" rates—banks advertising a tempting below-market introductory rate. These rates are often good for only three to six months, after which the rate is tied to the prime rate or to treasury bills.

Often, too, the rates on home-equity credit lines are readjusted more frequently than rates on the typical adjustable-rate mortgage. And they may not have a cap. Occasionally, the rate may vary from month to month.

Only protection: Read the fine print. Use a worst-case scenario to calculate how high your monthly payment schedule could get. If there's any doubt about your ability to meet those payments, don't take the loan.

General rule: Think of your home-equity credit line as a large pool of funds that can be tapped quickly at relatively attractive interest rates to help you meet an emergency or to finance truly worthwhile purchases, such as a college education. Don't use it simply to fund general household expenses. That's an invitation to overextend yourself.

Tax Considerations

From a tax standpoint, the advantage of home-equity borrowing is that the IRS doesn't care what you do with the money up to $100,000 in principal. This means that the IRS won't trace the investments you make with your home-equity borrowing and then tell you how much of your interest is tax-deductible. With a qualified home-equity loan, the interest is *all* tax-deductible.

Strategy: If you're going to borrow, it's better to borrow on a tax-deductible basis. Consider your whole financial picture, and then borrow carefully so that you will achieve the maximum tax-deductibility.

Bottom line: Use the home-equity line of credit to finance the car...but not the investments. Always remember, however, that if you can't meet the payments, it's not your car that you're going to lose—it's your home.

Real-Estate Purchases

Many people use the equity in their primary residence to help finance a real-estate purchase. That's fine if you're planning to use the place exclusively as a vacation home, or if that's the only way you can put together the down payment that banks may require to buy rental property.

You should understand, however, that when you own rental property, the IRS already gives you the right to deduct passive losses up to the extent of your passive (rental) income, so you don't really need the tax-deductibility of a home-equity loan.

What's more, if you can qualify as an active participant in the rental property (own at least 10% of it and meet certain other requirements), it may be smarter *not* to finance it with a home-equity loan. *Reason:* The tax law provides that so-called active participants can deduct up to $25,000 of losses against their income, until that income reaches $100,000 (excluding the loss), at which point the tax break gradually phases out.

Source: Steven M. Friedman, senior manager in the national tax department of Ernst & Young, 1225 Connecticut Ave. NW, Washington, DC 20036

Reap tax rewards renting to your parents

Turn Your Parents' Home Into A Great Tax Shelter

Real-estate deals are the best tax shelters left after Tax Reform. One of the safest is to buy your retired parents' home on the installment basis and *rent* it back to them.

The installment payments you make can be set to be:

- *Larger* than their rent, giving them extra cash each month.
- *Equal* to their rent, so cash payments offset it.
- *Smaller* than their rent, so you get extra cash each month.

Breaks for your parents: They get up to $125,000 of their gain on the sale tax-free (assuming at least one of them is age 55 or over and has used the house as a principal residence for three of the past five years). And they can get extra cash at a time they need it through the down payment and/or installment payments you make.

Breaks for you: You can deduct depreciation on the house as well as other expenses related to the *business* of renting your house (insurance, repairs, etc.). So you will probably be able to deduct *tax losses,* even if the deal is structured to give you cash flow.

Family tax-saver: If your retired parents are in a lower income-tax bracket than you, the interest that you pay on the installment sale will be tax-deductible at your *high* tax rate and taxed to them at their *low* rate, cutting family taxes overall.

Watch this: Your deductions from the rental are limited to $25,000 a year and are phased out completely if you are filing a joint return and your Adjusted Gross Income exceeds $150,000. Also, a sale of your parents' home in their lifetimes precludes a substantial family benefit at their deaths—that is, a stepped-up basis on the home—so the capital-gains tax need never be paid.

The IRS scrutinizes family deals very closely, so be sure you buy your parents' house for a reasonable market price and lease it back to them for a reasonable market rent.

Renting To The Folks

A dentist and his wife bought a townhouse for his parents. They paid him a fair market rental for the home, but the house had a negative cash flow. When he deducted losses each year, the IRS said they were personal and nondeductible. *District Court:* He charged a fair market rent, had a written lease, and kept a ledger and separate bank account for the property, which showed that he had an intent to make a profit. By renting to his parents, he knew he had good tenants who would take care of the property. The loss was allowed.

Source: *Robert Kuga,* No. 86-0022-A.

Mortgage rules to know

The Revenue Act Of 1987 And Mortgage Interest

The Tax Reform Act of 1986 generally limited the home-loan interest deduction to interest on an amount of debt equal to the home's original cost plus the cost of improvements, plus amounts borrowed to pay educational or medical bills. Because the Tax Reform Act also phased out the deduction for consumer interest, many people have borrowed against their homes up to this limit to finance consumer purchases (of cars, furniture, etc.).

The Revenue Act of 1987 sets up *new* deduction limits. First, only interest on debt to acquire, construct, or substantially improve your first or second residence up to *$1 million* is deductible, even if the mortgages on your first and second homes together are higher. Second, interest is deductible on a home-equity refinancing only to the extent that it doesn't increase your home-loan debt by more than $100,000.

Example: You bought a home for $500,000 and paid the mortgage down to $200,000. Under the Tax Reform Act of 1986, you could refinance the mortgage for up to $500,000 and get a full interest deduction. But under the 1987 Act, you can claim an interest deduction on a refinancing for only up to $300,000 ($200,000 on the existing mortgage plus $100,000 of new debt).

Impact: These new limits generally cut back on the opportunity to use home loans to finance consumer purchases and other expenses. In the future, home buyers who wish to use home loans to maximize their deductible borrowing should take out the largest mortgages possible (up to the $1 million aggregate) over the longest term.

Hidden benefit: There's *good news* in the new borrowing limits, too. Subject to the $1 million cap, you can deduct interest on up to $100,000 of increased financing against your home, *regardless* of the home's original cost. Thus, if the costs plus improvements of your home were $300,000 and you have paid the mortgage down to $250,000, you can borrow another $100,000 to make your total debt $350,000. Under the Tax Reform Act of 1986, you could borrow *only* another $50,000 so that debt equaled the home's cost (including improvements) of $300,000, unless amounts in excess of $300,000 were for educational or medical expenses.

Source: S. Theodore Reiner, director, tax client communications, Ernst & Young, 1225 Connecticut Ave. NW, Washington, DC 20036.

Type Of Trust Is Important

Title to my home is held by a revocable trust, of which I'm the sole trustee. Can I deduct the mortgage payments and property taxes that are paid on the house from the trust income?

It depends on the type of trust that is involved. If the trust is what the IRS calls a *grantor trust,* it is disregarded for tax purposes. All the trust's income is taxed to the person who set it up, and that person is entitled to claim a deduction for all deductible items that are paid from trust funds. If it is not a grantor trust, it is subject to a different set of rules. Generally, the trust is a separate taxpayer liable for its own taxes, and you can't claim a deduction for expenses that it pays.

To find out how these rules apply in your situation, you should consult with your accountant or with the lawyer who set up the trust.

Second Home

I own a second residence in the country that I plan to rent out this summer. How will this affect my deduction for the interest on its mortgage?

You can qualify the summer house as your personal second residence by using it yourself during the year for *more* than the greater of 14 days or 10% of the number of days you rent it out. As a second residence, the mortgage interest on it will be fully deductible under Tax Reform rules.

Alternative: By *not* using the home for the minimum number of days, you may qualify it as an income-generating business property. You could then claim deductions for related expenses such as depreciations, insurance, and maintenance. But your interest deduction could be limited by Tax Reform rules. Your tax adviser can work through the figures both ways to see which brings the bigger after-tax return.

Monitoring Mortgage Deductions

IRS Form 8598, for reporting home-mortgage interest deductions, requires taxpayers to list their *average balance* for each mortgage. Banks are required to report these balances to taxpayers and to the IRS on Form 1098.

Getting Around New Residence Interest Rules

New rule #1: Acquisition indebtedness. Interest on mortgages for acquiring, constructing, or substantially improving your principal residence and one second residence is deductible for loans of up to $1 million. A principal or second residence includes a house, condominium, cooperative, mobile home, boat, or similar property that has basic living accommodations, including sleeping space and toilet and cooking facilities.

If you borrow more than $1 million to buy your principal residence and a second residence, the interest on the amount over $1 million constitutes personal interest. (The deduction on personal interest is phased out.)

Note: Acquisition indebtedness also includes a mortgage resulting from a refinancing up to the remaining principal balance of the refinanced debt.

This rule went into effect on January 1, 1988. *Important exception:* The $1 million limitation does not apply to mortgages obtained on or before October 13, 1987. If you borrowed more than $1 million on or before October 13, 1987, you can still fully deduct your entire interest payment if you qualify under the Tax Reform Act of 1986.

New rule #2: Home-equity indebtedness. Interest on home-equity mortgages on your principal residence and a second residence is deductible for loans of up to $100,000. A home-equity mortgage is a loan secured by the present fair market value of your home, regardless of how the amount borrowed is used.

In addition to the $100,000 limitation, a home-equity mortgage isn't deductible if it's for more than the current fair market value of your home minus your present first mortgage.

Example: Suppose you purchased a home many years ago for $30,000 and finished paying off your mortgage. The house is now worth $225,000. You can deduct the interest on a home-equity mortgage for up to $100,000. You can use the money for whatever you choose. *Important details:*

■ Even if your original purchase price in this example was over $100,000, the interest deduction on the home-equity mortgage would still be limited to a loan of $100,000.

■ No special provision has been made for amounts specifically borrowed for medical or educational purposes as under the Tax Reform Act of 1986. Those rules have been replaced by this $100,000 cap. You are limited to deducting interest for loans of up to $100,000, even if you should borrow more than that amount to pay for medical or educational expenses.

Combination of rule #1 and rule #2. The maximum allowable debt on which you can deduct mortgage interest for your principal residence and a second residence is $1,100,000 ($1 million of acquisition indebtedness plus $100,000 of home-equity indebtedness).

Example: You take out a mortgage of $200,000 to purchase a home. After several years, when the house has a value of $300,000 and you have paid the mortgage down to $195,000, you refinance for a new mortgage of $250,000. All interest paid on the new debt is deductible, since $195,000 of the mortgage constitutes acquisition indebtedness and $55,000 of the mortgage qualifies as home-equity indebtedness.

Under the new law, mortgages on your principal residence or a second residence obtained on or before October 13, 1987 are grandfathered.

Example: On January 1, 1987, you obtained a home-equity loan for $150,000. The interest was fully deductible under the Tax Reform Act of 1986 because at the time you obtained the loan, the cost plus improvements on your home was $200,000 and you had an existing mortgage of $50,000. The total interest will continue to be deductible, even though the home-equity debt is in excess of $100,000.

Source: Lorin D. Luchs, tax partner, BDO Seidman, 1200 18 St. NW, Washington, DC 20036.

Real-estate investing and reinvesting

Deducting Real-Estate Losses

Deductions for real estate losses in actively managed property are limited to a maximum of $25,000, provided your Adjusted Gross Income is $100,000 or less. If it's more than $150,000, no loss deductions are permitted. For an AGI of between $100,000 and $150,000, you lose $1 in deductions for every $2 of AGI. (You must reduce the $25,000 amount by 50% of the amount by which your AGI exceeds $100,000.)

If you have real-estate losses and you can't claim them, one way to take advantage of them is to prepay your mortgage or to pay as much of it as is necessary to reduce the loss. In this way, you'll "earn" income equivalent to the interest rate on the prepaid mortgage. These earnings will be "tax-free" since they'll be sheltered by the real-estate losses you wouldn't be able to deduct otherwise.

Assume that you have a mortgage of $100,000 at 10% interest and your annual losses, including depreciation, amount to $4,000. Also, assume that your AGI is more than $150,000 so that no part of the loss is deductible. If you prepay $40,000 of the mortgage, you'll decrease the loss by $4,000 (10% interest times $40,000 reduction of mortgage). In effect, you'll be breaking even. You'll be saving the $4,000 in interest payments or "earning" that $4,000 on the $40,000 used to prepay part of your mortgage. That $4,000 is probably more than you would earn on other investments.

Source: Edward Mendlowitz, partner, Mendlowitz Weitsen, CPAs, Two Pennsylvania Plaza, New York 10121.

Tax Status Of Residential Lot

I purchased a vacant residential lot on which I intend to build a home. The former owner of the land is providing financing. How do I handle the interest on the loan? Can I treat the lot as a second residence?

The lot won't qualify as a second residence because you don't have a residence there. Your property purchase will be treated as an investment, and interest paid on the financing will be investment interest.

Investment interest is deductible to the extent that you have investment income, and another $10,000 of interest is deductible beyond that. However, Tax Reform phases out the deduction for interest exceeding investment income.

Reinvesting Pitfall

Lester Kahl sold investment real estate that was threatened by condemnation. He used the sale proceeds to set up a Costa Rican corporation that invested in real estate, among other activities. He then claimed tax deferral for his gain on the sale of the condemned property, stating that he had bought similar property in Costa Rica. *Tax Court:* Kahl had not reinvested the proceeds from the real-estate sale in "similar" property. Rather, he had used the condemnation proceeds to buy a corporation that was *not* primarily engaged in owning real estate. Thus, he was entitled to *no* deferral.

Source: *Lester Howard Kahl,* TC Memo 1986-240.

Charitable-giving tactics

Deductions For Appreciated Property

Charitable deductions are usually limited to the fair market value of the donation or cost at the time of purchase, whichever is less. If, however, you donate appreciated securities that you've owned for more than one year (more than six months, if bought before January 1, 1988), you get a deduction for the full market value of the securities.

If you donate appreciated assets other than securities—such as art or antiques—to a charity that will use them in connection with its activities and not subsequently resell them, you can get a tax deduction for the fair market value, even when it's greater than the amount you paid. You don't have to declare the difference or the profit as income—a double benefit. These deductions are limited to 30% of your current Adjusted Gross Income. Any excess profit can be carried forward for five years.

If the deduction you claim for charitable donations of appreciated property is more than $500, you must fill out Form 8283. If it's more than $5,000, you must get an appraisal, except that no appraisal is required for publicly-traded securities. For non-publicly-traded securities, you must get an appraisal if the value exceeds $10,000.

Source: Edward Mendlowitz, partner, Mendlowitz Weitsen, CPAs, Two Pennsylvania Plaza, New York 10121.

Old-Property Donations

There are two approaches to take in claiming deductions for donating old property to charity. You can take a deduction for the fair market value of clothing, furniture, and similar property that you give to a charity. However, it's often hard to determine what the fair market value is. *Suggestion:* Estimate the cost of the property when it was new. Then take 25% of that amount as the fair market value for the used property. For example, if you give away a suit that cost you $100, take a tax deduction of $25.

Use the following approach when contributing old books and/or magazines to a library that will use them for charitable activities. Get the items appraised by a used book or magazine dealer. You'll probably be charged a fee. For tax purposes, list separately each book or magazine issue and its value. You can chalk up thousands of dollars in deductions, which will far outweigh the cost of the appraisal.

For both types of donations, if you claim a deduction of more than $500, you must fill out Form 8283 and attach it to your tax return. If the deduction is more than $5,000, you must get an appraisal.

Source: *New Tax Traps/New Opportunities* by Edward Mendlowitz, CPA, Boardroom Special Report, Springfield, NJ 07081.

Rendering Services For Charity

If you perform services for a charity, you can't deduct the value of your services. However, you can deduct all out-of-pocket expenses that you incurred in the course of your service. *Examples:* Costs of coffee and cake for meetings in your house, money spent on supplies that you purchased in connection with charitable activities, and certain expenses of chaperoning a youth group on a trip. You're entitled to a deduction for the use of your car in connection with a charity.

Source: Edward Mendlowitz, partner, Mendlowitz Weitsen, CPAs, Two Pennsylvania Plaza, New York 10121.

Veterans' Break

Earl Weingarden donated a valuable building to a nonprofit veterans' organization and deducted his gift. But the IRS *limited* his deduction. It said the veterans' group was a membership organization, *not* a charity, so a charitable deduction resulting from a gift to it cannot exceed 20% of the donor's Adjusted Gross Income (AGI), instead of the 50% limit that applies to charities. The Tax Court agreed. *Court of Appeals:* For Weingarden and the veterans' group. A technical reading of the law indicates that the 50% limit *does* apply to veterans' organizations.

Source: *Earl Weingarden,* CA-6, No. 86-1681.

Unused Benefit Tickets

Unused benefit tickets are deductible at full cost as a charitable contribution. *Example:* You pay $100 for a top-of-the-line seat at the benefit performance. The box office price of the seat is $37. If you attend the performance, you can deduct only $63 ($100 cost minus $37 value received). But if you send back the ticket unused after paying for it, you can deduct the full $100.

Future Gift

A man who owns a house plans to give an irrevocable remainder interest in the house to a charity, thus giving the charity ownership of the house after he dies. *IRS ruling:* The owner of the house can claim a charity deduction for the value of the gift *now,* even though the charity won't receive the house until after his death.

Source: IRS Letter Ruling 8711038.

Charity Remainder Trusts

A charity remainder trust is a trust in which the grantor continues to earn income on the principal throughout his/her lifetime. He may also take a tax deduction based upon the full appreciated value of the property at the time of the donation. At a specified time, such as the death of the grantor, the principal becomes the property of the charity. Charity remainder trusts can be very effective tax-saving devices. As the grantor, you get an immediate deduction for the value of the remainder interest in the year that it's donated to the charity. The value of the gift is based on the present value of the principal. Accordingly, if you donate substantially appreciated assets, your deduction will be based on the current value of the asset, and you won't have to pay income tax on the unrealized gain.

Source: Edward Mendlowitz, partner, Mendlowitz Weitsen, CPAs, 2 Pennsylvania Plaza, New York 10001.

College Contribution

D. D. Palmer donated land with a Victorian mansion located on it to Palmer College and claimed a $300,000 charitable deduction. The college had already used the mansion as the hub of its activity. But the IRS and the Tax Court refused to give Palmer *any* deduction for the mansion, allowing a deduction only for the land and saying the land was worth more without the mansion than with it. *Court of Appeals:* For Mr. Palmer. Both the IRS and the Tax Court made the mistake of valuing the old mansion as a residence. But it was, instead, being used as a college building. It was much *more* valuable as such, so a higher valuation was proper.

Source: *Estate of D. D. Palmer,* CA-8, No. 86-2044.

Charitable Easement

A group of property owners were allowed to deduct *$1 million* in charitable contributions because an easement that they gave to the county decreased the value of their land by that much. The IRS tried to argue that the decrease in value to the land was $400,000 and, therefore, the amount of the charitable contribution was only about $400,000. *Tax Court:* The IRS appraiser calculated the value of the land inaccurately. The taxpayers' appraiser, on the other hand, had extensive experience and conducted a much more thorough investigation of the land's value. His determination of value was accepted.

Source: *Henry T. Stotler,* TC Memo 1987-275.

Painless Deduction

A farm owner plans to grant to a conservation group an easement that will prohibit the property from ever being developed for industrial, commercial, or residential use. *IRS ruling:* The value of the easement may be deducted by the farm's owner as a *charitable gift,* even though it cost him nothing out-of-pocket and there may never have been any intention to develop the property in the first place.
Source: IRS Letter Ruling 8711054.

Risks for charitable giving

New Trap For Charity Givers

The holding period for long-term assets has been increased by Tax Reform. Securities and other property bought in 1988 or later must be held for *more than one year* (rather than six months) to qualify as long-term. Taxpayers who make charitable donations of properties that have increased in value can get a deduction for full market value—but *only* if they owned the property for the long-term period. Otherwise, they can deduct no more than the original cost. *Smart giving:* Don't donate appreciated securities (or other property) bought after December 31, 1987, until you've owned them for at least a year and a day.

Investment Gift Scam

Myron Sammons bought a collection of American Indian artifacts for $140,000 and obtained *two* appraisals saying they were worth $540,000. He donated the artifacts to a museum and claimed a $540,000 charity deduction. *Tax Court:* The appraisals were worthless because the appraisers would not testify at the trial. Moreover, one of the appraisers was actually an officer of the museum that received the gift. Thus, the best evidence of the artifacts' worth was the price that Sammons actually paid for them—$140,000. He was entitled to a deduction in that amount.

Source: *Myron G. Sammons,* TC Memo 1986-318.

Audit Risk For Charitable Donors

Gifts of property valued at more than $500 may be challenged under new IRS procedures. The IRS will match the taxpayer's valuation (Form 8283) against the charity's report of sales proceeds (Form 8282). Discrepancies could trigger audits (as could the lack of a charity report).

New Charity Proof

Starting with your 1988 tax return, gifts of art to charity are handled differently than in the past. Deductions for charitable gifts of art valued at $20,000 or more must be accompanied by either an 8- by 10-inch color photo or a 4- by 5-inch color transparency. Form 8283 must be filed with an expert appraisal of the art object attached.

All about property transfers

Giving Away Real Estate Tax-Free

Real estate may be transferred free of gift tax. *Angle:* A series of annual transfers, each of which is equal to the annual *gift-tax exclusion*. This exclusion is $10,000 per year per recipient when the gift is made by a single person, and $20,000 per recipient when the gift is made by a married couple.

Example: A retired couple owns 80 acres of income-producing real estate appraised at $1,000 an acre. They wish to transfer this property to their two children. They can do so by giving each child 20 acres a year for two years. The couple will owe no gift tax.

Source: David S. Rhine, tax partner, BDO Seidman, 15 Columbus Circle, New York 10023.

Gift's Value

Thomas Kaplin donated six old buildings, and the land they were on, to the city of Toledo. The county appraiser valued the property at $860,000. The IRS said the gift's value equaled that of the land *minus* the cost of demolishing the buildings, or only $22,000. A developer later bought the property for $175,000. *Valuation fight:* The Tax Court first accepted the IRS's $22,000 valuation, but the Court of Appeals supported Kaplin. Then the Tax Court accepted the $175,000 figure, but the Court of Appeals supported Kaplin again and said "try again." *Final verdict:* The gift was worth $600,000, the figure that Kaplin had proposed as a reasonable discount from $860,000 in light of the buildings' poor condition.

Source: *Thomas Kaplin,* TC Memo 1987-337.

Property Transfer

A man gave his girlfriend a house in payment for household and secretarial services during their relationship. Later he went bankrupt and couldn't pay his taxes. The Tax Court voided the transfer as a fraudulent attempt to avoid selling the house for taxes. But a Court of Appeals ruled that it was valid. Both parties believed the girlfriend had a right to compensation for her services.

Source: *Susan J. Mayors,* CA-9, 785 F.2d 757.

8

TAX LOOPHOLES

EVERYTHING THE LAW ALLOWS

Estate-Planning
Tactics

The key word is planning

Tough-Minded Estate Planning

It may seem callous to even think about taxes when a loved one faces a life-threatening illness. But if tax planning is ignored at that point, assets carefully accumulated over a lifetime may be squandered unnecessarily. For many facing a final illness, dealing with these matters provides a life-oriented focus that helps them combat depression and achieve a sense of completion in seeing that their affairs are well-ordered. *Some things to consider:*

Gifts by the patient. In many cases, estate taxes can be saved by making gifts to family members and other intended beneficiaries. An unlimited amount may be transferred gift-tax-free provided no single person receives more than $10,000. The maximum tax-free gift per recipient can increase to $20,000 if the patient's spouse is still alive and consents to treat each gift as having been jointly made.

Under the old law, gifts made within three years of death were figured back into the taxable estate. The 1981 Tax Act repealed this "contemplation-of-death" rule in most cases. *One major exception:* The old rule still applies to gifts of life insurance.

Gifts to the patient. This tactic may seem useful when the patient doesn't have enough property to take full advantage of the estate-tax exemption of $600,000. *Reason:* Property that passes through the decedent's estate gets what's known as a stepped-up basis. That is, the person who inherits it is treated for income-tax purposes as though he/she bought it and paid what it is worth on the date of death (or what it was worth six months after the date of death, if the executor chooses this alternative date to set the value of the taxable estate).

Example: Mr. Jones, a cancer patient, has $150,000 worth of assets. His wife has a large estate, including $75,000 worth of stock that has a tax basis of $10,000. That means there's $65,000 worth of taxable gain built into the stock. Mrs. Jones gives the stock to her husband. (There's no tax on gifts between spouses.) He leaves the stock to the children. The children inherit the stock with the basis stepped up to $75,000. So if they turn right around and sell it for $75,000, there's no taxable gain. With these shares, Mr. Jones's estate is still only $225,000—under the exempt amount. So the stepped-up basis is achieved without paying estate tax. And the property is taken out of Mrs. Jones's estate, where it might be taxed.

In most cases, it doesn't pay to use this tactic with property that will be bequeathed back to a spouse who gave it to the patient. *Reason:* Unless the gift was made more than a year before the date of death, stepped-up basis will be denied. But when the patient is expected to survive for substantially more than a year, this tactic can be quite useful.

Example: Mr. Smith owns a $150,000 rental property with a $25,000 tax basis. Mrs. Smith has a disease that will be fatal within two to five years. She has few assets of her own. So Mr. Smith gives her the building and inherits it back from her a few years later with the basis stepped up to $150,000. This substantially increases his depreciation deductions if he keeps the building and eliminates any taxable gain if he sells it.

Loss property. In general, there is a tax disadvantage in inheriting property that is worth less than its original cost. *Reason:* Its tax basis is stepped down to its date-of-death value, and the potential loss deduction is forfeited. If the patient has substantial income, it might pay to sell the property and deduct the losses. But it doesn't pay to generate losses that are more than $3,000 in excess of the patient's capital gains. *Reason:* These excess losses can't be deducted currently, and there's likely to be no future years' income on which to deduct them. *Alternative:* Sell the loss property at its current value to a close family member. *Result:* The patient's loss on the sale is nondeductible because the purchaser is a family member. But any future gains the family member realizes will be nontaxable to the extent of the previously disallowed loss.

Charitable gifts. In some cases, bequests to charitable organizations should be made before death. *Benefit:* Current income-tax deductions. But it's important not to give too much away. This tactic may generate more deductions than the patient can use.

Flower bonds. Certain series of US Treasury bonds can be purchased on the open market for substantially less than their full face value because they pay very low interest. But if a decedent owns these so-called flower bonds on the date of death, they can be credited against the estate tax at their full face value.

Timing: Flower bonds should be bought when death is clearly imminent. There's little point in holding them for substantial periods before death because they yield very little income. On the other hand, it does no good for the estate to purchase them after death because they won't be applied against the estate tax. In some cases, flower bonds have been bought on behalf of a patient in a coma by a relative or trustee who holds a power of attorney. The IRS has attacked these purchases. But the courts have so far sided with the taxpayer.

A power of attorney should be prepared early. If it's properly drafted, it can cover flower-bond purchases and authority for a wide variety of other actions that can preserve the patient's assets and allow for flexible planning.

A number of income-tax moves should be considered:

■ Income timing. If the patient is in a low tax bracket, it may pay to accelerate income. The key here is to compare the patient's tax bracket with the bracket his/her estate is likely to be in. In some cases, it will pay to accelerate income to make full use of deductions that would otherwise yield little or no tax benefit. Medical deductions, in particular, may be very high.

■ Choosing gift property. In making gifts to save estate taxes, it does not pay, from an income-tax standpoint, to give away property that has gone up in value. *Reason:* The tax basis of gift property is not stepped up. So the recipient will have a potential income-tax liability built into the gift. This potential is eliminated if the property is kept in the estate and passes by inheritance. For similar reasons, the patient should not give away business property that has been subject to depreciation. (There's a built-in tax liability for recapture of the depreciation deductions. This is eliminated if the property passes through the estate.)

■ Other moves. For owners of stock in an S corporation, it may pay to accelerate distribution of income, particularly if the ill shareholder has previously taxed income that wasn't distributed.

Where death is expected, but not clearly imminent, a private annuity may be a useful way of disposing of property. *Reason:* IRS regulations will key the required annuity payments to a healthy person's life expectancy.

An experienced estate planner can help you explore all aspects of these moves and other possibilities.

Source: G. William Clapp, partner, Bessemer Trust Co., N.A., New York City.

Beating the rules

Estate-Planning Traps

Who pays estate and inheritance taxes? If you don't specify in your will, taxes will be apportioned among your beneficiaries according to state and federal law, regardless of your wishes or anyone else's. The wrong person may end up paying...heavily.

Lack-of-proper-tax-apportionment-clause trap. Many states *require* beneficiaries to pay a share of estate taxes *unless* the will provides otherwise. To avoid having a beneficiary's share reduced by taxes, stipulate in your will that taxes are to be paid out of your residuary estate without apportionment. (Your "residuary estate" is what's left after all bequests.)

Example: Suppose you want a grandchild to get $100,000 of your $1 million estate. If your will doesn't have an "anti-apportionment" tax clause, your grandchild's $100,000 gift will be reduced by one-tenth of the total federal and state estate taxes levied on your estate. But if your will does have an anti-apportionment clause, your grandchild will get $100,000 free and clear of estate tax.

Making-so-many-specific-bequests-of-cash-that-your-residuary-estate doesn't-have-enough-left-to-pay-estate-taxes trap. The IRS can go after *any* of your beneficiaries for the unpaid estate tax. State law may specify the order in which bequests are used to pay unpaid taxes. *Another trap:* By wiping out the residuary estate to pay taxes, you may inadvertently eliminate bequests to your primary beneficiaries.

Avoidance: Make sure your executor has a sufficient reserve of funds for paying estate tax and paying the bequests to your residuary beneficiaries.

Shortchanging-charities-or-your-spouse trap. The standard tax clause, calling for taxes to be paid from your residuary estate without apportionment, can cause unfortunate results if you make tax-free bequests from your residuary estate—such as leaving part of the balance of your estate to your spouse (tax-free because of the unlimited marital deduction) or giving the residue to charity. If your will does not stipulate that taxes are to be paid from that portion of the residuary estate that does *not* pass to your spouse or to charity, what would otherwise be a tax-free bequest has to bear its portion of the taxes. This creates a round robin of tax problems, increasing the overall taxes on your estate.

Avoidance: Be sure your will specifies that taxes are to come from that portion of the residue of your estate that does *not* pass to your spouse or to charity.

Owning-property-jointly-with-a-beneficiary trap. You may have to pay gift-taxes at the time you put the property in joint names. And unless you can prove who paid what for the property, it could be fully includible in the estate of the first person to die (even if that person wasn't the one who made the gift). With certain exceptions, it's presumed that the joint owner who dies first owned 100% of the property (except married couples are presumed to own joint property 50/50). It's up to the estate and surviving owners to prove otherwise. This could be extremely difficult, especially if many years have passed since the property was originally acquired.

Example: Property is put in the joint names of a parent and a child. If the child should die first, property might be fully taxed in his/her estate and then taxed again when the parent dies.

Giving-the-family-home-to-your-children-while-you're-still-alive, while-keeping-the-right-to-live-in-it-until-you-die trap. You could end up paying *both* gift tax on the transfer of the house *and* estate tax. *First problem:* You've made a gift of the house to the children. Depending on the value of the house, you may owe gift tax on the transfer. *Second problem:* For estate-tax purposes, the IRS says you've retained a life estate in the house, even though there's nothing in writing, simply because you continue to live there. That makes your interest in the house fully taxable in your estate at its value on the date of your death. So you pay estate taxes in addition to the gift tax. *Avoidance:*

■ Don't give it to the kids during your life.

■ If you do give it to them, move out.

■ If you don't want to move out, reserve the right to live only in a small portion of the house, or pay a fair rental for your use of the house. For instance, reserve the right to live in one bedroom and share the use of the living room. All that would remain in your estate for tax purposes is the value of the room you retained the use of.

Leaving-everything-outright-to-your-spouse-or-holding-all-property-jointly-with-your-spouse trap. When you die, the estate will pass to your spouse tax-free. But when your spouse dies, the entire combined estate will be taxable except for your spouse's $600,000 estate-tax exemption. But your estate, too, could have been entitled to the $600,000 exemption, giving the combined estate a total exemption of $1,200,000. You could have left up to $600,000 to your children and the balance to your spouse.

Avoidance: Set up what is known as a credit-shelter trust, giving your spouse income for life from the $600,000 left to your children. In that way *both* estates, yours and your spouse's, can take advantage of the $600,000 exemption *and* your spouse can still have the income for life.

Forcing-your-beneficiaries-to-pay-tax-on-life-insurance-proceeds trap. Unless your will stipulates otherwise, estate taxes are paid by the beneficiaries of life-insurance policies. This is required by Section 2206 of the Internal Revenue Code.

Avoidance: Be sure your will has a provision specifying who pays all taxes, *including* taxes on life insurance.

Source: Peter Van Nuys, a New York tax, trusts, and estates attorney, 60 E. 42 St., New York 10165-0015.

The Revenue Act of 1987 And Estate Taxes

Under the rules of the Tax Reform Act of 1986, the maximum estate-tax rate was to be cut to 50% in 1988, and a tax credit effectively exempts the first $600,000 of an estate from tax.

Under the Revenue Act of 1987, however, the top estate-tax rate is 55%. Moreover, the tax benefit received from the credit is *phased out* for estates exceeding $10 million through the imposition of an *extra* 5% tax on estates between $10 million and about $21 million in size. Persons with large estates should review their estate plans now.

Source: S. Theodore Reiner, director, tax client communications, Ernst & Young, 1225 Connecticut Ave. NW, Washington, DC 20036.

How To Keep Estate Taxes Low

Failure to plan for your taxable estate could mean that a significant portion of money left to your heirs will end up fattening the IRS instead. *Basic techniques to reduce estate taxes:*

Learn the ground rules. Estates of single taxpayers worth over $600,000 and estates of married taxpayers worth over $1,200,000 must pay federal estate taxes.

Know the tax rates. The top official tax rate is 55%. *It gets worse:* Estates worth $10,000,000–$21,040,000 are subject to a 5% surtax, for a total estate tax of 60%.

Establish a program of annual gift-giving. The tax value of your estate can be reduced through such a program. But gifts must be planned carefully, or you may end up paying gift tax instead of estate tax. *How much you can give tax-free:*

■ *Single givers* can give gifts of up to $10,000 per recipient per year to as many people as they choose.

■ *Married givers* can give as many gifts as they choose of up to $20,000 per recipient per year, even if the entire $20,000 is from assets belonging to only one of the spouses.

■ *Medical or tuition bills,* if paid directly to the hospital, doctor, or school, can be made federal-gift-tax-free, in addition to a tax-free gift of $10,000–$20,000 made during the same year.

An annual gift-giving program based carefully on these rules will reduce your taxable estate by a substantial amount.

Example: You are a widow and you know the 60% rate will apply to your estate. By giving each grandchild a $10,000 gift each year and paying his/her high school or college tuition of $5,000 per year, you'll remove $15,000 *per grandchild* per year from your estate. If you left the money in your estate, only 40% of it would actually go to your grandchildren after taxes.

Take life insurance out of your estate. All life insurance that's paid in the event of your death is taxed to your estate, unless you give up all control and ownership rights in the policy.

How to give up your rights: Set up an irrevocable life-insurance trust that owns your insurance policy and will pay the proceeds to the beneficiaries you have chosen. This includes life insurance that is paid for by your employer. An independent trustee must be given all your ownership rights in your life insurance policies, including the right to change beneficiaries.

Set up a credit-shelter trust. All property left to your spouse in your will passes tax-free. But if your estate is worth over $600,000, leaving everything to your spouse is the worst thing you could do. *Reason:* Every individual can leave up to $600,000 to anyone tax-free. You and your spouse each get the $600,000 exemption, for a total of $1,200,000. By leaving *everything* to your spouse, you'll have wasted that opportunity to pass $600,000 estate-tax-free.

How the credit-shelter trust saves taxes: Let's say your estate is worth $1,200,000. Leave $600,000 of property in trust for your children or grandchildren, with your wife to receive income from the trust assets for her lifetime. The trust assets won't be taxed to your wife's estate because she has access only to the *income* from the trust. Your estate has used its $600,000 exemption, and your spouse's estate can later use its own $600,000 exemption. *Bottom line:* You avoid paying tax on $600,000.

Source: David S. Rhine, CPA, tax partner, BDO Seidman, 15 Columbus Circle, New York 10023.

Estate-Planning Alert

Irrevocable life-insurance trusts, a popular estate-planning tool, are an increasingly likely target for taxation. Under current law, if the insured has no ownership rights at death, the proceeds are not included in his/her estate. Estate-planning experts are advising clients to act quickly in setting up life-insurance trusts. *Trap:* If the insured bought the policy, or is deemed to have bought it, three years must pass after the trust is created in order to ensure exclusion of insurance proceeds from the estate. But there are ways to get around this waiting period. Consult your estate planner.

Tax traps after you die

How To Avoid State-Death-Tax Trap

■ Check with local counsel regarding the relevant laws of the state in which you live.

■ Sever all existing ties when you move to a different state. Establish a new church affiliation, club memberships, physicians, dentists, banks, safe-deposit boxes, and charities. Do not retain affiliations in a state where you had once lived because of purely sentimental reasons. A person may wish to keep up his/her church affiliation in a state where he had lived because he had been married there. There are less costly ways of remembering a marriage. A state can be alerted to an opportunity to assert its death tax by a newspaper item long after a former resident has moved. Typical was a news account about a man who lived thousands of miles away from the state where he had once been domiciled. The newspaper mentioned that he "still returns to...see his doctor and dentist." Predictably, the state made a follow-up notation in its records against the time of his eventual death.

■ When a person moves from one state to another, it is easy to overlook things. Check to see whether any active bank accounts have been left behind. Not only can such an account cause state death-tax complications, but the money forgotten can be forfeited. After a number of years (which varies from state to state), an inactive bank account must be turned over to the state by a process known as escheat.

■ Do not believe that because your attorney says you are now domiciled in State A, you are not also domiciled in State B for death-tax purposes. Or in States C and D.

Source: *Encyclopedia of Estate Planning* by Dr. Robert S. Holzman, Boardroom Classics, Springfield, NJ 07081.

Joint Ownership Isn't Always Desirable

There are some disadvantages to joint ownership of property:

■ A major shortcoming of joint ownership is that on the death of one co-owner, the IRS, as a matter of expediency, considers that the decedent really owned all of the property and will include its value in his/her gross estate, then let the executor prove the extent to which all of this property wasn't the decedent's—if possible. For failure of adequate proof, the total value of property in which the decedent was only one co-owner frequently winds up in his gross estate, even though the other co-owner(s) may actually have paid for their interests with their own funds. Proof of who had furnished how much of the consideration many years ago is difficult, especially if the property had been acquired piecemeal. This rule no longer applies to joint interests of husband and wife. Now one-half such property is included in the estate of the spouse who dies first.

■ The death of a co-owner may make all of the property unavailable to the survivor for a time. For example, in the case of a joint bank account, the funds will be frozen by the bank until the tax authorities unfreeze the account.

■ There can be serious practical problems in selling one's interest in property if co-owners are opposed to the idea.

■ If two or more persons own property, such as a business, in joint ownership, the IRS can shut down the enterprise for nonpayment of taxes by one co-owner.

■ If a husband and wife own property jointly and there is a divorce, or even if there are marital difficulties that haven't gone that far, management and administration of the joint property can prove difficult.

■ Where certain types of property are owned jointly, one owner can be heavily involved financially because of an act of the co-owner. For example, if a mother and son own an automobile jointly, and he is involved in an accident that entails more money than the insurance covers, she is confronted with the liability.

■ When there's a joint bank account, one spouse cannot logically argue that he/she didn't know what was in the account. This greatly weakens any claim that when the husband omitted income from a joint return, for example, the wife is not subject to tax, penalty, and interest on the unreported income because she is an innocent spouse.

Source: *Encyclopedia of Estate Planning* by Dr. Robert S. Holzman, Boardroom Classics, Springfield, NJ 07081.

Cash Found In Decedent's Safe-Deposit Box

What was the source of any cash in a safe-deposit box or in your home or office? In the absence of proof to the contrary, the IRS will consider any unexplained cash to represent previously untaxed income. This presumption can be refuted if there is credible evidence. For example, there may be a letter to your executor stating that Social Security checks or horse track winnings (reported) will be converted into cash, to be kept in the box as an emergency fund. Correspondence can identify cash as having been found money, which had been turned over to the police department and given back to the finder when no claimant appeared.

Source: *Encyclopedia of Estate Planning* by Dr. Robert S. Holzman, Boardroom Classics, Springfield, NJ 07081.

Scariest Tax Audit

It is standard operating procedure for the IRS to examine the federal income-tax returns of a decedent for the three years prior to his/her death. Unless clear and well-documented work papers can be shown and explained to the IRS by a knowledgeable person who's familiar with the facts, there are apt to be disallowances.

Can your returns be explained satisfactorily by someone else when you are not available? Information as to where records are located should be included in a separate communication to the executor in advance, or left among personal possessions.

Source: Dr. Robert S. Holzman, professor emeritus of taxation at New York University and the author of the *Encyclopedia of Estate Planning*.

Your will is crucial

The Biggest Tax-Related Mistake When Making A Will

Obviously, it's very important from a financial and legal standpoint to have a will. From a tax standpoint, there are a few very simple things you can do to drastically reduce the effect of taxes. Sound planning for making a will can save more money than a lifetime of income-tax planning and saving.

Everything left to a spouse is completely free of estate taxes during the lifetime of the spouse. However, when the spouse dies, all funds are subject to estate taxes.

Give your spouse the full benefit of your assets while saving your heirs from having to pay exorbitant estate taxes when your spouse dies. The IRS sets a limit to the amount an estate can be taxed. This is called the "equivalent exemption." If the total of your estate and that of your spouse (including life insurance proceeds) will be greater than the amount of the equivalent exemption, which is $600,000, follow these procedures:

Leave all your funds to your spouse, *except* for an amount equal to the equivalent exemption. This amount should be left in trust for your heirs as the principal beneficiaries and your spouse as the income beneficiary. Your spouse will be able to live on the interest of this amount and withdraw from the principal—as needed for the prudent maintenance of personal health or welfare or the children's education—by requesting withdrawals from the trustee. When your spouse dies, the amount in the trust will go to your heirs estate-tax-free.

Source: Edward Mendlowitz, partner, Mendlowitz Weitsen, CPAs, Two Pennsylvania Plaza, New York 10121.

Rewriting A Will

I'm rewriting my will in light of all the changes in the tax laws. Can I deduct my lawyer's fee?

The cost of drawing up a will, as such, is not deductible. However, the cost of tax advice *is* deductible as a miscellaneous item on your tax return. Thus, to get a deduction for your legal expenses, you should have your lawyer give you an *itemized* bill showing just how much of his fee was for tax planning. *That* part of his bill will be deductible.

Limit: Tax Reform allows a deduction for miscellaneous expenses only to the extent that their total exceeds 2% of Adjusted Gross Income.

Inadvertent Mistake In Will

A woman died leaving a will that placed in a trust some of the stock she owned in an S corporation. *Trap:* The tax code prohibits most trusts from owning S corporation stock. The mistake wasn't discovered for almost a year. *IRS ruling:* Because the mistake involving the trust was *inadvertent,* and because steps were taken to correct the mistake *immediately* upon its discovery, the corporation's S election would remain in force.

Source: IRS Letter Ruling 8703042.

Gift-giving and estate-planning

Deductible Bequest To Charity Goes To Relatives

If properly structured, a charitable bequest can serve a person's estate-planning objectives by making provision for the assistance of members of his/her own family. If the recipient organization is a *bona fide* religious, charitable, etc., body, a charitable bequest is deductible even though preference is to be given to relatives of the testator, provided that they qualify as objects of legitimate charitable purposes.

Deduction was allowed for a bequest to set up an educational loan fund to provide scholarships "first to relatives or other boys or girls" who lacked funds.

Recognition was given to a decedent's bequest to pay the annual income of a trust to persons in need of financial assistance, despite this language in the will: "It is my wish that in carrying out the objects in this trust fund, preference be given to my relatives and friends that are in need of such aid and assistance."

Bequests were deemed to be charitable when university scholarships were funded for high school graduates "in need of funds." Preference was to be given to applicants with the same surname as the grantor, who were related to him; but the scholarships could be awarded to other qualified persons if no applicant met the special qualification. Although the testator plainly expressed a preference that qualified persons with his surname who were relatives should benefit from the scholarships, his charity was not confined to such persons.

One decedent's will set up a trust to provide scholarships for students who wanted education in vocational or agricultural studies. The trustee was first to award scholarships to students who had been the decedent's employees or their descendants, a requirement that could be waived in favor of other students only if insufficient employees made applications. This bequest qualified for deduction, being for the benefit of a general class as distinguished from mere benevolence to employees, as long as the general class to be benefited (nonemployees) was not so small that the community did not benefit from the aid given to students.

Source: Dr. Robert S. Holzman, professor emeritus of taxation at New York University and the author of the *Encyclopedia of Estate Planning*.

Insurance Loophole

Gifts of life-insurance policies are valued at the "interpolated terminal reserve"—which is akin to the cash-surrender value. The insurance company will notify you (and the IRS) of the amount when you request transfer of ownership. No gift tax is due if the value is $10,000 or less ($20,000 if the donor is married). Giving away your policy can get the proceeds out of your taxable estate and beyond the reach of creditors.

Estate-Interest Costs

Ruby Sturgis died owning $7 million worth of timberland but not much cash. Her estate borrowed $2.6 million to pay estate taxes and deducted the interest on the loan. The IRS disallowed the interest deduction, saying that the estate could have sold enough timber to pay the tax. *Court:* Deduction allowed. Such a large timber sale could be imprudent for business reasons. It was not proper for the IRS to substitute its business judgment for that of the taxpayer.

Source: *Estate of Ruby S. Sturgis,* TC Memo 1987-415.

Owner's Estate

A major stockholder in a privately owned company died. His shares were subject to a legally binding buy-sell agreement that assigned them a price according to a fixed formula. The company would buy the shares back at the formula price. *IRS ruling:* The value of the shares for estate-tax purposes will be that set by the buy-sell agreement's formula, even if it differs from the real value of the shares.

Source: IRS Letter Ruling 8634004.

Late-Filing Penalty

An estate's tax return was filed late because the attorney handling it was killed in a plane crash. *Tax Court:* Late-filing penalties apply. The Supreme Court has specifically ruled that a lawyer's failure to file a return is not an excuse that will abate a late-filing penalty.

Source: *Estate of Sheila B. Gardner,* TC Memo 1986-380.

No Penalty

The IRS was wrong when it tried to penalize an estate and its executor for errors made by the tax return preparer. *Tax Court:* The executor acted in good faith, filed a timely return, and acted promptly to correct the return-preparer's mistake as soon as he realized it had happened.

Source: *Scott G. Martin,* No. CV 85-5512-AAH.

Use Year-End Gifts To Cut Estate Tax

Married couples with estates worth over $1,200,000 and individuals with estates over $600,000 will eventually pay federal estate taxes. But some of this tax can be avoided through a yearly gift-giving program to reduce the final value of your taxable estate.

Gifts, however, also have tax consequences and must be planned carefully. Every individual is allowed a maximum gift-tax exclusion that depends on marital status. *Exclusion amounts:* Single donors are allowed to give up to $10,000 per year to *each* recipient without incurring a gift tax. Married donors can give a combined gift of $20,000 to each recipient federal-gift-tax-free, even if the whole $20,000 stems from assets that belong to only one spouse.

Gifts of over $10,000 can be made tax-free if they are payments made directly for tuition or medical bills.

Problem: You may not want to give an outright gift of $10,000 per year to a very young person. *Alternatives to consider:*

■ *Custodial accounts* under the Uniform Gifts to Minors Act. The child can't get the money until age 18.

■ *2503(c) trust.* The child can't get the money until age 21.

■ *Crummey trust.* The child has a specific time period after age 18 (usually 30 or 60 days) to take the money. If the child doesn't exercise this right, the money goes back into the trust for a specified number of years.

Source: John R. Sanderson, office-managing partner and director of tax for the Buffalo office of Ernst & Young, 3000 Marine Midland Center, Buffalo, NY 14203.

Poor Excuse

An estate failed to file its tax return on time and was penalized by the IRS. It protested that it had relied on an accountant who said the filing extensions were properly in place. *Court:* It's every taxpayer's responsibility to see that any required tax return is filed on time. This duty can't be delegated to others. The penalty stands.

Source: *Estate of Robert Cox,* SD Fla., No. 84-8344-Civ-SCOTT.

9

TAX LOOPHOLES

EVERYTHING THE LAW ALLOWS

Treasury Of
Tax Deductions

Deduction magic

How To Keep Your Deductions And Exemptions Despite The New Tax Law

The 1990 Tax Act imposes new cutbacks on income-tax deductions and personal exemptions. The cutbacks are based on your level of taxable income. The higher your taxable income, the more deductions and exemptions you lose. *New limits:*

■ When your Adjusted Gross Income (AGI) goes above $114,700 in 1995, you must reduce your *deductions* by 3% of the excess.

■ When your AGI goes above $172,050 on a joint return (above $114,700 for singles), you begin to lose the benefit of your personal and dependent *exemptions*. These are reduced at the rate of 2% per $2,500 of AGI in excess of the limits.

Strategy: Keep your Adjusted Gross Income under the limits, and you'll keep all your deductions and exemptions. One way to do this is to invest in tax-exempt municipal bonds, which produce income that is not reflected in the AGI. A simple shift to make, if you're close to the cut-off point, would be to switch from taxable corporate bonds to tax-exempt municipals.

Source: Randy Bruce Blaustein, Esq., partner, Blaustein, Greenberg & Co., 155 E. 31 St., New York 10016.

Accelerate Deductions

Save taxes by taking as many deductions as possible this year or by deferring payments until next year. *Deductions to accelerate or defer:*

Medical expenses: Deductible only to the extent that they exceed 7.5% of your AGI. If you're going to reach the 7.5% limit this year, maximize your deduction in these ways:

■ Pay all outstanding medical and dental bills.

■ Have elective surgery done. *Caution:* Unnecessary cosmetic surgery is no longer deductible.

■ Pay your children's outstanding orthodontist bills.

■ Get medical checkups for yourself and your entire family.

Note: If you're *not* going to reach the 7.5% limit, defer payment of medical expenses until next year, when you may reach the limit.

Taxes:

■ Pay outstanding state and local income taxes by December 31.

■ Prepay property tax bills before the end of the year.

■ Pay contested state tax bills before year-end, even though you plan to continue your fight with tax people. The bill will be deductible this year.

Casualty losses: If you're close to settling with your insurance company for a casualty, wind up the settlement before December 31. *Reason:* The unreimbursed part of the loss is deductible in the year you settle.

Charitable contributions:

■ Make charitable donations to churches and charities *now.*

■ Satisfy next year's commitments with a contribution this year.

■ Look into setting up charitable trusts before year-end.

Moving expenses: If you're being transferred to a new job next year, take a house-hunting trip to the new area before year-end.

Miscellaneous expenses: Deductible only to the extent that they exceed 2% of your AGI. If you're going to get up to the 2% limit this year, increase your deduction:

■ Prepay business or professional association dues.

■ Prepay tuition bills for job-related courses.

■ Buy or renew subscriptions to business, professional, tax, and financial publications.

■ Get tax and investment advice before the end of the year.

■ Pay bills for holiday business entertainment and gifts before December 31. (Business entertainment is only 50% deductible.)

■ Have a new résumé prepared and printed before year-end. The cost of the résumé is a deductible job-hunting expense, even if you don't get a new job.

Business expenses: Some of these deductions apply to employees as well as business owners. *Employees* would include these costs under miscellaneous deductions—subject to the 2% of AGI limit. *Ways to accelerate business expenses:*

■ Buy new equipment and place it in service before year-end. You can deduct up to $17,500 of the cost immediately and depreciate the balance.

■ Have repairs and maintenance done before the end of the year.

■ Purchase supplies.

■ Prepay insurance costs.

■ Pay promotion and advertising expenses.

■ Give employees their bonuses by December 31.

Bad debts: Deductible in the year they become totally worthless. Be prepared to prove that you made a good-faith attempt to collect the debt you're deducting.

Source: Steven L. Severin, partner, Deloitte & Touche, 1633 Broadway, New York 10019.

The Credit-Card Ploy

There's an exception to the general rule that you can take a deduction only in the year you pay for a deductible expense. For tax purposes, payment made by credit card is considered to be made on the *date of the charge,* not on the date you actually pay the credit-card issuer. If you signed for the expense this year, you can deduct it on this year's return even though you don't actually pay for it until next year.

Medical and dental expenses paid by credit card are deductible in the year the charge is made (Revenue Ruling 78-39). So are *charitable contributions* made by credit card (Revenue Ruling 78-38).

Interest deduction self-defense

Interest Deductions: New Traps And Opportunities

Tax Reform imposed strict limits on interest deductions, breaking interest payments into five distinct categories, each with its own separate and complex rules.

Personal Interest

Interest payments that don't fit into any of the categories that are given special treatment under Tax Reform (i.e., mortgage interest, business interest, investment interest, passive-activity interest) are considered *personal interest* and are not deductible.

Interest charges that you might not think of as "personal" interest are included in this dramatic phaseout of deductibility. *Surprises and solutions:*

Interest owed to federal and state tax authorities on contested tax bills is personal interest.

Interest paid on a car loan by an employee who uses the car for business is personal interest, even if the car is used solely for business. The same rule applies to interest paid on the financing of any other type of property that an employee might use for business, such as a personal computer.

Loophole: Have the company buy the car (or other property) that you use for business. A corporation's interest costs are 100% deductible as *business* interest. To square things up, the company can charge you for personal use or reduce your salary accordingly. (You will be taxed to the extent that you use the car for personal purposes.)

Interest paid for borrowing against life-insurance policies is personal interest.

Loophole: Pay off the existing loan, take out a new one, and use the newly borrowed money to buy stock or other investments. Since the deductibility of interest depends on what you spend the borrowed money on, your interest payments will now be investment interest, deductible up to the amount of your net investment income for the year.

Interest on loans from your employer is also considered personal interest.

Loophole: To increase your interest deduction, borrow from the company *pension plan*. Use your *house* as security for the loan. Use the proceeds to pay back the loan from the company. Interest on the pension-plan loan will be fully deductible home-mortgage interest, since it's secured by your house—it's the same as a home-equity-loan. (Check with your tax adviser as there are limitations on your right to borrow from pension plans.)

Interest on credit-card balances, car loans, and other consumer loans is personal interest.

Loophole: If you have large credit-card balances, consider taking out a home-equity loan and using the proceeds to pay the credit-card companies. Interest on home-equity loans (up to $100,000) secured by your home or vacation home is fully deductible *mortgage* interest, regardless of what you spend the money on.

Investment Interest

If you borrow money from your margin account and use the money for personal purposes (for instance, to take a vacation), the interest is personal interest. But if you use the money to buy stock, the interest is investment interest (fully deductible up to the amount of your investment income for the year).

Loophole: To get full deductions for interest on money borrowed for personal use, sell some of the stock you currently own, use the proceeds to take your vacation, and buy the stock back on margin. Your margin interest charges will be fully deductible investment interest (assuming you have enough investment income to cover it).

Caution: Keep records that clearly show where borrowed money came from, what it was spent on, and all interest payments you make.

Real Estate

Rental property. Mortgage interest on a "passive activity," such as a house you rent out, can't be deducted separately. It's part of the overall expense of the property and part of any annual rental loss. If your Adjusted Gross Income (AGI) is under $100,000, you can deduct up to $25,000 of loss against your other income. You can get a partial loss deduction if your AGI is between $100,000 and $150,000, but you are not entitled to a deduction if your AGI is over $150,000.

Loophole: Suspended losses from passive activities (e.g., those you can't use because your AGI is too high) can be carried forward to future years. And you will be able to deduct them when you eventually sell the property.

Co-op apartments. If you give stock in the co-op corporation to a bank as collateral for a loan, your interest payments are fully deductible mortgage interest.

Home buyers: Get as big a mortgage as possible when you buy. The Revenue Act of 1987 imposed new limits on interest deductions for mortgages taken out after October 13, 1987. Interest is fully deductible on mortgages of up to $1 million spent to acquire, construct, or substantially improve a principal or second residence. But if you need to borrow further, through refinancing, second mortgages, or home-equity loans, interest will be fully deductible on only $100,000 additional. Since interest on additional borrowing is so severely restricted, it's wise to take out as large a mortgage as you can when you buy a house, especially if you know you'll be needing money in the future, e.g., for your children's college education.

Source: Edward Mendlowitz, partner, Mendlowitz Weitsen, CPAs, Two Pennsylvania Plaza, New York 10121.

Vacation-Home Loophole

Here is a planning strategy that will cut your tax bill substantially...

Pay-down-the-mortgage-on-your-vacation-home loophole: If you pay down the mortgage on your vacation home, the reduced interest deductions should give you a net cash flow from rent payments. This cash flow from the rent payments can be sheltered by depreciation deductions.

Big, Big Interest Deductions Are Still Possible

Interest comes in five different varieties, each with its own deduction rules:

■ *Mortgage interest:* Fully deductible on your personal residence, and one other residence, on up to $1 million of acquisition debt used to purchase, construct, or improve the residence, plus an additional $100,000 of home-equity debt used for any purpose whatsoever. *Note:* Interest on mortgages taken out before October 13, 1987, is fully deductible without regard to the dollar limits.

■ *Business interest:* Fully deductible if incurred for use in your trade or business if you "materially" participate.

■ *Investment interest:* Deductible up to the amount of net investment income. (Formerly the limit was net investment income plus $10,000. But the extra $10,000 was phased out gradually and totally eliminated in 1991.)

■ *Passive-activity interest:* Not deductible as interest, but may be used to figure income or loss from the passive activity for which the money was borrowed. Passive activities include investments in limited partnerships, businesses in which you don't materially participate, and *all* rental activity.

■ *Personal interest:* No deduction is allowed. Personal interest includes all interest that doesn't fit into any of the other categories (e.g., interest on car loans, tuition loans, credit-card interest charges on personal purchases, and interest on late payments of taxes).

Key New Rules

■ Deductibility depends on what you spend the money for. For instance, if you use your margin account to buy stock, the interest is investment interest. But if you use the money to take a vacation, the interest is personal interest. *Exception:* Mortgage interest—first and second homes—is fully deductible no matter what the loan is spent on. If you take a second mortgage out on your house and take the family to Disney World with the money, the interest is fully deductible (as long as the limitations under mortgage interest are met).

■ If you put borrowed money into your personal bank account, the use of the money will be determined under the IRS's "ordering rules." The money that you take out of the account *first* is considered to come from the borrowed funds. *Example:* You borrow $10,000 and add it to your personal account. A month later you withdraw $5,500 to buy a fur coat for your wife. The next day you withdraw $8,000 to buy stock. *Result:* $5,500 of the loan is deemed to have been used for personal reasons (giving you limited interest deductions) and only $4,500 (the balance of the borrowed $10,000) for investment. Had you made the investment first, the full $8,000 would have been deemed investment use and only $2,000 personal use.

■ *Exception to the ordering rule:* If you spend borrowed money within 15 days of receiving it, the IRS will consider it spent for the purpose you claim.

Ways To Maximize Your Interest Deductions

■ Refinance your home mortgage and use the money to pay off personal debt. *Reason:* Home-mortgage interest is fully deductible, subject to the limitations previously discussed, and personal interest is only partly deductible.

■ If you need money in the future for personal use, take out a second mortgage or a home-equity loan.

Source: Sharon Virga, partner, Deloitte & Touche, CPAs, 1900 M St. NW, Washington, DC 20036.

The Two Most Forgotten Deductions

1. Contributions to a Simplified Employee Pension (SEP). Many taxpayers with self-employment income don't realize that they can make last-minute deductible contributions to a pension plan even though they missed the December 31 deadline for opening a Keogh plan for the first time. *Opportunity:* Taxpayers have until April 15 to establish SEPs and make contributions that are deductible on *last year's* return.

2. Deducting the full amount of state and local income taxes that you paid last year. Don't limit your deduction for state taxes to the amount that you paid through salary withholding as shown on your W-2 Form. *Add to that figure:*

■ The amount you sent the state in April of last year for the balance of the previous year's state and local tax bill, and...

■ Fourth-quarter estimated tax payments that were made by December 31 of the tax year, and...

■ Payments sent with last year's request for an extension of time to file your state income-tax return.

Source: Barry Salzberg, partner, Deloitte & Touche, CPAs, One World Trade Center, New York 10048.

Smart Way To Deduct Interest On Personal Loan

There are three perfectly legal ways to deduct interest on a personal loan without borrowing on home equity:

■ Instead of simply borrowing money to make a consumer purchase, you make the purchase *first*—with bank savings, for example. Then you borrow the money to restore your savings balance. The loophole here is that interest on money borrowed for investment purposes is fully deductible (up to certain limits that depend mainly on investment income). Since your savings account is legally an investment, the money you actually borrowed goes toward investment rather than consumption, and you take a neat tax deduction with the blessings of the IRS.

Source: Barry Salzberg, Deloitte & Touche, CPAs.

■ Sell some stocks and use the money for consumer purchase. Then buy the stock back on margin. Your interest payments will be fully deductible (assuming you have enough investment income to cover it).

Source: Edward Mendlowitz, partner, Mendlowitz Weitsen, CPAs, Two Pennsylvania Plaza, New York 10121.

■ Pay for consumer purchases with the money you've set aside for your IRA. Then take out a bank loan to fund the IRA. The interest on that loan will be tax-deductible.

Source: Charles J. Givens, a financial planner who specializes in accumulating wealth while minimizing risk. He heads the Charles J. Givens Organization, 921 Douglas Ave., Altamonte Springs, FL 32714, and is the author of *Financial Self-Defense*, Simon & Schuster, 1230 Avenue of the Americas, New York 10020.

Medical deductions—some new surprises

Making The Most Of Medical Deductions

You can only deduct medical expenses that exceed 7½% of your Adjusted Gross Income, but the IRS and court decisions have expanded the definition of deductible medical costs. Plan ahead to take advantage of as many medical expenses as possible.

Medical deductions can be taken for the costs of diagnosis, the treatment or prevention of a disease, or for affecting any structure or function of the body (except for unnecessary cosmetic surgery). *Limitation:* Treatment must be specific and not just for general health improvement.

Example: The IRS successfully denied taxpayers deductions for the cost of weight-control and stop-smoking classes that were designed to improve general health, not to treat a specific ailment or disease. On the other hand, someone with a health problem specifically related to being overweight, such as high blood pressure, might be allowed the deduction.

If an employer tells an overweight employee to lose weight or leave, and the boss has previously enforced such a rule, the plump employee can deduct the cost of a weight-loss program, because money spent to help keep a taxpayer's job is deductible. The IRS says it will allow a deduction if a physician prescribes a weight-reduction program for the treatment of hypertension, obesity, or hearing problems. The same could go for someone whose doctor certifies that a stop to cigarette smoking is necessary for a specific medical reason (such as emphysema).

The same logic applies to home improvements. The cost of a swimming pool might be deductible if it is specifically necessary for someone who has polio, as would the cost of an elevator for a heart patient.

Caution: Only the actual cost is deductible. The IRS makes taxpayers subtract from the cost of an improvement the amount that the features add to the value of the residence.

Example: If a swimming pool costs $10,000 but adds $4,000 to the value of the property, only $6,000 would be tax-deductible. To determine the value, have the property appraised before and after the improvement. (The appraisal fee is deductible as a miscellaneous itemized deduction to the extent allowed by the Tax Reform Act of 1986.)

Medical or business? Because medical costs are deductible only after they exceed 7½% of a taxpayer's Adjusted Gross Income, it is tempting to declare them as business expenses. *Trap:* The IRS rarely allows those business deductions. But there is a sizable gray area. A professional singer was once not allowed to deduct the cost of throat treatments as a business expense, but an IRS agent did allow a deduction for a dancer who found it necessary to her career to have silicone breast implants.

Medically unproven treatment is generally deductible, since the IRS has taken the position that it cannot make judgments in the medical field. *Example:* Laetrile treatments are deductible if the taxpayer receives them legally.

Deductions for nondependents are sometimes possible if a person cannot be claimed as a dependent solely because he/she earned more than the allowable amount or filed a joint return with a spouse. *How it works:* The daughter of a highly paid executive ran up medical bills of more than $5,000. She married later that year. Because she filed a joint return with her husband, her father could not claim her as a dependent. Nevertheless, he was allowed to deduct the cost of treatment on his return for the year.

Education: The IRS draws a hard line on deductibility of special schooling for children with medical problems. *Not deductible:* The cost of attending a school with smaller classes, even for a child with hearing or sight problems. To be eligible to make such a claim, the school would have to offer special programs for the children with specific disabilities. *Approved by the IRS:* A deduction for the full cost of sending a child to a boarding school equipped to handle deaf children with emotional problems. *Denied by the IRS:* A deduction for extra costs, including travel, that was claimed by a parent who sent his deaf child to a distant public school that was better equipped than the local public school to handle such students.

Other deductible costs: Birth-control pills and other prescription drugs, vasectomies, legal abortions.

Source: Sidney Kess, tax partner, retired, KPMG Peat Marwick, 55 E. 52 St., New York 10055.

Medical-Expenses Savvy

■ *Deduct medical expenses without subtracting percentage of income:* One of the healthiest tax benefits you can provide for yourself or your key employees is a corporate medical reimbursement plan under Section 105(b).

You get full reimbursement of medical expenses without reduction for the 7.5 % of Adjusted Gross Income limitation on medical expenses. For example, if you are currently earning $40,000, the first 7.5% or $3,000 you spend on medical expenses is lost forever as a deduction.

Medical expenses that are reimbursed to you or are paid directly for your benefit are fully deductible by the corporation as compensation.

The amounts reimbursed to you or paid for your benefit are not included in your gross income.

Simply put, all medical expenses for you and all your dependents can be paid by your corporation and are fully deductible by the corporation without your having to pay one penny of income tax on the benefits.

Uninsured (self-insured) medical-expense reimbursement (pay) plans have to meet the breadth-of-coverage requirements applicable to qualified pension plans. In order for medical-expense reimbursements to be excluded from the employee's income, the plan must not discriminate in favor of key employees (highly compensated individuals and certain stockholders).

Unusual Medical Deductions

Medical expenses are deductible only to the extent that they exceed 7½% of your Adjusted Gross Income, so it's important not to miss a single deductible item. Here are some unusual deductions that have been upheld by the courts and the IRS.

- **Acupuncture.**
- **Addiction therapy.**
- **Clarinet and lessons** bought on a doctor's advice to correct tooth defects.
- **Companion** hired to escort blind children to school.
- **Contact lens insurance.**
- **Dentures,** hearing aids, orthopedic shoes.
- **Detachable home installations** such as air conditioners, heaters, humidifiers, air cleaners, used for the benefit of a sick person.
- **Dust-free room** for allergy sufferer.
- **Elastic stockings** ordered by a doctor to alleviate varicose veins.
- **Extra rent** for a larger apartment required to make room for a nurse/attendant.
- **Fluoridation device** installed at home on a dentist's recommendation.
- **Legal fees** incurred for the commitment of a mentally-ill spouse.
- **Long-distance telephone** counseling for someone with a drug problem.
- **Maintenance costs** of a home swimming pool for someone suffering from emphysema.
- **Mattress and boards** to alleviate an arthritic condition.
- **Mobile phone** installed in a car to enable someone with heart disease to reach a doctor in an emergency.
- **Payment of lump-sum fee** for lifetime care of a mentally-retarded child.
- **Sex counseling** by a psychiatrist for a husband and wife.
- **Special diets**—salt-free diets, high-protein, etc., for treatment of specific conditions (but only to the extent that the special diet exceeds the cost of a normal diet).
- **Stop-smoking programs** if prescribed as treatment for a specific disorder (e.g., emphysema), but not just for improvement of general health.
- **Trained cat** to alert its hearing-impaired owner to unusual sounds.
- **Transportation costs** to Alcoholics Anonymous meetings.
- **Weight-loss programs** if prescribed by a doctor for treatment of a specific disorder (e.g., hypertension).
- **Wig** to alleviate mental stress caused by hair loss.

Deducting Vitamins And Aspirin

There's a perfectly legal way that just about everybody overlooks. Only prescription drugs can be deducted as medical expense. But there is nothing to stop you from asking your doctor to give you prescriptions for vitamins, aspirin, or any other over-the-counter drugs he wants you to take. The cost as a prescription may be higher—but if you use a lot of them, and shop around for the best price, this strategy could be well worth following.

Deduction For Special Diet

My doctor put me on a low-cholesterol diet consisting of fish, vegetables, certain breads, and fowl. If I keep receipts, can I deduct these items on my tax return as a medical expense?

A medically-prescribed diet is deductible only to the extent that its cost *exceeds* that of a regular diet. Since fish, vegetables, breads, and poultry are common elements of a normal diet, it is highly doubtful that the IRS would allow you a deduction for them.

Taxpayers on special diets may be able to get some kind of deduction under certain circumstances, however. *Example:* When a person who was traveling was required to have a salt-free diet, the Tax Court *did* allow him to deduct charges imposed by restaurants for preparing such meals, as well as *taxi fares* that he had to pay to get to the restaurants that were willing to prepare them.

Source: *Lee R. Cohn,* 38 TC No. 387.

Deduction For The Self-Employed

I understand self-employed people can deduct 25% of their medical insurance. Where on the tax return is the deduction taken? Is it subject to the 2% limit on miscellaneous expenses?

The deduction is taken as an "Adjustment to Income" on page 1, line 25 of Form 1040. It's deducted directly from gross income. You get the deduction whether or not you itemize, and it is not subject to the 2% limitation.

Nursing-Home Fees

An entrance fee and monthly fees are charged by a nursing home that provides both medical and residential services. *IRS ruling:* The fees qualify for deduction as a medical expense to the extent that the home allocates a reasonable portion of them to medical services, and to the extent that they are not covered by insurance.

Source: IRS Letter Ruling 8748026.

Taxed Reimbursement

A person had medical bills for which he was reimbursed by his company's medical plan. But the IRS later found that the plan discriminated in favor of top executives, so the reimbursement was included in taxable income. *IRS ruling:* Normally, reimbursed medical expenses aren't deductible. But because this reimbursement was *taxed,* the related medical bills *could* be deducted.

Source: IRS Letter Ruling 8733002.

Motive is key

Deducting Guests' Expenses

A title insurance company that depended on referrals from selected attorneys and realtors invited them to take periodic trips as guests of the company to Las Vegas, New Orleans, and Dorado Beach when the company's board met at those places. Board members would then mix and discuss business with them. The IRS disallowed the company's deduction for its guests' expenses, saying the trips were primarily social and weren't necessary, since none of the firm's competitors sponsored similar trips. *Tax Court:* Deduction allowed. The trips promoted further referrals from the company's guests. The fact that other title insurance companies pursued business in a different manner was irrelevant.

Source: *United Title Insurance Co.,* TC Memo 1988-38.

Horse Shelter

Alice Jane Snyder was a doctor who had a sideline of breeding horses. Over six years, the sideline generated $200 of gross income and $32,653 of expenses, which she deducted. The IRS disallowed her deduction, saying the sideline obviously had no profit motive. *Tax Court:* Snyder put significant effort into her horses, kept excellent records, dealt with recognized professionals, and acted in a businesslike manner. Moreover, it often takes years to make a horse-breeding business profitable. Thus, while her efforts may have been "misguided," the evidence showed that she *did* have a profit motive, so her losses *were* deductible.

Source: *Alice Jane Snyder,* TC Memo 1987-539.

Entertainment Deduction

Michael Bernard was a salesman whose territory covered the entire state of Ohio. His company did not reimburse him for lodging, meals, or auto costs, so he deducted these expenses on his own return. Bernard had receipts, canceled checks, and notes showing *how much* he spent. But he did not have records indicating the *business purpose* of most of the expenditures. *Court:* Bernard's records were good enough to support most of his deductions. Because most of his trips were clearly business-motivated, the expenses incurred on them had a business purpose.

Source: *Michael J. Bernard,* Cl. Ct., No. 205-84T.

A Writer's Write-Offs

Wilford Burrhus, a data processing manager for Sears, wrote short stories on the side. He claimed he was in business as a writer and deducted an assortment of related business expenses, even though he had never sold a story or made any money from writing. *Tax Court:* Burrhus hadn't shown that there was any profit motive behind his writing, so he wasn't in business as a writer and his deductions were disallowed. *Worse:* Burrhus was hit with *negligence penalties* for wrongfully claiming deductions in disregard of the law.

Source: *Wilford F. Burrhus,* TC Memo 1986-430.

Yacht-Club And Charter-Boat Deductions

A doctor purchased a yacht club and a motorboat to use as a charter boat. He sold 25 memberships in the yacht club. *Tax Court:* Both activities were entered into with a real profit motive, even though the expectation of profit may have been unreasonable. The deductions he took were allowable.

Source: *Paul P. Slawek,* TC Memo 1987-438.

Loan To A Client

John Bowers, the sole owner of a real-estate agency, made a personal loan to one of his major clients. When he wasn't repaid, he deducted the loan amount as a bad business debt. But the IRS disallowed the deduction, saying Bowers wasn't in the business of making loans. *Court:* For Bowers. He made the loan to get future business from the client, so there was a clear business motivation behind it.

Source: *John N. Bowers,* 716 F2d 1047.

Job-related expenses can benefit workers

Teacher's Expenses

A teacher was selected to participate in a program located 600 miles from her home. She originally expected the program to last for only one year, but it was extended for a longer period. She continued to receive her regular pay while in the program. *IRS ruling:* She is on a temporary assignment with full expectation of returning home when the job ends, so she is allowed to deduct ordinary and necessary travel expenses.
Source: IRS Letter Ruling 8730050.

Deductible Volunteer Expenses

A New York doctor/professor took a sabbatical from the school where he taught in order to work as an unpaid adviser to a US Senate subcommittee. *IRS:* He was allowed to deduct expenses incurred for rent and substantiated trips between New York and Washington. Since he was advising in his own field of expertise, all relevant expenses were treated as if they were ordinary and necessary business expenses.
Source: IRS Letter Ruling 8727045.

Education Deduction

A financial consultant could deduct the cost of enrolling in an advanced-degree program concentrating on taxes and financial planning, even though he was *not* required to take the courses for work. The education was job-related because it *enhanced* the skills used by the consultant in his current job.
Source: IRS Letter Ruling 8706048.

Tax-Free Subsidies

Mass-transit subsidies can be given to workers tax-free under federal tax law. *How they work:* Companies buy vouchers from local transit authorities and distribute them to workers, who can apply them to whatever form of mass transit they use. *Limit:* $21 per month. The vouchers are completely tax-deductible for companies and not taxable to individuals.

Benefit-Plan Fees

A company that sponsors retirement plans on behalf of its employees now wishes to charge each employee a *fee* to cover administration and bookkeeping costs. *IRS ruling:* The fee will be *deductible* by the employees who pay it and will *not* count as an extra contribution to an employee's benefit-plan account. *Exception:* The IRS refused to rule concerning the portion of a fee that may be attributable to brokers' commissions.

Source: IRS Letter Ruling 8704058.

Your car holds big deductions

Getting The Most Mileage From Your Auto-Expense Deductions

You can get big tax deductions if you use your car for business (or for investment purposes, such as meeting with your stockbroker or checking on rental property you own). Even some personal use of the car is deductible (going to the doctor, doing volunteer work for charity).

To take full advantage of your deductions, you have to be aware of some complicated rules and comply with stiff recordkeeping regulations. Here's how to protect yourself.

Make The Right Choice

You can deduct your actual expenses, including depreciation, insurance, license fees, parts, tools, repairs, and operating expenses. If you use the car only partly for business (or investment), you can deduct a proportionate part of the expenses. Or you can elect to take the IRS mileage allowance of 30¢ per mile, plus tolls and parking.

Which is better? The mileage allowance is easier, but actual costs often add up to a higher deduction. The only way to tell for sure is to work out the deduction both ways and use the higher figure.

Can you switch? If you ever deducted *accelerated depreciation* or *first-year expensing,* you cannot switch from the actual-cost method to the mileage allowance. You *can* switch from the mileage allowance to the actual-cost method, but you are then limited to *straight-line* depreciation (rather than accelerated).

Claiming your deductions. *Self-employed* taxpayers deduct business expenses on Schedule C. *Employees* claim business (and investment) expenses as itemized deductions, subject to the 2%-of-AGI limit on miscellaneous expenses. (Nonitemizers get no deduction.)

Medical transportation is an itemized medical expense, subject to the 7½%-of-AGI limit on medical expenses. Deduct either actual *out-of-pocket* costs (gas, oil, etc., but not depreciation, insurance, general maintenance)...or the IRS mileage allowance of 9¢ per mile, plus tolls and parking fees.

For *charitable use* of the car, deduct either *out-of-pocket* costs or the IRS mileage allowance of 12¢ per mile, plus tolls and parking fees.

Keep Fail-Safe Records

Record every cent you spend on your car. Make it easier by paying everything you can by credit card—gas, oil, repairs, tires. Keep receipts for car payments, insurance, licenses, and plates. If you pay by cash, write it down as soon as possible in a daily record or log book. Don't forget parts, tools, inspection, tolls, parking fees.

Mileage records: You must be able to prove your allocation of costs between business and personal use of the car. *Best way:* Keep a daily log book. Write down every trip you make (or at least every business trip). Record the mileage and why the trip was made. Also record other deductible uses of the car—investment, medical, and charitable.

Commutation costs: You cannot deduct the cost of traveling from your home to your workplace or of returning to your home at night. However, if you have two jobs, you can deduct the cost of traveling from one to the other. And you can deduct the cost of transportation to and from your office on business trips, such as visiting customers or purchasing supplies.

Depreciation Traps

For cars bought in 1987 or later, the depreciation period is lengthened from three years to five years. (For older cars, you can continue to use the depreciation schedule you used on previous tax returns.)

Percentage test. The car must be used more than 50% for business in order to qualify for accelerated depreciation. *Caution:* Use of the car for checking on your investments is deductible, but it does *not* count toward meeting the more-than-50% test.

Depreciation "recapture." If business use drops to 50% or below in later years, you must switch to straight-line depreciation. Moreover, you must add back all the extra deductions you got from accelerated depreciation and pay tax on that amount.

Depreciation limits. Under the so-called "luxury car" rules, you can deduct no more than $3,060 in the year you buy the car, $4,900 the next year, $2,950 the third year, and $1,775 each year in succeeding years. These are the figures for cars placed in service in 1995. If you use the car only partly for business, the limits are reduced proportionately.

Example: You use your car 60% for business. The maximum depreciation deduction in the year of purchase is $1,836 (60% × $3,060), in the second year $2,940 (60% × $4,900), and so on.

First-year expensing. Generally, purchasers of depreciable business property are allowed to deduct up to $10,000 of the purchases as ordinary business expenses in the year of purchase. The balance, if any, must be depreciated. For cars, however, the $3,060 limit applies to the *total* of first-year expensing *plus* first-year depreciation.

Example: You buy a business car for $15,000. Normally you could deduct $10,000 as ordinary expense and take depreciation on the remaining $5,000. Because of the special limit, however, you can deduct a *total* of only $3,060.

Source: Howard A. Rabinowitz, tax partner, and Lawrence W. Goldstein, tax principal, Ernst & Young, 277 Park Ave., New York 10172.

No-Records Loophole

Rudolph Barnes regularly drove between several job sites for business. But he didn't keep very good records, so the IRS disallowed his deduction for auto costs. *Tax Court:* It was clear that Barnes *had* to drive between these sites for work. Further, the cost could be estimated by measuring the distance between jobs and the number of trips he had to make. Thus he *was* entitled to a deduction. *Catch:* Because Barnes had no records, the Court allowed only the minimum deduction that was reasonable under the circumstances.

Source: *Rudolph J. Barnes,* TC Memo 1986-585.

Auto Deductions Without Records

Rose Fabbo claimed deductions for the use of her van in the family business. The IRS disallowed her deduction because she had *no records* documenting the use of the van. *Tax Court:* Although Fabbo had no records, it was undisputed that she had used the van for business, so she was entitled to some deduction. Thus a deduction of $250 per year was allowed. However, a negligence penalty was also imposed for claiming the deduction without adequate records.

Source: *Rose C. Fabbo,* TC Memo 1987-402.

Car-Expenses Loophole

A taxpayer's employer had a formal policy of reimbursing employees for any business expenses they incurred. His immediate supervisor, however, followed a policy of never approving car expenses. So he deducted the costs as a business expense instead. The Tax Court okayed the deduction. Theoretically, the expenses were reimbursable, but as a practical matter they were not.

Source: George Kessler, TC Memo 1985-254.

Auto Accidents

When a driver made a payment to settle an accident claim that arose while he was driving his car on business, the payment was held to be a deductible business expense.* As one court said in a similar case, accidents "seem to be an inseparable incident of driving a car. Costs incurred as a result...are just as much a part of overall business expenses as the cost of fuel."**

*Plante v. US, 226 F. Supp. 314.
**Harold Dancer, 73 TC 1103.

Personal Auto Accident= Business Deduction

It may be possible to claim a *business deduction* for the cost of settling a lawsuit arising from *personal* use of a car. *Example:*

A company owner allowed his son to use a company car for personal business, and the son was involved in an accident that severely injured another motorist. The injured person filed a multimillion-dollar lawsuit against the owner, the son, *and the company*. As a result, the firm's line of credit was frozen, and its financial viability was threatened. The company quickly settled the lawsuit and deducted the cost.

There was a *business reason* for settling the lawsuit quickly, so the deduction was allowed.

Source: *Koop's Co. v. U.S.,* 46 AFTR2nd 80-6018.

Gambling—fun and deductible

Gambler Wins

The Supreme Court ruled that someone engaged in gambling on a full-time basis was *in business* as a gambler, even though he had a net loss for the year. *Key legal issue:* The Court rejected the IRS's argument that an individual has to provide goods or services to others in order to be in business. *Impact:* An individual who is "in business" can deduct a multitude of related expenses, such as the cost of a home office, travel, entertainment, depreciation on equipment, etc. These deductions may now become available to other persons, such as *investors,* who act to earn income for themselves without actually providing goods or services to others.

Source: *Robert Groetzinger,* S. Ct. No. 85-1226.

Tax Break For Gamblers

Deductions for gambling losses are not subject to the 2% limitation placed on deductions for *miscellaneous expenses.* Under Tax Reform, those expenses (subscriptions to investment or tax-advice publications, tax-preparation fees, etc.) are deductible only to the extent that they exceed 2% of Adjusted Gross Income. *Catch:* Deductibility of gambling losses is limited to the amount of winnings, as under the old law.

Source: Mark Sellner, tax manager, Ernst & Young, 1225 Connecticut Ave. NW, Washington, DC 20036.

Full-Time Gambler

Charles Rusnak was a full-time racetrack gambler. He was also a heavy player in state lotteries. On his tax return he reported $27,000 of gambling winnings and $31,000 of losses, for a net loss of $4,000. The IRS disallowed Rusnak's net loss, saying he could deduct losses only in an amount *equaling* his winnings. *Court:* Since Rusnak was engaged in gambling full-time as a *business,* he *was* entitled to the loss deduction.

Source: *Charles C. Rusnak,* TC Memo 1987-249.

Unknowing Gambler

A lawyer who was also a lottery dealer deducted the cost of unsold lottery tickets as a business expense. *Circuit Court:* The loss was only *partially deductible* under the less favorable *gambling losses* rule. That is, he could deduct his losses only to the extent of his winnings. *Reason:* If any of the unsold tickets had been winners, he could have kept the winnings as if he had purchased the ticket himself. If he sold the tickets at a discount or donated them to charity, it would have been impossible for him to win—and then he could have deducted the unsold tickets as a business expense.

Source: *Gregory E. Miller v. Leroy A. Quinn,* No. 85-3353.

A Real Prize

Gambling winnings are subject to income-tax withholding and are reported to the IRS. But when the sponsor of high-stakes bingo games offered valuable *door prizes* as a promotion, the IRS conceded that the door prizes *weren't* subject to withholding because they weren't won as the result of a wager.

Source: IRS Letter Ruling 8642002.

All about loans and bad debts

Tax Angles Of Unrepaid Loan

My company went out of business owing the Small Business Administration $18,000 on a loan. I had to give the company the money to pay it off and will never be repaid. Can I take a bad-debt deduction?

The normal rule is that a loss on this kind of loan is deductible only as a short-term capital loss. That means that only $3,000 can be deducted against your ordinary income in any single year. However, you can use the loss to offset any capital gains you might have, and losses exceeding $3,000 can be carried forward and used in future years.

You might be able to get *full* deductibility by treating your payment as a *business* loss. But the IRS will say that you were not in the business of lending money. Thus, to get the deduction, you will have to show that you had a pressing business reason for paying off the loan.

Example: In a recent case, a lawyer was able to deduct the debts of a company he invested in when he showed that his law practice would have suffered if he hadn't done so.

Source: *Warren F. Young, 57 AFTR2d 86-985.*

Bad-Debt Deduction

I placed a phone order for $8,000 worth of Krugerrands and paid for them with a cashier's check, but the company I ordered from filed for bankruptcy without delivering. The entire matter is now bogged down in legal proceedings. Can I deduct the $8,000?

A bad debt becomes deductible only when your loss is *final.* Since this case is still being heard by the Bankruptcy Court, there is still a chance (however small) that you may recover some or all of your $8,000. Thus, you can't deduct your loss yet. You'll have to wait until the court issues a final ruling and the amount of your loss becomes certain.

Alternative: You can fix your loss *now* by selling your claim against the coin dealer for a small amount of money to a friend or acquaintance who's willing to take a small risk for the chance of gaining $8,000. Your loss will then be $8,000 *minus* what you get for the claim.

Bad Business Debt

William Pierce, a professional writer, put up $25,000 when he formed a partnership with Ray Henry to produce a newsletter. Pierce would write the newsletter while Henry would publish it. When the partnership broke up, Pierce could have gotten his money back but took a promissory note instead, hoping that he'd get writing assignments from Henry on future projects. When Henry failed to pay off the note, Pierce claimed a *business* bad-debt deduction. *IRS position:* Pierce had suffered an investment loss, not a business loss. *Tax Court:* Pierce had a business reason for taking the note—his hope of getting future writing work. Thus, he was entitled to the deduction.

Source: *William L. Pierce,* TC Memo 1986-552.

Takeover Trap

Roth Steel bought 62% of the stock of Remco, Inc., a financially troubled toy maker, and advanced large amounts of cash to Remco, which needed operating funds. When Remco's business finally failed, Roth tried to claim a *bad-debt deduction* for the cash. *Court findings:* No loan documents had ever been drawn up between Roth and Remco. Moreover, Remco had been unable to get a loan from any other source because it was so badly undercapitalized. *Conclusion:* The advance to Remco wasn't a loan but a contribution to capital. Therefore, Roth wasn't entitled to the deduction.

Source: *Roth Steel Tube Co.,* CA-6, No. 85-1656.

Legitimate Loan

Formal loan documents aren't necessary for a loan to be deemed legitimate, even if it's made by one company to another with the same owners. The key is the intent, a recent court ruling says, overturning the position of the IRS and the Tax Court. Because the borrowing company paid back borrowings when it could, the rest of the debt became a legitimate bad-debt deduction when the borrower went bankrupt.

Source: *Mills v. Commissioner,* USCA Fourth, 2/16.

Losers in the deduction game

Time Bomb

A doctor greatly overstated the value of artwork that he donated to a museum in order to get a charity deduction. But when the IRS finally challenged the deduction, the doctor said that the statute of limitations for the year had expired so he was safe. *Tax Court:* The deduction claimed by the doctor was so large that he had carried it forward into a subsequent year to save more taxes. And this later year was within the limitation period. *Result:* The IRS could challenge the deduction, it was disallowed, and the doctor was held liable for back taxes and underpayment penalties.

Source: *Joseph S. Angell,* TC Memo 1986-528.

Tax-Free Damages = No Deduction

A high-school teacher was fired for publicly criticizing the local school district. When he sued, the district was found to have violated his right to free speech and was ordered to pay $24,000 in damages. The teacher didn't include the award in his income but did deduct $8,000 that he paid to the teacher's union, which had provided his lawyer. *Tax Court:* The $24,000 award was tax-free because it was compensation for harm, not back pay. On the other hand, costs incurred to receive tax-free income can't be deducted, so the $8,000 the taxpayer paid the union wasn't deductible.

Source: *James Edward Bent,* 87 TC No. 15.

Other Cases Don't Matter

Edward Schlecter made and deducted voluntary contributions to his employer's pension plan. The IRS audited Schlecter and, because the employer hadn't met certain technical pension-plan requirements, disallowed the deduction. Schlecter protested that this wasn't fair because other employees who hadn't been audited had kept their deductions. In fact, the deductions of two other employees who *had* been audited had been allowed. *Tax Court:* How the IRS handled other cases didn't matter as long as it handled Schlecter's properly—which it had. His deduction was disallowed.

Source: *Edward F. Schlecter Sr.,* TC Memo 1987-528.

Deducting Work Clothes

A club tennis pro could not deduct the cost of tennis clothes that he *had* to wear for work. *Reason:* Clothes are deductible as a business expense *only* when they are not suitable for everyday wear away from work. The club pro could have worn the tennis clothes on informal social occasions when he wasn't working, so he *couldn't* deduct their cost.

Source: *Cecil Mella,* TC Memo 1986-594.

Strike Benefits

Randall Gregory received strike benefits from his union during a labor action against the telephone company. Gregory claimed that the benefits were a tax-free *gift* from the union. *Court:* Such benefits obviously *aren't* a gift. They're taxable like any other income.

Source: *Randall T. Gregory,* ED NC, No. 84-1124-CIV-5.

Lobbying Costs

A land developer needed zoning changes to develop a certain tract. He lobbied the local authorities to enact the changes, but his effort failed. He then deducted the lobbying costs. *IRS ruling:* No deduction. The Tax Code *prohibits* a deduction for costs incurred to promote the enactment or defeat of specific legislation.

Source: IRS Letter Ruling 8715006.

Religious Deduction?

An avowed sun worshiper could not deduct the cost of a trip to Puerto Rico as a religious contribution deduction, even though he claimed in Tax Court that the primary purpose for taking the trip was to be closer to the "sun god."

Source: *Lewis Hanford Kessler,* 87 TC No. 75.

Big changes in miscellaneous deductions

Fully Deductible—Or Not?

The Tax Reform Act of 1986 changed the rules for deducting miscellaneous expenses.

Miscellaneous deductions include all deductible items not in the categories of medical, taxes, interest, charitable contributions, or casualty losses.

They're further subdivided into two groups. Some miscellaneous deductions are deductible in full. Others are deductible only to the extent that they total more than 2% of a taxpayer's Adjusted Gross Income (AGI).

Here's a rundown of the major items in each group:

Fully deductible:

■ Moving expenses.
■ Gambling losses, up to the amount of gambling winnings.
■ Special job-related expenses of the handicapped (readers, aides).
■ Estate taxes already imposed on the same taxable income.
■ Unrecovered cost of annuities (on a decedent's last return).
■ Amounts previously included in income but since repaid.

Subject to 2% floor:

■ Investment expenses.
■ IRA or Keogh custodial fees.
■ Cost of a safe-deposit box.
■ Tax preparation or other tax-assistance expenses.
■ Employee business expenses, including travel, 50% of meals and entertainment, supplies, professional books and journals, home-office deductions (where applicable).
■ Depreciation on equipment purchased for business use—cars, tools, etc.
■ Job-hunting expenses.
■ Job-related educational expenses.
■ Professional and union dues.
■ Appraisal fees (for charitable donations or casualty losses).
■ Hobby expenses, to the amount of hobby income.

Moving-Expense-Time-Test Trap

Don't overlook the tricky time-limit rules when you're taking a deduction for the cost of a job-related move.

General rule: Moving costs are deductible only if you work as a full-time employee at the new location for at least *39 weeks* in the *12-month period* following your arrival. *Caution:* You don't have to have a job waiting for you at the new location—but if you don't find one within 13 weeks after moving, you can't possibly meet the 39-week test.

If you do have a job (or find one) but lose it before meeting the time test, the law relaxes the rules. *Major exception:* The time test will *not* apply if you expected the job to last 39 weeks but lost it because of "involuntary separation—other than for willful misconduct."

Other exceptions: Death, disability, retransfer by your employer.

Taxpayers who can't meet the 39-week employee test may be able to meet the alternative 78-week test. You can deduct moving expenses if:

■ You work as a full-time employee and/or *self-employed person* for 39 weeks of the first 12 months at the new location, *and also*

■ You work as a full-time employee or *self-employed person* for at least *78 weeks* of the first *24 months* at the new location.

Moving A Sailboat

John Fogg was an avid sailor who owned a 36-foot sailboat. When his employer transferred him from Florida to South Carolina, he claimed a moving-expense deduction for the cost of moving his boat. The IRS disallowed the deduction. *Tax Court:* A person required to make a job-related move can deduct the cost of moving "personal effects." The sailboat *was* a personal effect because Fogg's frequent use of it was intimately associated with his lifestyle. Thus the cost of moving the boat *was* deductible.

Source: *John R. Fogg,* 89 TC No. 27.

Tax consolation in losses

Taxpayer Sunk

William Shields paid $13,000 for a repossessed fishing boat that was in a state of general disrepair. Shortly thereafter, the boat sank when a power outage on the dock caused an on-board pump to stop working. Shields claimed a casualty-loss deduction for the boat. The IRS denied the deduction. *Reason:* Dockside power failure was not an event (such as a storm) that could cause a deductible casualty. *Tax Court:* The power failure was sudden and unexpected and led directly to the sinking of the boat, so the loss *was* a deductible casualty.

Source: *William D. Shields,* TC Memo 1987-495.

Casualty Loss

The Finkbohners' house wasn't damaged during a flood, but many neighboring houses had to be razed. As a result, the market value of the Finkbohners' house decreased. *IRS:* The decline in market value was only temporary and, therefore, was not deductible. *Circuit Court:* The removal of the surrounding homes was a *permanent* change. Deduction allowed.

Source: *G.W. Finkbohner, Jr.,* 788 F2d 723.

10

TAX LOOPHOLES

EVERYTHING THE LAW ALLOWS

Dealing With
The IRS

Protecting your assets

When Not To Trust A Bill From The IRS

When the IRS comes up with a deficiency as the result of an audit, the taxpayer is given a waiver to sign and mail back to the Service. It's called *Waiver of Restrictions on Assessment and Collection of Deficiency of Tax,* either a Form 870, a Form 4549, or a form in the 1902 series. (These are not to be confused with waivers to extend the statute of limitations, Form 872, or with a waiver issued by the appeals office, Form 870AD, which does not stop the interest from running until it is approved.)

By signing one of these forms, you give up your right to contest the deficiency in Tax Court. According to the tax law, interest on the deficiency stops running 30 days after the waiver is received by the IRS. They can't start charging interest again until they issue you a written demand for payment of the tax.

Problem 1: **Wrong date.** The IRS has been known to charge taxpayers interest from the due date of the return right up to the date of the notice demanding payment, which is often several months after the date the waiver was received by them. This extra interest can be a lot more than you should pay.

Problem 2: **Timing question.** It's very difficult to determine whether the IRS has billed the correct amount of interest on a deficiency. They don't tell you the specific dates interest was charged for or the interest rates that were used in the calculation. They just give you a total interest figure. Over the last few years, the IRS interest rate has varied from 6% to 20%. *More complications:* If you're dealing with a deficiency on a tax-motivated transaction (for example, a tax shelter) the interest is 120% of the going rate. Furthermore, interest in recent years is compounded daily.

What to do:

■ Carefully check the interest period before paying the deficiency bill. Interest should be charged for the period beginning with the due date of the return and ending 30 days after the IRS receives the waiver form. If the IRS delayed sending you a demand for payment, interest can't pick up again until you received the written demand. So the first thing to do is check the dates carefully to determine the period for which interest should have been charged.

■ Check the interest calculations. You really need a calculator with a financial mode including compound tables. Your friendly banker could check it for you. *Better:* Have the figure checked by an accountant who has a computer program designed to calculate IRS interest.

■ Pay the tax you owe and the interest you determine to be correct. Clearly explain in an accompanying letter how you arrived at your figures, including a detailed computation of the correct interest.

Warning: Pay the deficiency bill within 10 days. If you don't, interest will start again. To be on the safe side, mail your check return-receipt-requested.

Source: Peter A. Weitsen, partner, Mendlowitz Weitsen, CPAs, 2 Pennsylvania Plaza, New York 10001.

Lien Loophole

People who owe money to the IRS often find that tax liens have been placed on their homes. The IRS files the lien to get a preferential interest in the proceeds from the sale of the house. *Catch 22:* Banks usually won't lend money to homeowners while an IRS lien is outstanding. And the IRS won't release the lien until the taxes are paid. *Inside information:* You can remedy this situation by taking advantage of a little-known IRS procedure. Ask for a "Certificate of Discharge of Property from Federal Tax Lien." Under this procedure the IRS agrees to release the lien simultaneously with the payment of the money you owe it. The bank can then register a mortgage that takes priority over the interests of all other creditors, including the IRS. The mortgage will give you the money you need to pay the back taxes.

Source: Ms. X, Esq., a former IRS agent, who is still well connected.

Collection Tactic

Here's a strategy to use when the collection division is threatening to seize your home. You may not be in a position to refinance your home because the bank isn't satisfied of your ability to repay the loan. *Helpful:* Present the revenue officer with this proposal: "Until such time as I can refinance my house, I'll increase my monthly payments to the IRS by the amount that I would have otherwise paid to the bank had it granted me a mortgage." Keep in mind that the revenue officer won't be interested in a 20-year payment arrangement. Impress on the officer that you'll try to refinance your home again in six months when, hopefully, your financial situation will have improved.

Source: Ms. X, Esq., a former IRS agent, who is still well connected.

Avoiding Fraudulent Conveyance

When you owe the IRS money and then make a gift or transfer of an asset to another person for *less* than its fair market value, the IRS will claim that you have made a fraudulent conveyance. The IRS can take the property from the person you gave it to. One way to avoid this is to negotiate the property's fair market value with the revenue officer and agree to pay that amount to settle the case. *Caution:* Make sure that the IRS gives a release to the person you gave the property to. Otherwise it may go back later and assert its claim that the transfer was fraudulent.

Source: Ms. X, Esq., a former IRS agent, who is still well connected.

Owing Money To The IRS

After the IRS has made an assessment, you have 10 days to pay the owed amount in full or be subject to collection action. The collection division at the IRS has the responsibility of collecting delinquent accounts. Although an account is technically delinquent after 10 days, no one will show up at your door on the eleventh day. A series of threatening notices will be mailed to you, and eventually you will be contacted in person by a revenue officer.

What Power Does the IRS Have?

Can you merely tell the revenue officer that you can't pay the tax right now? Can you avoid seeing or speaking to the officer? You can, but it won't do any good. Unlike other creditors, who must go to court to obtain a judgment against you and then go back to court to have that judgment enforced, the IRS is vested with the power to seize your property without a court order. The only requirement is that it have a valid assessment, give notice with a demand for payment (which has to be sent to your last known address), and give notice of intent to seize.

The IRS can also place a levy on your bank accounts and on your salary. This means that both your bank and your employer must turn over to the IRS all funds being held for you, to the extent of the levy. (*Note:* Special rules apply to salary.)

Certain types of property are exempt by law from levy:

■ The taxpayer's principal residence (in most cases).

■ Apparel and schoolbooks. (Expensive items of apparel such as furs are luxuries and are not exempt from levy.)

■ Fuel, provisions, furniture, and personal effects, not to exceed $1,650 in value (for the head of household).

■ Books and tools used in your trade, business, or profession, not to exceed $1,100 in value.

■ Unemployment benefits.

■ Undelivered mail.

■ Certain annuity and pension payments (including Social Security benefits).

■ Workers compensation.

■ Salary, wages, or other income subject to a prior judgment for court-ordered child-support payments.

■ An amount of weekly wages equal to the sum of your standard deduction, plus personal exemptions for the tax year in which the levy occurs, divided by 52.

Can the IRS put you in jail because you owe it money and have failed to pay, even though the debt has been outstanding for years? The answer is no. Unless you fraudulently conceal your assets or otherwise conspire to beat the government out of its money, you have committed no crime by being unable to pay your taxes.

The best way to approach the situation of having fallen behind in the payment of taxes is to respond immediately to all notices sent you requesting payment. Make every attempt to speak to someone at the IRS and follow up the conversation with a confirming letter. Depending upon the facts and circumstances involved, the IRS may be willing to enter into an installment agreement for payment of the outstanding taxes. Usually, such a part payment agreement requires a down payment, followed by monthly payments over a year or 18 months. If you fail to comply with the terms of the part payment agreement, which also requires that all current taxes be paid on time, the agreement becomes void and your property is then subject to levy seizure.

The best time to try to get the IRS to offer you an installment agreement is at the beginning of the collection process. If you have ignored IRS attempts to work out an arrangement and it is now at your door with a Notice of Seizure, it is extremely unlikely that a part payment agreement will be offered.

How to Negotiate a Settlement When You Owe Money

The first step in negotiating a settlement of taxes owed is to provide the IRS with a current financial statement. Without a statement it can verify, the IRS will not even consider a settlement. What should you do if you don't want the IRS to know about certain assets you own? Just don't furnish the financial statement. It's better to offer no statement at all than to offer one that is misleading or fraudulent.

If the IRS already knows about all of your assets and there is no disadvantage in providing a financial statement, go ahead and submit the statement. The IRS will be interested in knowing how much money you receive each month, how much is spent, and where. When you complete the personal living expense portion of the form, it is generally a good idea to arrange for some money to be left over each month to pay taxes. The IRS is more inclined to go along with a part payment offer if it feels confident there is money available to make the agreement work.

If you have no assets and no income, there is nothing the IRS can levy. If you are in this desperate predicament, you can discuss an Offer in Compromise with the IRS.

An Offer in Compromise is a little-publicized procedure whereby the IRS will accept a one-time payment of as little as 10¢ for each $1 owed in settlement of your tax debt. If the IRS feels it will receive more money from you in the long run by entering into an Offer in Compromise and a collateral agreement (an agreement whereby you agree to pay a certain percentage of your income for five to 10 years), it may agree to the compromise.

The best chance of successfully using the Offer in Compromise route is when the tax debt has been on the books for a number of years. The IRS must be convinced that conventional collection procedures won't work. That's why a relatively recent tax obligation will not be settled this way. But if the IRS has had a chance to collect and hasn't succeeded, it is likely to accept your compromise offer. *Advice:* Always use a tax pro to get you through the Offer in Compromise procedure.

Source: *How to Beat the IRS* by Ms. X, Esq., a former IRS agent, Boardroom Classics, Springfield, NJ 07081.

Wrongful Lien

Once in a while the IRS files a tax lien against the property of an individual who has absolutely no idea why such drastic action has taken place. Here's how to get the lien released if you should happen to be the unfortunate victim of such a mistake. Contact the IRS's Special Procedures Staff (SPS). They will ask you to mail in copies of canceled checks along with any other documents that prove you don't owe any tax. If you can prove that all your tax has been paid, you can expect to have the lien lifted within days.

Source: Ms. X, Esq., a former IRS agent, who is still well connected.

Your money and the IRS

Applying Refunds To Next Year's Tax Bill

If you file the short form, 1040A or 1040EZ, and claim a refund, the IRS will send you a check for that amount (provided you haven't made any errors on your return). But if you file the long form, 1040, you are offered an alternative to getting a check. The back of the form, down at the bottom, asks if you want to let the IRS keep your refund and apply it to your next year's estimated tax bill.

Advice: Don't do it! Never, ever let the IRS hold on to your refund.

Why not? Because it won't really help you in the long run—and it may end up hurting you.

Example: You fill out your return and discover that you had a $900 refund coming. You decide to let the IRS hold on to it and apply it to your next year's estimated tax bill.

But what if the IRS finds a math error on your return? Or your employer made a mistake on your wage statement? Or you forgot to include in your income the interest you earned on a bank account?

These things happen all the time. And any one of them would affect your tax return.

Let's suppose that the bottom line is this: After correcting your return, the IRS sends you a bill for an additional $400.

You already have $900 sitting in your estimated tax account. As far as you're concerned, the IRS can go ahead and take the $400 out of that. Right?

Wrong. You told it to credit the $900 to your estimated tax account, and you're stuck with that decision. In other words, you'll have to come up with the extra $400 on your own.

What if the IRS audits a recent return and finds that you owe additional taxes plus interest? You still can't touch your $900.

To make matters worse, the money you left in your estimated tax account doesn't even earn any interest.

If you really want to earmark your refund for your future tax bill, let the IRS send you your check. Then deposit the money in a savings account or invest it for a year. Don't let the IRS have it for nothing.

IRS Reimburses Bank Charges

The IRS will reimburse taxpayers for up to $1,000 in bank charges resulting from erroneous IRS levies on bank accounts. To get reimbursement, file Form 8546 within one year after being charged.

Advantage Of Informal Payment Arrangements

Entering into an informal arrangement to pay your tax over a number of months may be the way to buy extra time from the IRS. The collection division has a formal procedure whereby a taxpayer must submit a financial statement and formally request permission to pay his tax liability in installments over a period of time. If your financial statement shows that you own assets, the IRS will generally request that you sell them. By avoiding the formal route of an official installment payment plan, you may be able to gain the time you need to gather enough money together to pay the tax bill *without* having to sell or liquidate assets you would rather keep. *Suggestion:* Tell the revenue officer that you will pay at least 40% of the bill *immediately* and the balance in equal payments over two or three months. His initial reaction may be negative, but his bark may be worse than his bite. Give him the down payment anyway. He will privately be happy that your case can be closed in so short a time without extra work on his part.

Source: Ms. X, Esq., a former IRS agent, who is still well connected.

Extending The Float On Tax Checks

The IRS service centers are quick to get your check into their bank. During tax filing season, when thousands of envelopes are received every day, the IRS strives for what it calls "zero day deposit"...all checks are deposited within 24 hours. Computerized mail processing machines can tell which envelopes contain checks by detecting, through the envelope, the magnetic ink on the check inside. *To extend the float:* Mail your check in an oversized envelope. The machines can only process standard, letter-sized envelopes; oversized ones must be handled individually. Human processing, especially during busy periods can add as much as 10 days to your float.

Source: Ms. X, Esq., a former IRS agent, who is still well connected.

Making A Deal With The IRS

The IRS collection people prefer to get money up front when they agree to settle a back tax bill for less than the full amount owed. But they may accept other arrangements, such as being named as the beneficiary of the taxpayer's pension plan or life insurance policy. For instance, in some cases they may be willing to give up 80 or 90 cents on the dollar in return for an irrevocable assignment of a taxpayer's life insurance policy or an irrevocable designation of the IRS as beneficiary of a taxpayer's pension plan.

Source: Ms. X, Esq., a former IRS agent, who is still well connected.

Avoid Paying Interest To The IRS

A little-known provision of the Tax Reform Act of 1986 gives the IRS a power it never had before. The Service can now waive interest charges generated by an IRS employee's error or delay in performance of his/her official duties. Taxpayers who paid IRS interest under such circumstances can apply for a refund. *Examples:*

■ Delay in transferring a case to another IRS district office after the taxpayer's request for a transfer has been approved.

■ Delay in issuing a notice of deficiency after a final decision to issue such a notice has been made.

■ Delay in crediting full payment of tax due.

■ Demand for payment sent to the wrong address when files indicate the proper address.

Retroactive effect: The power to waive interest is retroactive to payments made after December 31, 1978.

How to Apply for a Refund

To request a refund of interest previously paid, file Form 843 (Claim) to the director of the service center where you filed your tax return. *In completing Form 843 state the following on line 7:*

■ The type of tax involved (income, estate, gift, or excise tax).

■ The period for which you're asking interest to be abated.

■ When you were first contacted in writing by the IRS concerning tax owed.

■ The circumstances of the case—the nature of the error or delay.

■ Why failure to abate interest could be widely perceived as grossly unfair.

At the top of the form, write "Request for Abatement of Interest Under Rev. Proc. 87-42." [Code Section 6404(e)]

Right to appeal: If your claim for abatement of interest is denied, you can appeal to the director of appeals.

Ministerial Acts Only

Don't expect the IRS to be too forgiving. Its interpretation of the law to have interest abated is very strict. *Fine points:*

■ The law says interest can be abated if it's attributable in whole or in part to any error or delay by an IRS employee acting in an official capacity in performing a "ministerial act."

■ The IRS defines this as a procedural or mechanical act that does not involve the exercise of judgment or discretion on the part of the employee.

■ The procedure is intended to be used in situations where the failure to abate interest would be widely perceived as *grossly unfair.*

■ Whether interest will be abated in a particular situation is at the discretion of the IRS.

■ The interest must have built up because of an error or delay happening *after* the service center contacts the taxpayer in writing about a deficiency or tax payment.

■ No significant part of the error or delay can be attributed to the taxpayer.

Delay in auditing a taxpayer's return will rarely be grounds for interest abatement. Nor will an IRS employee's decision about the proper application of the tax law give rise to interest abatement because the decision involves judgment.

Source: George S. Alberts, former director of the Albany and Brooklyn IRS districts.

Keep The IRS And The State Happy

Many taxpayers who owe back taxes to both the IRS and the state have a hard time keeping both happy. The IRS usually comes knocking before the state does, since the IRS is better staffed and has more sophisticated collection procedures. As a result, taxpayers who negotiate agreements to pay the IRS in installments are unlikely to have much money left over to pay the state. *Suggestion:* Arrange to give the IRS only about half of the money available to pay back taxes. Point out to the IRS that if a fair share is not paid to the state, it will enforce collection by attaching your salary.

Source: Ms. X, Esq., a former IRS agent, who is still well connected.

Fighting IRS Math And Clerical Errors

Not all tax disputes may be heard in Tax Court. The Tax Code specifically *prohibits* the Tax Court from hearing disputes that arise from the IRS's "mathematical or clerical errors." When such a mistake inflates your tax bill, you must either straighten it out within the IRS's administrative channels, or pay the tax and sue for a *refund* in District Court or Claims Court.

Source: *Alan F. Segal,* Tax Ct. Dkt. No. 13786-83.

Bankrupt Taxpayer Gets Refund

Michael Crabtree filed for bankruptcy, and the court approved a financial reorganization plan for him. The IRS objected to the plan because it wanted to offset Crabtree's refund against an overdue tax bill from an earlier year, and the plan required the IRS to *pay* the refund. *Court:* The plan required Crabtree to pay the tax bill *in full* over time, so the IRS had to pay the refund now.

Source: *Michael Crabtree,* Bankr. MD Fla., No. 85-316-BK-T.

Preventing The IRS From Seizing Your Salary

What are your options if the IRS tries to collect back taxes by serving your employer with a notice of levy garnisheeing your wages? The IRS is authorized to seize almost all your take-home pay. You get to keep less than $100 a week for yourself, plus about $40 a week for your spouse and for each dependent. *The best way to avoid having your salary seized:* Make a sincere effort to work out a voluntary payment schedule for back taxes with the collection division. Revenue officers generally resort to enforced collection tactics only when they meet continued resistance or procrastination by the taxpayer.

Source: Ms. X, a former IRS agent, who is still well connected.

Answering Unreported Income Notices

The IRS recently mailed over 1.6 million computer-generated notices to taxpayers whose returns did not show dividend or interest income as it was reported to the IRS by banks and financial institutions. The notice recalculates the tax due, adds interest charges…and imposes a *negligence* penalty.

How should taxpayers handle these notices? What can they learn from them that will help in preparing this year's returns? *Here's the procedure:*

First step: Study the notice carefully and define the problem. Discover precisely which item, or items, of income the IRS says you did not report. You'll find this information on a separate page of the multipage notice.

Second step: Review your copy of the return and the 1099 forms you used to fill it out. Determine whether the IRS notice is right or wrong. *Never* automatically write out a check for the amount the IRS says you owe. The notice could be dead wrong—many are.

Third step: Answer the notice, in writing, within the time limit given—usually 30 days. Write to the IRS service center at the address given in the notice.

If the IRS is right and you did accidentally fail to report an item of income: Pay the tax and interest but ask that the negligence penalty be waived.

Sample letter:

IRS Service Center
City, State

> Re: John and Sally Connell
> Social Security Nos…
> Form 1040-198__

Gentlemen:

In response to your notice, a copy of which is attached, you will find enclosed a check payable to the IRS in the amount of $x, consisting of tax of $y and interest of $z.

The item in question was inadvertently omitted from our return as filed under the following circumstances: *(Give the reason for the accidental omission of the income.)* It is contended that this constitutes reasonable cause for the inadvertent omission of this item. It is respectfully requested that the negligence penalty assessed in your notice be abated.

> Sincerely yours,
> John & Sally Connell

When you did report the income or the notice is otherwise wrong: Review the notice and your return to discover the cause of the discrepancy. One of several things may have happened. The IRS may be working with an incorrect 1099. Or the 1099 may be right and you reported the income but not as you should have.

Sample letter:

Gentlemen:

In response to your notice, a copy of which is enclosed, I am submitting the following in explanation of the alleged omission. *(Examples follow.)*

1. The dividend of $1,200 reported on my return as being received from General Motors should have been reported as being received from Merrill Lynch as nominee. A copy of my Schedule B is enclosed. *(Circle the item where it appears on your Schedule B to show that you reported it.)*

Lesson: Report dividends from stock held in street name by your broker as dividends received from the *broker* as nominee and not from the company. That's the way the 1099 will show them.

2. Dividend of $400 from Dreyfus Liquid Assets Fund was reported as interest income of $400 from Dreyfus. A copy of my Schedule B is enclosed. *(Circle the item.)*

Lesson: Most money-market funds report their income as dividends and not as interest. Report the income as it is reported to the IRS on the fund's 1099.

3. Interest of $600 from Citibank was on an account owned jointly by myself and my brother. I reported only one half of the interest—$300. A copy of my Schedule B is enclosed.

Lesson: The correct way to report interest from a joint account would be: "Interest, Citibank, $600, *less* amount reported by others, $300. *Net amount:* $300."

4. Interest of $500 from Wells Fargo Bank was reported on my return as $100, per corrected Form 1099, a copy of which is enclosed.

Lesson: Review all 1099s when you receive them. Immediately request corrected copies of any that are wrong. Report the correct information on your return. If the IRS doesn't pick up the correction, you'll have it in your files should you need it.

5. Interest of $2,140 from American National Bank was nontaxable income distributed from my IRA account and immediately reinvested in another IRA. I enclose a copy of a corrected 1099 from American National showing $0 taxable interest in this account.

How to end the letter:

If there are any further questions, please contact me.

If you get a second notice that seems to have ignored your letter:

Gentlemen:

In response to your notice dated March 28, I received a similar notice dated February 23. I answered the first notice with the enclosed letter. It would appear that my response was not received in time to prevent the second request for payment from being issued. *(Enclose photocopies of both notices and a copy of your original letter.)*

Sincerely yours,
John & Sally Connell

Don't Borrow Too Much

Before the collection division will agree to an installment arrangement for paying back taxes, it generally requires the taxpayer to borrow up to the entire equity in his/her home and other assets. During negotiations with the IRS, it is common for a revenue officer to overstate the fair market value of property. *Aim:* To force the taxpayer to borrow the maximum amount possible. *Caution:* Do not accept an undocumented IRS statement that your assets are worth what the revenue officer says they are. Rather, tell the officer that you'll borrow the most the bank will lend. *Key:* People who owe the IRS money are not generally candidates for conventional bank loans. To protect their position, most banks that give mortgages without credit checks will loan significantly less than the fair market value of assets.

Source: Ms. X, Esq., a former IRS agent, who is still well connected.

Can the IRS solve your problem?

Resolving Tough Problems

In most instances, tax problems involving misreported income, lost documents, and other administrative errors will be resolved after sending one or two letters of explanation to your local IRS service center. However, once in a while the nightmare problem arises. You receive one threatening notice after another and just can't get things straightened out through normal channels. That's when it's time to turn to the IRS's Problems Resolution Office (PRO).

The PRO is assigned the task of helping taxpayers who have been frustrated by the IRS bureaucracy. The phone number of the local PRO office can be obtained by looking among the government listings in the phone book, or by calling and asking the local IRS district office.

When you go to the PRO, you must be able to show that you've already tried to resolve your problem through normal channels. You should have copies of at least two letters that you've sent to the local IRS service center or district office, plus copies of all the correspondence the IRS has sent to you.

The PRO handles administrative problems only. It won't get involved in legal issues or the merits of your case. But when it agrees to deal with your problem, you'll be given the name and phone number of the agent helping you, so you'll no longer be dealing with an anonymous bureaucracy.

The PRO gets things done. IRS statistics indicate that on average, paperwork problems involving IRS service centers are resolved in 22 days after referral to the PRO, while problems involving district offices are resolved in 27 days.

Source: Charles Pomo, former IRS appeals officer, now tax principal with Ernst & Young, 277 Park Ave., New York 10172.

Phone Savvy

The phone number the IRS lists in telephone directories is usually the taxpayer assistance number. But the IRS personnel answering questions at that level are generally inexperienced. *To get more reliable help:* Ask the person who answers the phone at taxpayer assistance for the number of the district director's office. By explaining your problem to the secretary at the district director's office, you have a better chance of being referred to the right person in authority at the IRS than you have with taxpayer assistance.

Source: Ms. X, Esq., a former IRS agent, who is still well connected.

Taxpayer Rights

The IRS has issued a set of "taxpayer rights" guidelines for collection division personnel to follow. The guidelines, which have been formally incorporated into the Internal Revenue Manual, require revenue officers to be sensitive to taxpayer problems and to take the initiative in explaining how the IRS arrived at the amount of tax it claims is owed. In real life, however, unless you remind the revenue officer of your rights, he/she isn't likely to follow the spirit of the guidelines. *Best:* Don't deal with the collection division without professional help.

Taxpayers are now allowed to record their audits, too.

Source: Ms. X, Esq., a former IRS agent, who is still well connected.

Protection From IRS Abuse

When Congress criticizes the IRS, the IRS takes notice. Hearings in recent years on the subject of IRS abuses led to legislation to protect taxpayer rights and have made higher-level management personnel sensitive to irate taxpayers who are frustrated by the system. If you feel you're being treated unfairly by lower-level IRS employees, get in touch with the *chief* of the examination or collection division in your local IRS district office. There's a good chance the chief will attempt to accommodate you.

Source: Ms. X, Esq., a former IRS agent, who is still well connected.

Best Times To Call The IRS

The best days to call the IRS (and not languish on hold) are Wednesday, Thursday, and Friday. Avoid midday calls, since most taxpayers phone at lunchtime.

Source: Study by the General Accounting Office.

IRS Truthfulness

The IRS manual bars the use of *pseudonyms* by IRS personnel who deal with taxpayers (except for personnel working in the *criminal* division). The rule requires all field-level IRS correspondence to bear the *real* name and telephone number of an IRS agent who can respond to a taxpayer inquiry.

Tracking Down Your Refund

If it's been at least 10 weeks since you filed your tax return and you *still* haven't received your refund, you *can* do something about it.

Step 1. Get out the copy you kept of your tax return. Be sure you know your Social Security number, your filing status, the exact amount of the refund you claimed and the service center to which you sent your return.

Step 2. Call the IRS's *automated refund information service* to find out the current status of your refund check. Call the *IRS Federal Tax Questions* telephone number for your area that's listed in the back of the Form 1040 instruction booklet. Or call 800-829-1040, a national toll-free number for taxpayer assistance.

Step 3. If there's still a problem, *write* to the IRS service center where you filed your return. Include your name, address, Social Security number, the tax year involved, and an explanation of your problem. Keep copies of the letters you send.

Step 4. If you've done all of the above and *still* haven't gotten your refund, it's time to call the IRS's *Problems Resolution Office (PRO)*. Have a record of the *names* of IRS agents you've talked with, along with copies of all your correspondence with the IRS. Shortly after a PRO officer is assigned to your case, you'll get either your refund or a full explanation of what's holding it up.

The Right-Person Problem

Finding the right person at the IRS to solve your problem is often the biggest problem. Many taxpayer difficulties occur at the regional service centers where tax returns and tax payments are processed. *Advice:* If you don't know whom to write to, address your letter to *Chief, Taxpayer Service*. If you are responding to correspondence received from the service center, put the *stop number* on the envelope. (The stop number appears after the zip code in the service center's address; for example, IRS Service Center, Holtsville, NY 11742, STOP: 422.) The stop number will direct your letter to the right area in the service center complex.

Source: Ms. X, Esq., a former IRS agent, who is still well connected.

Fight Fire With Fire

There are rare situations when a revenue agent will use his position to intimidate a taxpayer or intimidate his/her representative. A taxpayer can be intimidated by an agent who threatens to disallow all the deductions on his/her tax return. A tax accountant or attorney can be intimidated by an agent who threatens disciplinary action for delay or procrastination. The best defense in these situations is to take an offensive position. Immediately write to the agent's group manager setting forth all the facts and requesting that the intimidation cease. Such letters get immediate attention and are generally made part of the agent's permanent personnel file.

Source: Ms. X, Esq., a former IRS agent, who is still well connected.

Psychological Warfare

How do you make a revenue agent see something your way when the agent continues to hold a position that you believe is unreasonable? One technique is to try to make the agent feel guilty that if he doesn't budge you'll have to take the case to court and that will cause you an unreasonable amount of anxiety and cost a lot of money. By getting the agent to feel sympathetic and guilty at the same time, you may be able to work toward a negotiated settlement.

Source: Ms. X, Esq., a former IRS agent, who is still well connected.

Appeals Made Easier

In the past, taxpayers who decided to appeal the IRS's findings at a field audit had to file a formal written protest if the disputed amount was over $2,500. *New rule:* Written protests are required only for disputed amounts over $10,000. A brief written statement will suffice for disputed amounts between $2,500 and $10,000. Oral requests are sufficient for amounts of $2,500 or less.

IRS quirks you should know about

Differing Opinions

In 1992 the IRS examined my return and allowed certain deductions. In 1993 it examined my return and disallowed the same deductions. Is the IRS now allowed to be completely arbitrary and subject to no rules?

Of course the IRS *is* subject to rules. But on an examination of an individual return it is the examiner's *opinion* of your deductions that counts, and one IRS agent's opinion may differ from another's on an unclear issue.

If you think the IRS examiner has been *unfair,* you are entitled to ask for a meeting with his supervisor. You can also take the matter to the IRS appeals division or go to Tax Court.

However, your search for consistent treatment could prove costly. An appeal might lead the IRS to conclude that the examiner for 1992 made the error, and you could lose your deductions for *both* years.

IRS Can Ignore Its Own Rules

When the IRS tried to levy against a person's IRA account, the trustee protested that the IRS manual *forbids* any levy against an IRA, unless the taxpayer "flagrantly disregards requests for payment," which wasn't the case here. *Court:* The procedures in the IRS manual do not have the force of law, so the IRS is not legally bound to follow them.

Source: *First Federal Savings and Loan Ass'n of Pittsburgh,* WD Pa., 644 F. Supp. 101.

Don't Rely On The IRS

Harold Turney retired early from government work with a disability pension. IRS agents *twice* told him that his pension would be tax free until he reached age 65, when regular (nondisability) pension payments would begin. Later, however, a third IRS agent told him that the first two agents were wrong, and that he owed *three years'* worth of back taxes. *Tax Court:* The first two agents *had* been wrong, so Turney *did* owe the tax. Reliance on an IRS agent's poor advice will not free you from paying a tax that's required by law.

Source: *Harold A. Turney,* TC Memo 1987-74.

Wrong Information From The IRS

The IRS Taxpayer Service answers telephone inquiries. But—only 79% of the answers they gave were correct, according to the latest analysis by the General Accounting Office. *Trap:* One answer out of five was wrong overall…and in response to tax reform questions, one answer out of three was wrong. *Best way to get a correct answer:* Make sure that your question is clear and precise. The survey showed that IRS telephone answers were right 90% of the time when the staffer immediately understood the question the taxpayer posed. But they were right only 56% of the time when they were unsure at first what the question was about.

Benefit From Agent Transfer

An opportunity to settle almost any case with the IRS arises whenever the agent you are dealing with tells you he's being transferred to another group. Most group managers discourage agents from bringing their old work with them to new assignments. Thus the agent who has been dwelling on unsubstantiated minor expenditures may be willing to reach a quick settlement once he learns he's being transferred. One way to keep on top of this opportunity is to chat with the agent about his IRS career plans each time you meet. When he tells you that a transfer is in the works, waste no time in suggesting that the two of you agree on a reasonable figure so that the case can be closed.

Source: Ms. X, Esq., a former IRS agent, who is still well connected.

"Unagreed" Cases

Before closing a case "unagreed" (meaning the taxpayer doesn't agree with the agent's assessment), the IRS tries to make sure that the agent assigned to the case has developed the facts as completely as possible. In practice, revenue agents tend to rush through unagreed cases and, thereby, fail to identify all the facts that favor the taxpayer's position. An agent tried this on one of my clients recently, closing the case without giving my client the opportunity to explain his side of the issue. As soon as I became aware of that, I filed a protest with the IRS appeals division and had the case returned to the agent. The agent's instructions from his boss were to listen to, and properly evaluate, the facts the taxpayer was prepared to submit. *Caution:* This tactic can backfire if you wind up providing new ammunition for the agent's case against you.

Source: Ms. X, Esq., a former IRS agent, who is still well connected.

Winning the IRS game

Winning The Fight After Losing The Audit

Taxpayers who disagree with an auditor's findings can appeal the decision both within the IRS and beyond...to the courts. The end of the audit may, if you choose, just be the beginning of your fight with the IRS.

Round One

Actually, it's the IRS that really starts the fight—with what is called its *30-day letter*. That contains a copy of the audit report showing the examiner's proposed adjustments to your tax bill. You have 30 days to respond or request an extension.

Important: Never ignore a 30-day letter. If you don't respond in time, you'll get a notice of deficiency (a 90-day letter) and you'll have to file a court petition to continue your fight. *Best:* Try to settle the case without going to court. It's quicker that way and much cheaper.

How to get to the IRS appeals office: Send a protest letter. This will move your case from the audit division to the IRS appeals office. *Advantages:* The hearings officers at the appeals office have more authority to settle a case than the IRS auditor did. They can use their discretion to judge by the facts and circumstances of the case what the chances are of each side winning in court.

Example: If the hearing officer thinks that you have a 60% chance of winning your argument about the disallowance of a certain deduction, he can decide to allow you to take 60% of the deduction.

If you haven't had one before, it's a good idea to get a tax professional to help you at this stage. He will know what the best legal arguments are in support of your case. He will also know what information to include in your protest letter. *A protest letter should include:*

■ A statement that you want to appeal the findings of the examiner to the appeals office.

■ Your name and address.

■ The date and symbols from the letter transmitting the proposed adjustments and findings you are protesting.

■ The tax periods or years involved.

■ An itemized schedule of the adjustments with which you do not agree.

■ A statement of facts supporting your position in any contested factual issue, declared true under penalty of perjury.

■ A statement outlining the law or other authority on which you rely.

Appeals Conference

You will be notified by the IRS when the appeals conference will take place. You may have to wait six months to one year. While you can represent yourself at this conference, it's a better idea to be represented by a professional who is qualified to practice before the IRS. These experts have experience in presenting your side of the issue to the IRS.

There is a very high rate of settling cases at this point. Usually the cases that aren't settled involve issues that the IRS has decided it isn't going to compromise, such as abusive tax shelter cases. On these issues, the IRS usually wants to test the cases in court in order to set a precedent for the future rather than settle at appeals. *Advantage of settling at this point:* Court proceedings are costly, time consuming, and should be conducted with legal counsel.

Continuing the Fight

If you can't reach agreement with the IRS at the appeals level, you don't have to give up. You have the option of fighting it out in court. The IRS at this point will send you a notice of deficiency (also known as a 90-day letter). You have 90 days from the date of the notice to file a petition with the Tax Court.

Important: Never ignore a notice of deficiency—or fail to answer it within the 90-day period. If you do ignore it, the IRS will automatically make an assessment and bill you for what it thinks you owe. You will forever lose your right to argue your case in Tax Court.

Major disadvantage: If you lose your right to go to Tax Court, you can still sue in District Court or Claims Court. However, for either of these two courts, *you must pay the tax first,* and then sue. In Tax Court, you don't have to pay the tax until the trial is over.

How To Gain Bargaining Power

The collection division usually holds all the cards in negotiations with taxpayers who owe the IRS money. But you may be able to gain some bargaining power by using a technique that has worked well for me. *Real case:* One of my clients owed the IRS more than $100,000. I came into the revenue officer's office with a $25,000 check made payable to the IRS. I put the check on his desk and said, "It's yours…just let my client pay the rest in reasonable installments." A large up-front payment has a real impact. Most revenue officers won't want to see it slip through their fingers.

Source: Ms. X, Esq., a former IRS agent, who is still well connected.

How To Get Fast Action

Making waves at the IRS is an effective way to move a case along. Often, the hardest part of dealing with the IRS is getting an IRS employee to do his/her job. The thing to do if you suspect an employee is taking too long to complete a task, is to confront the employee and, if necessary, speak to his/her supervisor. Don't be too concerned that you are alienating the employee. The threat to go over the employee's head may be enough to get action.

Source: Ms. X, Esq., a former IRS agent, who is still well connected.

IRS Dirty Tricks

Revenue agents have been known to use unauthorized bullying tactics and costly delaying strategies to collect taxes. Here are some measures you can take to protect yourself...

IRS GAME: Foot dragging. The IRS can be terribly inefficient when inefficiency serves its best interest.

Example: A Dallas couple was audited over a complex tax shelter issue involving $50,000 in taxes. The revenue agent was only too happy to put the audit on hold pending receipt of a technical advice memorandum on the issue from the IRS's National Office in Washington. The agent told the couple that it would probably take a year or more for the memo to be issued. What he didn't tell them was that during that time interest would continue to build up on the disputed tax.

Best protective measure: Stop interest from piling up on tax deficiencies by making an advance deposit of the tax the IRS says you owe (it's called "payment in lieu of bond"), but make sure you have professional tax counsel first. If you lose the case, at least no more interest will have accrued. If you win, you get your money back...but without interest.

Alternatives: Pay the disputed tax, appeal within the IRS, and, if turned down, sue for a refund. Or, proceed directly to the Tax Court without paying any of the disputed tax if you've received a deficiency notice.

IRS GAME: Last known address. When you owe the IRS back taxes, the Service will utilize its vast resources to find you. But when it's in the IRS's best interest to lose track of you, it will. Every year the Service sits on millions of dollars of "undeliverable" refunds.

The IRS does, however, publish in the newspapers the names of taxpayers it can't find. Look over the list. You may be pleasantly surprised. *Advice:* Keep track of your refund claims. When more than two or three months have passed without a word, contact your local IRS office.

IRS GAME: Insidious inefficiency.

Example: The Service sends an audit notice to the address shown on the tax return you filed for 1990. Since then, you've moved to another state (and properly filed your 1991 and 1992 returns). When the audit notice goes unanswered because it was not forwarded from your old address, the IRS will settle all tax issues in its favor and charge you with a deficiency. Then, next April rolls around and you file for a refund with your 1993 return. *You won't get it.* The IRS will magically locate you at your new address and apply the current year's refund against the 1990 deficiency...plus penalties and interest it says you owe. *Solution:* Once you learn of the problem, work through the unresolved audit so you won't be unjustly penalized.

To prevent this from ever happening to you, send the IRS and state tax authorities registered letters informing them of your new address.

IRS GAME: Refunds. The IRS hates to pay interest on tardy refund checks but enjoys charging you interest whenever possible. The Service encourages taxpayers to file early in the filing season, but you don't get any reward for filing early. The rule is that the IRS has 45 days from the date of the return or its due date, whichever is later, to process the refund. The IRS says a refund is on time and no interest is payable as long as the check is approved at the IRS within 45 days after April 15.

IRS GAME: Intercept tax refunds. Before sending out a refund, the IRS checks your name and Social Security number against lists that it receives from various government agencies of persons who owe unpaid child support, outstanding student loans, and overdue Small Business and Veterans Administration loans. Your refund automatically goes to cover these outstanding debts, no questions asked. It doesn't matter that there may be a question about the validity of the debt.

Self-defense: The obvious way to avoid interceptions is to avoid refunds. Don't overpay your taxes. Adjust your salary withholding and estimated tax payments so that you break even with the IRS at year-end (or owe them no more than $500). That way the refund intercept program can't touch you. What's more, lack of a refund shows that you've done some effective tax planning.

IRS GAME: Delay release of lien. When you owe back taxes, the IRS is quick to place a lien against your property to ensure that it gets its money. But after you've paid what you owe, the Service can be infuriatingly slow to remove the lien. *Solution:* Nag until the IRS lifts the lien. Don't rely on the Service to automatically remove it even though it says it will.

IRS GAME: Bad tax advice. Taxpayers who rely on incorrect advice given by IRS employees or in IRS publications are just out of luck. The IRS insists that it's not responsible for its own bad advice. The courts have upheld the Service on this point. *Some help:* Do your own research by reading tax books, magazines, and newsletters. And hire a professional tax adviser if your return involves complex issues.

IRS GAME: Terrorize tax preparers. Preparers save taxpayers too much money. The IRS knows that most taxpayers who file without professional assistance overpay their taxes and will try to avoid the confrontation of an audit at all costs. But tax professionals help calm a taxpayer's fear of confrontation with the IRS and open up new tax-saving opportunities.

To fight the tax drain caused by private tax advisers, the IRS has instituted a program that can effectively drive a preparer out of business. If a preparer strays too far from the IRS-approved path, he can be fined, penalized, barred from practicing before the IRS, and even have all his clients audited. That's something the preparer can't afford, even if he has been meticulous with the returns. *Result:* Many preparers have become overly cautious in handling tax returns. Some fear the IRS more than they fear losing your business.

Source: Paul N. Strassels, a former IRS tax-law specialist, Box 195, Burke, VA 22015.

Buying Time

Just because a case has been assigned to the collection division, it does not necessarily mean that collection activity will begin right away. In a great many cases enforcement action will not start until after the taxpayer has failed to respond to a series of letters from the collection division requesting payment. Even after personal contact has been made by a revenue officer, it is still possible to squeeze out a few more months before you are in serious jeopardy of losing your house and business. The way you can really get in trouble with the IRS is to completely ignore the collection division. Sooner or later, time will run out.

Source: Ms. X, Esq., a former IRS agent, who is still well connected.

A word to the wise...

Danger Of Suspected Fraud

If the IRS suspects fraud it can ruin your business and reputation even if it later finds that the suspicion was unfounded. In the course of a criminal investigation, the IRS will be concerned with how customers, clients, patients, etc., pay their bills. They generally suspect that checks and cash payments were received but never recorded by the taxpayer. They can send summonses to third parties to obtain this information. Blocking enforcement of an IRS summons is very difficult, since you must prove to a court that it is an unnecessary invasion of privacy or a threatened injury to your reputation. However, even if your privacy will be invaded and your reputation injured, the court will order the summons enforced if the IRS can show a legitimate investigative purpose for it.

Source: Ms. X, Esq., a former IRS agent, who is still well connected.

Good News For Tax Evaders

Convicted tax evaders can reduce prison time by making every effort to pay what they owe as soon as possible after conviction. Recent experience shows that sentencing judges are impressed by tax evaders who agree to pay the tax they owe. Those defendants who are still able to generate income from their businesses should be encouraged to enter into a meaningful agreement with the IRS to pay what is owed as soon as possible to avoid disruption of the business and to favorably influence the sentencing judge.

Source: Ms. X, Esq., a former IRS agent, who is still well connected.

Travel Alert

The IRS has beefed up its Office of International Operations, heeding the concern of Congress over the amount of revenue lost through the use of foreign entities (corporations, partnerships, etc.) in tax haven countries. Domestic corporations that transact business with foreign entities are under closer scrutiny. Special attention is being given to business transactions between foreign entities and US corporations that are owned by the *same* person. Especially suspect are business owners who regularly travel to a foreign country and then return home *via* Switzerland.

Source: Ms. X, Esq., a former IRS agent, who is still well connected.

Warning To Accountants And Tax Preparers

Sooner or later in your practice you are likely to encounter a special agent or an assistant US attorney who will ask how you obtained the information you used to prepare a client's tax return. The client in these cases is typically the subject of a criminal investigation and the government will be seeking your cooperation as a witness against him. *Caution:* Any statements that you make in explanation of what was done, and why, can be used against you if the government later charges that you were part of a conspiracy with your client to evade tax. Before making any statements to investigators, insist that you be granted immunity from prosecution...even if you sincerely believe you have nothing to be afraid of.

Source: Ms. X, Esq., a former IRS agent, who is still well connected.

Not So Immune

Eldridge Black was involved in a kickback scheme being investigated by a federal grand jury. He was given immunity from criminal prosecution in exchange for providing information to the grand jury. Later though, the IRS sent him a bill for taxes owed on the kickback income. Black protested that the immunity agreement protected him. *Court:* The immunity agreement applied only to *criminal* prosecution. The IRS's demand for back taxes was a *civil* action.

Source: *Eldridge Black,* TC Memo 1987-212.

Crime Gets Taxed

Frank Signorile ran a sandwich shop while conducting a loan-sharking operation on the side. The IRS took action when it noticed that he seemed to have much more income than he could have earned selling sandwiches. *Tax Court:* He owed not only income tax on his unreported earnings, but also *self-employment taxes* for running his illegal business.

Source: *Frank Signorile,* TC Memo 1986-565.

IRS Insider Goes Bad

Lawrence Weisensee learned all about prosecuting tax evaders while working as an IRS attorney. But this did not stop him from failing to file *his own* tax returns for several years after he left the IRS and started his own practice. *Court:* Weisensee was guilty of tax *fraud.* He, of all people, knew what his legal obligations were, and his avoidance of them had to be intentional.

Source: *Lawrence Weisensee,* TC Memo 1987-206.

Informants and investigations

All About Whistle Blowers And Tax Cheats

If everyone paid their fair share of taxes, we'd all have a lower tax bill. The tax fraud economy runs into the billions of dollars. It's a national scandal and without public cooperation, the IRS doesn't have a fighting chance against it.

No one, *including the IRS,* wants a society where everyone is spying on everyone else. On the other hand, it's adolescent to believe that there is something dishonorable about revealing to the IRS that a person is deliberately, systematically, and substantially evading taxes. *Here's what you can do:*

A Reasonable Personal Policy for Giving Information

If you have information you believe will be valuable to the IRS, it can be given in person, or in writing, to:

Head of the Criminal Investigation Division, Internal Revenue Service, Washington, DC 20224.

If you're not claiming a reward for the information, you can use an assumed name. But if you are claiming a reward, you must give your name.

Section 7623 of the Internal Revenue Code authorizes payment of a reward to anyone who provides information leading to the detection and punishment of anyone who violates federal tax law. *To claim a reward,* you need to complete Form 211, available through the IRS's toll-free forms number.

Mail the completed form to *Informant's Claim Examiner* at the office of any IRS service center director...or you can deliver the form in person to a representative of the Criminal Investigation Division at your local IRS district director's office.

What to Expect

The IRS does not disclose the identity of an informant to any unauthorized person. And it takes heroic procedural steps to prevent mistakes.

Informants are *not* kept posted on the progress of investigations. They can, however, check to see if their claim for a reward is still under active consideration by the IRS.

Rewards are paid only *after* tax is recovered from the subject of the investigation. This can take five years—or more.

Informant's Rewards

Rewards are based on the value of the information given and the amount recovered from the target of the investigation. There are three reward scales:

1. For *specific* and responsible information that caused an investigation and resulted in recovery of taxes, fines, and penalties: 10% of the first $75,000 recovered; 5% of the next $25,000; 1% of any additional amounts. The maximum reward: $100,000.

2. For information that caused an investigation and, although not specific, was of value in determining tax due and of direct value in recovering tax, the reward is: 5% of the first $75,000 recovered; 2½% of the next $25,000; ½ of 1% of additional amounts recovered. Maximum reward: $100,000.

3. For information that caused an investigation but was of no value in determining tax due, the reward is: 1% of the first $75,000; ½ of 1% of additional recovery. Maximum reward: $100,000.

More Valuable Information

Don't waste the IRS's time and the taxpayers' money by using the informant process to get even with people you're feuding with. Frivolous reports are easily spotted by the IRS, and no action will be taken. The IRS is looking for real tax cheats and needs specific information to work with.

If you have specific knowledge of deliberate, systematic evasion, tell the IRS how you came by the knowledge—from a bank employee, bookkeeper, former partner, etc.

Informant's rewards are fully taxable. The IRS checks every case to be sure informants have declared rewards.

There are several reasons why the IRS might reject your claim for a reward:
- Your information was of no value.
- It was already known to the IRS.
- The information is available in public records. For instance, the alleged tax cheat bought a $500,000 yacht.
- Payment of a reward would be inappropriate. *Example:* The informant participated in the scheme to cheat the government out of taxes.

Testing the waters: If you're not sure whether the information would be of value to the IRS, talk to a representative of your local district director's office. You'll get an informed opinion of the value of the information. But that opinion won't be binding on the ultimate decision to pay or not to pay a reward.

Source: George S. Alberts, former director of the Albany and Brooklyn IRS districts.

Can You Trust Your Accountant?

The IRS makes no secret of the fact that it will pay a reward of up to $100,000 for information that leads to the collection of money owed by tax cheats. It turns out that most informants are disgruntled employees, ex-lovers, and former husbands and wives. But your former *accountant,* who usually has more knowledge of your finances than anyone else, could actually be the person you should be *most* concerned about. *Recent case:* An accountant, who felt he had been cheated out of a fee by a client, turned in revenge to the IRS Criminal Investigation Division.

Source: Ms. X, Esq., a former IRS agent, who is still well connected.

Joint Investigations

In a program that may be a model for other states, the IRS and Massachusetts entered into an agreement to conduct joint criminal tax investigations and audits, and to exchange more information in the hopes of catching tax cheaters and delinquents. *Information to be shared:* Interest and dividend payments, audit findings, federal estate-tax-return information, and federal out-of-state audits.

The IRS doesn't always get its way

How To Sue The IRS

The IRS has to pay your litigation expenses in certain situations. Don't miss the opportunity to collect if you qualify. The expenses that will be paid include fees for attorneys, accountants, expert appraisers, expert witnesses, and court costs. The maximum amount that can be recovered is $25,000. *When the IRS must pay:*

■ When the result of the litigation is that you've "substantially prevailed" over the IRS, and,

■ You can prove that the IRS has taken an unreasonable position in the case, and,

■ You have tried all available methods within the IRS to dispose of the issue, such as talking to an IRS supervisor or using the IRS Appeals Office.

Winning Tax Fight Fees

When IRS auditors disallowed some of Paul Plowman's deductions, he incurred substantial legal fees while appealing the matter *within* the IRS. Finally, he was forced to take his case to court. When the IRS's lawyers got the case, they immediately realized that Plowman was right and conceded without going to trial. Plowman then asked to have the IRS pay his attorney's fees. But the IRS said that a taxpayer can collect attorney's fees only if he wins his case *in court*, and Plowman's case hadn't gone to court. *Verdict:* Plowman had incurred expensive legal bills as a result of the IRS's *unreasonable* behavior, regardless of whether the case actually went to trial. Thus, he *was* entitled to reimbursement.

Source: *Paul Plowman,* WD Okla, No. CIV-85-2334-W.

IRS Loses Through Unreasonableness

The IRS misplaced an organization's return and imposed late-filing penalties and interest when the organization sent a copy to the IRS. *Claims Court:* The IRS had to pay the organization's attorney fees. *Reason:* The IRS was unreasonable when it delayed investigating the claim that the return had been filed on time.

Source: *Tax Analysts v. US,* No 440-85T.

IRS Pays Attorney's Fees

C.H. Golden managed a hotel for a corporation that was entirely owned by Albert Lawson, who ordered Golden not to pay employment taxes owed to the IRS. The IRS held Golden *personally* liable for the unpaid tax and collected it out of a refund owed to him. Golden sued to get his money back. *Court:* The IRS acted unreasonably when it pursued Golden instead of Lawson, so it had to refund the tax to Golden *and* pay $6,905 in attorney's fees for Golden's lawyer.
Source: *C.H. Golden,* WD Mo., No. 85-0741-CV-W-5.

Unreasonable Again

A woman was penalized by the IRS for not withholding federal taxes from employees at the company where she worked. The company's president had signed an affidavit stating that she was not the person responsible for withholding these taxes. *District Court:* The IRS had to pay her attorney's fees. *Reason:* The IRS acted unreasonably when it failed to further investigate the situation in light of the affidavit.
Source: *Brenda Brigham,* No 85-60478-AA.

A Refund And More

When a corporation owned by Willard L. Coon owed back taxes, the IRS wrongfully held up a $50,000 refund that was due on his *personal* return. Coon had to sue to collect. *Court:* Because Coon had won the case, and the IRS's denial of the refund was *unreasonable,* the IRS owed Coon $11,594 in attorney's fees and accountant's fees *in addition* to the amount of the refund.
Source: *Willard L. Coon,* S.D. W. Va., No. A: 85-0366.

IRS Pays The Bill

The IRS accused a company of failing to report the profits from two large sales of silver. It sent a tax bill for a year that would be protected by the statute of limitations *unless* the IRS could prove fraud. But when the case went to trial, the IRS couldn't prove when the sales took place. *Tax Court:* Since the IRS couldn't prove fraud, the company was safe all around. Moreover, the IRS had acted *unreasonably*—it should never have brought the case, unless it *could* prove fraud. *Result:* The company could collect its litigation costs from the IRS.
Source: *Don Casey Co., Inc.,* 87 TC No. 54.

IRS Loses By Giving No Explanation

Richard Beebe received a letter from the IRS saying that an investigation of his tax liability had ended. *Then* he received a court summons ordering him to produce records for the same liability. When he challenged the summons, the IRS said that its earlier letter had been an "administrative error." *Court of Appeals:* The IRS's argument was "disingenuous" for it had no explanation of *how* the earlier letter could have been sent by mistake. The summons was voided *and* the IRS had to pay $10,144 for Beebe's lawyer's fees.

Source: *Richard L. Beebe,* CA-6, No. 86-4141.

Safe Silent Partner

A firm had three officers, all of whom could sign checks. Two were responsible for withholding and paying employment taxes. When the firm failed to pay these taxes, the IRS held all three officers personally liable. The officer who had no payroll authority protested that she shouldn't be liable because she had nothing to do with payroll matters. The other two officers agreed, even though this admission meant they would have to pay the whole tax liability. Eventually the court freed the officer who had no payroll responsibilities from all liability. *Bonus:* Because the IRS's action against this officer was unreasonable from the start, *it* had to pay *her* legal bills.

Source: *Marcia Lindt,* Ed Ill., No. 85-C-4146.

Offshore Loan

Kenneth Rogers sold a small business and some Florida land to Braulio Vila for $250,000—cash. At the same time, Vila sent an additional $50,000 to the Netherlands Antilles bank account of a Panama corporation that Rogers had set up. Soon after, the $50,000 was forwarded to Rogers' *personal* account in Florida. Rogers and Vila said the $50,000 was a loan, but the IRS said that Rogers was trying to hide future revenues from the sale. *Tax Court:* For Rogers, because the $50,000 *was* a loan. *Key facts:* The loan had been *documented* with a note, and Rogers had actually made payments of both principal and interest on the note.

Source: *Kenneth A. Rogers,* TC Memo 1986-529.

Written Limitations Stick

A taxpayer and the IRS signed an IRS form extending the time for the Service to assess his tax. The taxpayer wrote on the back that the extension applied only to certain issues and not his entire tax return. *Tax Court:* The IRS had to abide by the taxpayer's written limitations, even though the agent claimed he never saw the restriction.

Source: *Arthur C. Schwotzer, et al.,* Tax Ct. Dkt. No. 14474-84.

Important Definition

Anthony Laglia raised fruit-bearing jojoba plants for their oilseed, which he sold. He deducted his costs as a business expense. The IRS denied his deduction because the Tax Code prohibits an expense deduction for the cost of raising fruit-bearing trees in a "grove or orchard." Laglia said that he wasn't selling fruit, he was selling oil. Further, the jojoba plant is a shrub, not a tree. The IRS replied that the plants could be pruned to resemble a tree, so that a number of pruned plants constituted an orchard. *Tax Court:* The IRS was ignoring the plain sense of the law. A shrub is not a tree. Laglia's deduction was allowed.

Source: *Anthony G. Laglia,* 88 TC No. 48.

No-Win Situation

Don Walker pleaded guilty to various tax offenses. The IRS and Walker's lawyers then met to decide which of Walker's assets would be used to pay his tax bill and which to pay his legal fees. After this meeting Walker attempted suicide. While he was recovering, the IRS couldn't interview him about the location of some of his assets, so it seized everything it could find, including property that had been pledged to pay his legal bills. Walker's lawyers challenged the seizure. *Court:* The seizure was unreasonable given the fact that both Walker and his lawyers had been *cooperating* with the IRS.

Source: *Don E. Walker,* ED Tenn., No. 3-86-480.

IRS Double Cross

A business filed for bankruptcy, and the IRS filed a claim for unpaid employment and withholding taxes. Finally a settlement with the IRS was reached, approved by the creditors as part of a reorganization plan, and paid by the business. Then the IRS sent another $21,000 bill for taxes that it said weren't covered by the settlement. *Court:* Both the business and its creditors had relied on the belief that the settlement covered the *full* tax bill. The extra taxes were disallowed.

Source: *La Difference Restaurant, Inc.,* SD NY, No. 83 Civ 3946.

Don't panic if your return is late—very late

What To Do If You Can't File On Time

The IRS will automatically give you until August 15 to file your tax return. All you have to do is notify the Service in writing by filing Form 4868 with your local IRS service center no later than April 15.

Caution: An extension of time to file your return isn't an extension of time to pay your tax bill. Write out a check for the estimated amount of tax you owe, attach it to Form 4868, and mail it by April 15. You will be charged penalties and interest for paying late taxes if you wait until the extended due date to pay the tax.

Calculate the tax as accurately as possible. When you do file your return, interest is due on the amount by which you underestimated your tax bill. If you underestimated by more than 10%, a penalty will be charged in addition to the interest.

Extensions beyond four months must be approved individually by the IRS. Use Form 2688 to give the reason why you need more time. If your request is approved, you get two more months to file your return. Attach this special approval to your return. *Important:* The IRS generally won't consider your request for an additional extension unless you had first filed a Form 4868.

Talking Your Way Out Of Late-Filing Penalties

Showing the IRS that you had a good reason for filing your tax return late may get you off the hook for penalties *even if you didn't file an extension form.* You must convince the IRS that it wasn't your fault that you filed late, and your excuse must be reasonable. *Excuses that have worked:*

■ Records were destroyed or lost due to a casualty, fire, or theft.

■ The taxpayer received incorrect information from the IRS. *Important exception:* The IRS has held that receiving wrong information from the IRS Federal Tax Questions telephone number is not an acceptable excuse for filing a tax return late.

■ Tax forms that you requested in time from the IRS were never received.

■ You filed your return on time but sent it to the wrong service center.

■ You filled your return out incorrectly because it was your first time filing and you were ignorant of the law.

■ You or someone in your immediate family was seriously ill or died.

Note: The IRS is not *required* to accept any of these excuses.

Source: Irving Blackman, partner, Blackman Kallick Bartelstein, CPAs, 300 S. Riverside Plaza, Chicago, IL 60606.

A Late-Filing Excuse That Worked

When the IRS tried to penalize William Haden for not filing a tax return, he claimed that he *had* filed a return at the post office on April 15. He said that the post office was so crowded on filing day that he had given the return to a postal worker who had been stationed on the street to accept returns, and he concluded that the worker must have *lost* the return. Both Haden's wife and a friend supported his story as witnesses. *Tax Court:* Although Haden's story was "shaky" on a few details, it was believable overall. The penalty was set aside.

Source: *William F. Haden,* TC Memo 1986-539.

Hope For Delinquent Filers

People who haven't filed tax returns for a couple of years are hounded by the thought that failure to file tax returns is a crime—and that's very nerve-racking. The best way to clean up the mess is to file the delinquent returns *before* the IRS comes after you. As a practical matter, if you file before the IRS contacts you, there's hardly any chance at all that criminal charges will be brought. *Tactic:* Mail the return for each delinquent year in a *separate* envelope. This reduces the chance that the person processing your return will realize that you also failed to file other returns.

Source: Ms. X, Esq., a former IRS agent, who is still well connected.

Intentions count

Fraud Defense

Albert Friedman was an independent insurance agent. On his tax return, he reported commission income that was much less than the amount that was reported as being paid to him on 1099 forms filed by the insurance companies he dealt with. When the IRS discovered the discrepancy it charged him with tax fraud. *Tax Court:* Understating income by itself is *not* fraud. Friedman *hadn't* acted to *hide* his income, and the IRS was bound to find out about it because of the 1099s. Thus, he hadn't committed fraud.
Source: *Albert C. Friedman,* TC Memo 1987-6.

Second Chance Given

Dr. John DeTar filed an accurate tax return every year but never paid any of the taxes he owed, letting a liability of over $100,000 build up. Finally the IRS brought criminal charges against him. He argued that personal problems kept him from paying. *Jury:* Guilty of a felony—willful tax evasion. *Court of Appeals:* Conviction overturned. The trial judge had not informed the jury about the *lesser* offense of intentionally failing to pay taxes that are due, which is merely a misdemeanor because it doesn't involve a plan of tax evasion. An informed jury might have found this verdict more appropriate, so DeTar was entitled to a *new trial.*
Source: *John N. DeTar,* CA-9, No. 86-1199.

Saved By The Calendar

Jerry Greenway greatly understated his income by failing to report benefits that he received from his company. Several years later the IRS came after him for back taxes. Greenway said he was safe because the three-year statute of limitations had run out. But since the IRS had accused him of *fraud,* it said the statute wouldn't apply. *Tax Court:* Greenway *was* safe. Failure to report income by itself is *not* fraud. Since Greenway had taken no steps to hide his income or deceive the IRS, he hadn't committed fraud and the limitation period *did* apply.
Source: *Jerry G. Greenway,* TC Memo 1987-4.

Negligence Wasn't Fraud

The IRS tried to assess the fraud penalty against a contractor who didn't report all his income. He relied totally on others to keep his books and prepare his tax returns. He never examined them carefully. And, he never questioned the fact that his business receipts were sometimes deposited into his personal savings account and weren't taxed. *Tax Court:* The *intentional* wrongdoing necessary for fraud wasn't proved.

Source: *Wendell W. Vaughn,* TC Memo 1986-578.

Embezzlement Defense

The IRS charged Robert Elmore with embezzling $450,000 from his employer when it discovered that he had made false entries in the company's books to cover that amount. It assessed him for back taxes on the sum. *Elmore's defense:* He had made the entries to cover kickbacks that the company's president had made to public officials. He hadn't taken any of the money for himself. *Tax Court:* The IRS had no proof that Elmore had gained from the scheme *personally,* so it could collect no tax.

Source: *Robert A. Elmore,* TC Memo 1987-72.

Fraud Vs. Negligence

Charlie Clark filed a tax-protest return that didn't include any income information. He didn't cooperate with the IRS during the audit, either. *Tax Court:* The IRS was wrong to try to assess the *fraud* penalty, because he didn't try to conceal his identity or his address. Clark, however, did have to pay the *negligence* penalty.

Source: *Charles Thomas Clark,* TC Memo 1986-586.

When it isn't your fault

Ignorance As An Excuse

Jackson Buster Wells failed to file tax returns for four years in a row and was convicted by a jury of criminal tax evasion. Wells had argued in his defense that, as he understood the law, he wasn't required to file a tax return. *Court of Appeals:* The verdict will be set aside. A person will not be convicted of *criminal* tax evasion unless he *knowingly* breaks the law. So a sincere belief that he wasn't required to file a return was a valid defense, even if that belief was unreasonable and wrong.
Source: *Jackson Buster Wells,* CA-10 790 F2d 73.

Bad Advice Loophole

A couple underpaid their taxes as the result of advice from their tax attorney. The IRS tried to charge them with the negligence penalty. *District Court:* They didn't have to pay it because they relied in good faith on the attorney's advice.
Source: *Alan G. Mack,* CD, CA, No. CV 85-3779-FFF(JRx).

Out Of The Country

A Tax Court petition usually has to be filed within 90 days after the taxpayer receives a notice of deficiency. However, Mrs. Mohamed was out of the country when the IRS mailed the notice. *Tax Court:* Taxpayers who are out of the country when the notice is mailed have 150 days to answer a notice of deficiency. Mr. and Mrs. Mohamed filed within 139 days so their petition was valid.
Source: *Zaid A. Muthala Mohamed,* TC Memo 1987-132.

Deadline Loophole

The 90 day deadline for appealing a deficiency notice to the Tax Court is extended to 150 days if you're out of the country. One taxpayer won the extension by showing the court his travel reservations in Mexico for the day the notice was delivered, and a passport stamp proving when he reentered the US.
Source: *William D. Blaine,* Tax Ct. Dkt. No. 28249-856.

IRS Loses Through Laziness

William King, television personality in Dallas, Texas, changed his address in 1980. But after he moved, his accountants continued to send King's correspondence to the IRS bearing his *old* address. Eventually, the IRS sent a deficiency notice to the old address. The notice was returned as undeliverable, but the IRS said it was still valid because it had been sent to the address King had given them. King didn't find out about the notice until the deadline for answering it had passed. *Tax Court:* When the notice was returned, the IRS should have realized something was wrong. It could easily have found King's right address had it tried, but it didn't try, so the notice was invalid.

Source: *William L. King,* 88 TC No. 58.

Fraud Insurance

The Borowieckis were charged with fraud when they moved $50,000 from their family business to their personal bank account without reporting it on their tax return. They said they hadn't reported the money because their return preparer told them that there was no need to. *Tax Court:* Fraud occurs only when a person *hides* income. The Borowieckis had disclosed all their income to the return preparer. Thus they couldn't be guilty of fraud even though the preparer had made a mistake.

Source: *Robert Borowiecki,* TC Memo 1987-23.

Appeal Postponed

The Tax Court decided against Don Newman, but the court clerk misaddressed the notice of decision to Newman's lawyer. As a result, the time for appealing lapsed before an appeal was made, and the Court issued a final order. Newman protested, but the IRS said that the order should stand. *Decision:* The Court will vacate the previous order and reissue proper notice of the decision. Newman will get his chance to appeal.

Source: *Donald Newman,* Tax Ct. Dkt. No. 21585-83.

Sloppy Records

Pierce Marshall received a few different notices from the IRS at his correct post office box. The IRS then sent a notice of deficiency to his street address. But it was returned to the IRS by the post office. The taxpayer didn't actually receive the notice until a year later. *Tax Court:* Case dismissed. The IRS should have used the address that had worked in the past.

Source: *E. Pierce Marshall,* TC Memo 1986-582.

Timing is everything

The Statute Of Limitations

The limitations period is the time within which the IRS must act to make any adjustment to your tax liability for a given year. When the period expires, you are safe from the IRS. There are *three* basic limitation periods:

■ *Three years* is the standard limitation period that applies to most returns; however...

■ *A six-year* limit applies to any return that omits reporting 25% or more of a taxpayer's income; and...

■ *No limit* applies when a person fails to file a tax return, or commits *fraud* by taking active steps to hide income from the IRS.

The limitation period normally runs from the due date of your return or the date you actually filed it, whichever is *later*.

Taxpayer Edge

Josephine Margolies received an IRS deficiency notice that was dated August 16 but which came in an envelope bearing an August 21 postmark. On November 15, she filed a Tax Court petition to protest the deficiency. The IRS said the Court should reject the petition because it wasn't filed within the 90-day period after the date of the notice. But Margolies said the filing period should begin only when the notice was mailed. *Tax Court's decision:* The 90-day rule is capable of both interpretations, and in ambiguous situations it should be read in the *taxpayer's* favor. Thus, the Court *will* hear the case.
Source: *Josephine Margolies,* Tax Ct. Dkt. No. 42058-85.

Second Notice Was Too Late

During an IRS audit, Charles Hubbard agreed to extend the statute of limitations that applied to his return. The IRS sent Hubbard a deficiency notice before the extended period ran out. *Problem:* It was mailed to the wrong address, and Hubbard didn't get it. Some time later, the IRS sent a copy of the notice to Hubbard's correct address. *Court:* The second notice was sent *after* the extended limitation period had expired, so Hubbard was safe.
Source: *Charles E. Hubbard,* TC Memo 1987-575.

Postmark Trap

Mr. and Mrs. Gerl had to mail a petition to the IRS by the deadline of July 25 for it to be valid. They did mail it by July 25 but since they mailed it after the post office closed, it wasn't postmarked until the next day. *Tax Court:* The petition was dismissed because it was postmarked one day late.

Source: *Wayne A. Gerl,* TC Memo 1987-289.

Too Late For The IRS

The IRS sent a deficiency notice to a couple for the year 1983 by mistake. The notice should have been for 1982. When the IRS realized its error, the statute of limitations had run out and it was too late for the IRS to collect. *Tax Court:* Case dismissed. The IRS was out of luck.

Source: *Rosario W. Tromp,* Tax Ct. Dkt. No. 14737-86.

Time Runs Out

Louis Roszkos signed a consent agreement that extended the statute of limitations until the IRS sent him a deficiency notice. But the IRS sent the notice to the wrong address. Roszkos found out about the notice only *after* the 90-day period for answering it had expired. He protested—and the Tax Court dismissed the IRS's case because the notice had been misaddressed. The IRS sent *another* notice. *Tax Court decision:* Too late. The limitations period expired when the *first* notice was sent. To give the IRS even *more* time to assess taxes would be to reward it for its lack of diligence.

Source: *Louis E. Roszkos,* 87 TC No. 72.

Extra Time For The IRS

During an IRS examination of the company's books, the president signed a consent form that extended the statute of limitations period, giving the IRS extra time to complete the audit. But the form was never *dated* and the president later claimed that it was totally invalid. *Court:* The important thing was that the form was signed. The date on which it was signed could be figured out from other records. Thus, the IRS got the extra time for the audit.

Source: *James H. Rutter,* TC Memo 1986-407.

Don't invalidate
your return

Tax Trap In
Altering Your Return

A taxpayer deleted the words "under penalty of perjury" from his return and then signed it. *Tax Court:* The return is treated as an unsigned return and isn't valid. *Result:* The taxpayer had to pay penalties for failure to file and negligence as if no return had been filed at all.

Source: *William J. Morgan,* TC Memo 1987-184.

Unsigned Return Trap

The IRS usually has three years to send a deficiency notice after a tax return has been filed. *Trap:* Michael Kelly had to pay tax penalties even though the IRS didn't send the notice until more than four years after Kelly filed his tax return. *Reason:* He didn't sign his return, and the IRS treats an unsigned return as if no return were ever filed. So, the IRS has all the time it wants to issue a deficiency notice to the taxpayer.

Source: *Michael R. Kelly,* TC Memo 1987-352.

Losing A Defense

Charles Daigle sent his tax return to the IRS, but refused to sign it and crossed out the statement on the bottom that attests to the return's accuracy. Several years later the IRS assessed back taxes, but Daigle said he was protected by the three-year statute of limitations. *Tax Court:* The statute of limitations protects only those taxpayers who file *valid* tax returns. Daigle's tax return wasn't valid as filed, so he *wasn't* protected.

Source: *Charles F. Daigle,* TC Memo 1986-558.

Getting trapped by the IRS

Sales Tax Liability

Darrel Shank, a retailer, owed state sales taxes. When his business failed, he declared bankruptcy. *Court:* The federal bankruptcy law could protect Shank from his *personal* tax liabilities. But he'd already collected these sales taxes from customers. The bankruptcy law won't protect him from this liability. Therefore, he has to pay the tax.

Source: *Darrel V. Shank,* CA-9, No. 85-4042.

Bankruptcy Trap

The Austin Insulating Co. filed for bankruptcy, but nobody notified the IRS. The bankruptcy court approved a plan for paying off creditors and discharged Austin's tax debts because the IRS hadn't filed a proof of claim. The IRS found out and protested. *Court:* The IRS could present its tax claim *now,* even though the bankruptcy plan had already been approved. Austin couldn't avoid paying its tax bill by hiding the bankruptcy proceedings from the IRS.

Source: *Austin Insulating Co. of Raleigh, Inc.,* Bankr. ED NC, No. S-85-00560-5.

IRS Revenge

Leslie Flaherty was an IRS auditor who *sued* the agency, claiming to be a victim of job discrimination. But Flaherty told the IRS he'd drop his suit if he got a disability pension. The Civil Service Commission then looked at his case, decided he was disabled, and gave him the pension. *Next:* Flaherty claimed the pension was *tax free* because damages from his lawsuit would have been tax free and he had taken the pension in their place. *Tax Court:* The IRS lawyer handling the suit didn't have the authority to grant the pension. Only the CSC could do that, and the CSC was an *independent* body. Thus, there was no connection between the pension and the suit, and the pension was *fully* taxable.

Source: *Leslie L. Flaherty,* TC Memo 1987-61.

Assessment Trap

The IRS and a taxpayer both signed a form that named the wrong tax year. As it turned out, the mistaken date would have been to the taxpayer's advantage, since it shortened the usual three-year period that the IRS is allowed for assessing taxes. *Tax Court:* The period of limitations cannot be made shorter than three years, even if the IRS signs a form to that effect. Taxes were assessed against the taxpayer.
Source: *Frances Rose Liles,* TC Memo 1987-16.

Late-Claim Pitfall

Charles Lemon went to District Court to get a refund for a tax claim that arose from his business. In court, Lemon claimed that he should get an extra $10,000 because the IRS had miscalculated his business income. *IRS objection:* Lemon had never mentioned this claim before. *Court:* Lemon hadn't mentioned the miscalculation during his audit, during the appeal from his audit, or in the papers he filed to bring the case to court. He *couldn't* bring the matter up for the first time at trial.
Source: *Charles Buck Lemon,* SD Ind., No. NA 83-178-C.

You could owe lots of money

Who Gets Paid First?

The late Alan Jay Lerner, the noted composer, owed back alimony to his wife, $75,000 to his publisher, and over $1 million to the IRS. The publisher obtained a court judgment against Lerner and filed a claim against him in June of 1981. Shortly thereafter, the IRS filed its claim. Lerner's ex-wife filed her claim in 1985, after Lerner reneged on an agreement to pay the back alimony. Everybody tried to collect from Lerner at once. *Court:* The claims would be paid off in the order that they were filed. First the publisher would be paid, then the IRS, and then (if any money was left) his ex-wife. *Moral:* When a debtor stops paying his bills, be the *first* one to reach the courthouse or you may wind up singing the blues.

Source: *Micheline Lerner,* SD NY, No. 85 Civ 6091.

Lawyer Gets Paid First

When James Nolan hired a layer, Bertram Polis, to represent him in a criminal case, Polis made Nolan hand over jewelry and cash as security for his legal fee. Ultimately, the IRS filed tax liens against Nolan's property and tried to collect the jewelry and cash Nolan had given to Polis. *Court:* Polis got his security interest *first,* so his claim gets *priority* over the IRS. If the value of the cash and jewelry in the end exceeds what's owed to Polis, the IRS will be able to claim the excess.

Source: *Bertram Polis,* D. Ariz., No. 85-066 TUC ACM.

What's An IRS Lawyer Worth?

When a taxpayer brings a meritless lawsuit against the IRS to delay the collection of taxes, the IRS can collect its lawyers' fees from the taxpayer *or* the taxpayer's lawyers. A District Court ruled that IRS lawyers' work could be fairly valued at *$125 per hour.*

Source: *London,* C.D. Ca., No. CV 85-2910-WJR(Px).

Refund Trap

The IRS can intercept your refund and use it to cover unpaid income taxes from previous years. *Recent case:* The IRS was allowed to get a refund even though the taxpayer had filed for bankruptcy. *Key:* The taxpayer didn't file for bankruptcy until after the date he was entitled to the refund.

Source: *Allen L. Eggemeyer,* Bnkr. SD Ill., No. 86-0261.

Tricks and excuses that don't work

Procrastination Is No Excuse

A recent IRS study concluded that a large percentage of individuals who fail to file tax returns say that the cause of their failure to file was simply procrastination. Although most nonfiler cases are handled routinely by an IRS notice that prompts individuals to get their returns in, a handful of failure-to-file cases are prosecuted. Failing to file a tax return is a crime, even if the reason is as innocent as not having enough time to put the numbers together.

Source: Ms. X, Esq., a former IRS agent, who is still well connected.

Unreliable Accountant

Earl Gose's petition to have a case heard in Tax Court was filed late. Gose said the late filing wasn't his fault, because he had relied on his accountant to file the petition. *Court:* Excuses aren't acceptable. The case won't be heard by the court.

Source: *Earl Gose,* Tax Ct. Dkt. No. 5714-86.

Unfair Tax

There was a typographical error on Lon Bleak's W-2 form. As a result he got a refund for $13,212 more than he should have received. Soon afterward, he declared bankruptcy. *Court of Appeals:* Debtors are not released from *tax* liabilities during bankruptcy, and this refund that was sent by mistake was in fact a tax liability. Bleak had to repay the refund.

Source: *Lon Lawrence Bleak,* CA-9 No. 85-2917.

Rule Avoidance Backfires

Splitting up currency deposits so each is below the $10,000 reporting threshold doesn't work. The IRS requires banks to report "related deposits" in determining when a currency transfer report is needed. When two or more $5,000 deposits are made on consecutive days, a report must be filed even though no single transaction was more than $10,000. *Danger:* If the IRS spots an attempt to skirt the reporting regulation, an investigation is *more* likely than if the reports had been properly filed.

Source: *How to Defend Yourself Against the IRS* by former federal prosecutor Sandor Frankel, Simon & Schuster, New York.

Delayer's Trap

When the Tax Court concluded that Randy Barber filed a meritless case simply to *delay* the time when he would have to pay his tax bill, it made him pay $5,000 in damages to the IRS *in addition* to his tax bill.

Source: *Randy Barber,* Tax Ct. Dkt. No. 41713-85.

Capitalize on IRS errors

Questions of Valuation

The IRS maintains its own staff of appraisers who are called on to provide a valuation for everything, from businesses to registered Holstein cows. The problem is that few members of the IRS valuation staff are true experts in any one field. They often need to consult outside experts. My recent experience with the IRS valuation people leads me to believe that the manner in which they put together a case to support their appraisal is often very weak and full of conclusions that are unsupported by facts. *Strategy:* Use the IRS's own appraisal against it in the appeals division. Argue that the valuation job was sloppy and incorrect. Hire your own valuation expert, one who can make a more credible presentation than the IRS staff.

Source: Ms. X, Esq., a former IRS agent, who is still well connected.

Refund Not Refunded

A misplaced comma in the IRS computer resulted in the Bruces' getting a tax refund of over $49,000 instead of $4,900. They notified the IRS of its mistake but were assured that they were entitled to the money. More than two years after the Bruces got the check, the IRS tried to get the money back. *District Court:* The IRS had two years from the date it made the mistake to correct its error. Since it waited so long, the Bruces were allowed to keep the money.

Source: *Alice A. Bruce,* SD TX, G-84-220.

IRS Overwhelmed

A company filed for bankruptcy, and the bankruptcy court set a date by which all creditors had to prove their claims. The IRS, a creditor, missed the date but said its claim should be allowed anyway. *Its excuse:* It couldn't process the company's tax return on time because the IRS Atlanta service center had been "overwhelmed." *Court:* The IRS's own procedural failures were the problem, so its claim would *not* be allowed.

Source: *Norris Grain Co.,* Bankr., MD Fla., No. 86-314.

IRS Embarrassed

The IRS has been rattled by the publicity given to cases where it has seized small children's bank accounts. *New procedures:* The IRS will not seize any account with a balance under $100. And when a seizure *is* contemplated, an account bearing more than one name will first be *frozen* for 21 days, during which time the IRS will try to determine the true owner. If the bank doesn't receive instructions within the 21 days, the account will be released.

IRS Uses Wrong Citation

During a Tax Court trial, an IRS attorney cited a wrong section of the law, and as a result had to concede certain points. After the trial, but before the court rendered its opinion, the IRS tried to revoke the concessions by citing a different part of the law. *Court:* If the IRS had made the right argument at trial, the taxpayer's lawyer would have had a chance to *answer* it, but now it was too late. The IRS was bound by its error.

Source: *Frank F. Foil,* Tax Ct. Dkt. No. 39599-84.

Notices and letter rulings

Opportunities In Private Letter Rulings

Before you go ahead with a deal that has complicated and unclear tax consequences, find out how the IRS will treat it. Ask for a *private letter ruling,* which is a written statement from the National Office on the tax effect of the proposed transaction.

You can do it yourself, although you should hire a tax professional when the impact of a *completed* and very complex transaction is in doubt. It's usually worth the fee to have your own tax pro's opinion on the legal ramifications of the transaction, how to report it on your return—and whether to ask for a letter ruling.

Effect of a ruling: If you get a favorable ruling in advance, your tax position is protected, and you can go ahead with the transaction. For all practical purposes, you may place full reliance on the ruling. Although the IRS does have the power to revoke a ruling at any time—even retroactively—this power is very seldom used.

When to Ask

You should ask for a ruling when the tax law is unclear on a major transaction that hinges on favorable tax treatment.

Types of transactions to ask for a ruling on:

■ You're considering an exchange of property, but only if the exchange is ruled tax free.

■ You're negotiating for the disposition of a valuable piece of property. All sorts of interesting variations are being proposed that will have an impact on your children and on your estate.

■ You want to give the government a right-of-way over your land, to be used as a hiking trail, but only if you get a charitable deduction for the gift.

When Not to Ask

Don't ask for a ruling when you feel that your chances of getting a favorable one are extremely doubtful. In such a situation it's better to rely on a tax professional's advice and proceed without a ruling. If your return isn't audited, the transaction may not be challenged. If it is challenged, your adviser will be able to argue your case without the handicap of an unfavorable ruling.

There are some issues the IRS will not rule on, especially...

■ Purely hypothetical questions. Never use "what if" in your ruling request.

■ Questions of fact—for instance, "What is the value of this piece of property?"

■ Reasonableness of compensation.

■ How estate tax will apply to the property of a living person.

■ Issues on which there are court decisions the IRS may be planning to appeal.

Tax Reform Barrier

My experience has been that the IRS is *hesitant* to issue letter rulings on questions involving new laws. It's best to stick to your unique situation and not try to extract interpretations of the Tax Reform Act of 1986 through private letter ruling requests.

What to Expect

It takes at least four to six months for the IRS to issue the written ruling. So you should submit your request well before you intend to complete the transaction the ruling relates to. Rulings are issued on a first-come first-served basis. This process may be speeded up if you can show real need for a quick response—but don't count on speed.

Within 21 calendar days after you request the ruling, an IRS tax law specialist will call you to discuss the issues involved. You may be asked to submit additional information. To check on the status of your ruling request, call the Director, Individual Tax Division, in Washington, D.C.

Before issuing an unfavorable ruling, the IRS generally permits a conference with a tax law specialist. If the specialist says he's going to rule against you, you can withdraw the ruling request. *Helpful:* Bring a tax professional to that conference, especially if the transaction you're asking about has been completed. The do-it-yourself approach is best left to prospective or contemplated transactions.

Dilemma: In my opinion withdrawing a request before a ruling is issued is a futile action. The local district director will get all the material anyway and will be watching for the transaction. If you receive a ruling and go ahead with the transaction, attach a copy of the ruling to your return being filed; it will likely result in an examination, but this probably will be confined to a comparison of the facts upon which the ruling was predicated with the facts as they actually happened.

Information Letter

You will get an *information letter,* rather than a letter ruling, if your request sought information that either was too general or did not meet the requirements for a formal ruling, e.g., the facts weren't unique. *An information letter* is a statement by either the National Office or your local district director pointing out established tax law, without application to a particular set of facts.

Source: George S. Alberts, former head of the Albany and Brooklyn IRS district offices.

Fees For IRS Rulings And Opinions

The Revenue Act of 1987 established fees for IRS rulings and opinion letters. The fees range from $50 (for computing the nontaxable portion of a taxpayer's annuity) to $1,000 (for various rulings on employee pension plans).

Source: *Revenue Procedure* 88-8.

How To Get An IRS Ruling

To apply for a private ruling, *write to:* Internal Revenue Service, Associate Chief Counsel (Technical), Attention: CC: IND-S, Room 6545, 1111 Constitution Ave., Washington, DC 20224.

Include in the request:

■ Names, addresses, and taxpayer identification numbers of all the people involved.

■ District director's office that has jurisdiction over the return.

■ Statement of the business or economic reasons for the transaction. *Important:* You will not get a favorable ruling unless a bona fide business or economic reason exists for the deal. So even if it is obvious, spell it out.

■ Detailed description of the transaction. Include copies (not originals) of any documents pertaining to the transaction.

■ Statement of what ruling you are asking for.

■ Your arguments in favor of your position, including any law, court cases, IRS regulations, revenue rulings, etc., that support your position. *Note:* Private letter rulings issued to other taxpayers on similar facts, while useful in determining what stand the IRS is likely to take in your case, may *not* be used as precedent.

■ Request for a conference to discuss the matter if an adverse ruling is expected.

■ Statement that the facts are true and that you are signing the request with the knowledge of the penalties for perjury.

New Power In Informal Notices

Informal IRS notices and announcements are now regarded as authority equivalent to official revenue rulings and procedures for purposes of avoiding penalties imposed on substantial understatements of income. Tax reform imposes heavy penalties on taxpayers who substantially understate their income, except when the taxpayer can show "substantial authority" to justify his position. Taxpayers can cite IRS notices and announcements as such authority.

Source: *Revenue Ruling* 87-138.

Stuck With Bad Agreement

A couple made a closing agreement with the IRS that they would follow a decision that was about to be made in the trial of a very similar case. But when the case was decided unfavorably, they tried to fight it. *Claims Court:* They were bound by their agreement.

Source: *Charles B. Temple,* Cl. Ct., No. 637-85T.

Going to Tax Court

Winning Tax Court Strategy

When a case is pending in the US Tax Court, the IRS attorney assigned to it usually doesn't know (and doesn't care) about the financial solvency of the taxpayer. You may be able to take advantage of this if the tax controversy involves a corporation that has since become defunct, and its shareholders, who have assets. *Perfectly legal strategy:* Compromise with the IRS so that the bulk of the tax burden is incurred by the insolvent corporation. When the dust settles, the shareholders will have to deal only with a small bill for tax and interest. The corporation, which has no assets, will never have to pay the agreed-upon liability.

Source: Ms. X, Esq., a former IRS agent, who is still well connected.

Advantages Of The Small Case Division

The Tax Court's Small Case Division provides a fast, simplified, informal handling of tax disputes. The amount involved in dispute can't exceed $10,000 in any taxable year. *Loophole:* If a dispute exceeds $10,000, taxpayers can get into the Small Case Division by conceding a portion of the bill. *Example:* One taxpayer was assessed a deficiency of slightly over $12,000. He conceded just over $2,000 and disputed $9,999. He was allowed to use the Small Case procedure.

Source: *Duke and Betty Kalich,* 89 TC No. 46.

Tax Court Trap

Bill Frisbie filed a case in Tax Court. However, at the start of the trial he asked to have his case dismissed so that he could bring it in a *different* court where he thought he'd get a more favorable hearing. *Decision:* Too late. Once you file a case in Tax Court you have to *stay* there. Moreover, since Frisbie wasn't prepared to present evidence on the issues, he was deemed to have conceded them, and the IRS got its tax.

Source: *Bill R. Frisbie,* TC Memo 1987-423.

Self-Representation Trap

Representing yourself before the IRS may not be such a good idea if you are an attorney. *Reason:* Lawyers can't collect attorney's fees for the value of their own services. *Recent case:* A lawyer spent some time working on a tax case he was involved in. The Tax Court eventually awarded attorney's fees to all the other taxpayers, but he wasn't allowed to collect for his own time.
Source: *Victor I. Minahan,* 88 TC No. 24.

No Attorney Fees For Attorney

The IRS challenged a lawyer's charity deduction for the value of a painting that he had donated to a college. The lawyer went to court, represented himself at trial, and won. Moreover, the judge found that the IRS had acted *unreasonably* by trying to harass the lawyer into conceding the case in disregard of its merits. So the lawyer asked the court to make the IRS pay his costs, *including* the value of the work he put into the case as an attorney. *Tax Court:* The lawyer could collect $1,800 from the IRS to cover litigation costs and witness fees. But he couldn't collect attorney's fees because he hadn't paid any. He could *not* collect for the value of the work he did himself.
Source: *E. Roger Frisch,* 87 TC No. 53.

Original Receipt Needed

When Thomas Schmidt's Tax Court petition was received five days late and bore a postmark indicating that it was mailed two days late, Schmidt brought in a *copy* of his certified mail receipt indicating that the petition had been mailed on time. But he couldn't produce the original certified mail receipt. *Tax Court:* A copy wasn't good enough. The petition was rejected.
Source: *Thomas G. Schmidt,* Tax Ct. Dkt. No. 20042-86-S.

Burden Of Proof

John Tokarski made large cash bank deposits without reporting corresponding amounts as income, so the IRS hit him with a back tax bill. Tokarski argued that the money was tax free because he had received it from his deceased father, but he offered no proof of this. He said it was up to the IRS to prove otherwise. *Tax Court:* Wrong. The IRS only had to show that Tokarski had received the money. *He* had to show *how* he got it.
Source: *John J. Tokarski,* 87 TC No. 5.

Does the IRS know where you are?

Address Changes

It pays to notify the IRS when you move. *Recent case:* The IRS sent a notice of deficiency to the Madsens' last known address, but they never received it. *After* their time to contest the notice had expired, the IRS sent the notice to their attorney, as listed on the IRS files. *District Court:* The Madsens had to pay the deficiency even though they never received the notice. The IRS was not obligated to send a copy to the attorney before it was too late to contest.

Source: *Kenneth J. Madsen,* DC Ca., No. 86-5361.

Vacation Travel And The IRS

When you travel, advise the IRS, *in writing,* to forward all correspondence to you and to send copies to a designated accountant or lawyer. If you don't, you could miss deadlines on IRS notices that require prompt action, or be hit with penalties, interest, liens, or the loss of the right to appeal.

11

TAX LOOPHOLES

EVERYTHING THE LAW ALLOWS

Audit
Secrets

Ways to avoid an audit

What IRS Computers Look For

Tax returns are selected for examination by a combination of computer and human factors. It is possible to improve the odds slightly against having your tax return selected by doing what the tax pros do for their own clients. Be aware, though, that there is nobody around (at least nobody who is talking) who knows the IRS computer program used to determine whose tax return is a candidate for audit.

What is public knowledge about the computer side of the selection process is that the computer determines the likelihood of a particular tax return generating additional tax dollars, if it is examined, by using a scoring system known as the Discriminant Income Function (DIF). Each tax return processed by the computer is assigned a DIF score. The higher the score, the more likely the return will be audited. The formula used to arrive at the DIF score is updated on a regular basis with information gathered by IRS examiners. Data is compiled from the thousands of tax returns actually audited, and the highly guarded and secret DIF formula is then modified. No public information is available on the factors that go into the DIF scoring.

Another scoring factor used by the IRS computers is known as Total Positive Income (TPI). TPI is the sum of all positive income values appearing on a return, with losses treated as zero. The purpose of this system is to eliminate or minimize the use of Adjusted Gross Income as a factor in deciding the potential for additional tax dollars if a return is audited.

The IRS found that it was not getting a true reading of tax returns when it relied on Adjusted Gross Income. An Adjusted Gross Income of, say, $15,000 can represent either a salary of $15,000 or a salary of $150,000 with tax write-offs that bring the Adjusted Gross Income down to $15,000. High-income taxpayers are less likely to escape audit now that the IRS computers have a second method to check for high audit potential.

The human process of tax return selection is much less scientific but just as important. After a tax return has been identified by the computer as having audit potential, it is shipped to the district office and manually screened by the classification division. An IRS examiner assigned to the classification division gives most tax returns a quick "once over" to determine if the computer has made an obvious error in selecting it or if there is a special item to be brought to the attention of the examining agent ultimately assigned to the return.

If at this initial human level of contact there is adequate explanation or proof of a particular deduction attached to your return, the classifier may decide that an audit is not in order. For example, receipts attached to your tax return that prove property was donated to a charity may satisfy the classifier and eliminate the need for an audit to document the claims.

If your return reaches the classifier at the end of the day, he or she may be bleary-eyed and less concerned about what you reported, and the special attention that might have been given to a particular issue will not be given. When your return actually reaches the classifier is, of course, out of your control.

Know Average Deductions

Some tax professionals attach great importance to the latest statistics correlating deductions claimed with Adjusted Gross Income, in an effort to determine the degree of risk of an audit their clients face. The latest numbers released by the IRS concerning personal income tax returns reflect only average amounts. An assumption is made that the computers use average numbers to determine if your particular tax deductions are likely to be disallowed if they are higher than average.

Reduce Your Chances of Being Audited

You may have the impression at this point in the discussion that the IRS computers are quite sophisticated and that it is virtually impossible to do anything legally to divert their eagle eyes from your tax return. By and large this is true, but there are at least two things that may help minimize the effect of the IRS's high-tech capabilities.

First, how income is reported on the return may make a difference. Suppose you have free-lance income. If it is merely reported as "Other Income" with an appropriate description as to its source, chances of having the return selected for audit may be smaller than if the same income is reported as business income on Schedule C (Income from a Sole Proprietorship).

Second, you can minimize your chances of being audited by filing as late as legally permissible. A tax return filed around April 15 generally has a greater chance of being audited than one filed on October 15 (the latest possible date). This is because the IRS schedules audits more than a year in advance. As returns are filed and scored by the computer, local IRS districts submit their forecasted requirements for returns with audit potential. The fulfillment is made from returns already on hand. If your return is filed on October 15, there is less risk that it will be among the returns shipped out to the district office in the first batch. As a result of scheduling and budget problems that are likely to develop in the two years after your return has been filed, it may never find its way into the second batch slated for examination.

Although the IRS is wise to this ploy and has taken steps to make sure that the selection process is as fair as possible, inequities invariably result. Why not try to be part of the group that has the smallest chance of being audited?

The *best* way to reduce your chances of being audited is to avoid certain items universally thought to trigger special IRS scrutiny. There are also some common-sense considerations that should be thought about before you mail in your return. They are often overlooked by the very people who can least afford to be the subject of an audit. *Here are a few examples:*

Some people who are in cash businesses are not content with merely skimming some of their income. They also want to get every possible tax deduction—which is where the potential for audit comes in. When a business owner reports only a modest income, the IRS naturally becomes suspicious if that person also claims many business expenses and has high interest expense deductions. Two immediate questions are raised in the mind of the IRS examiner: Where does this person get money for personal living expenses and how is he or she able to make the principal repayments to justify the interest expense? When you are preparing your return, step back and think like an IRS auditor. If you can spot questions, so can the IRS.

What else can be done to minimize the chances of being audited? *The following items should be reviewed carefully:*

■ *Choose your return preparer carefully.* When the IRS suspects return preparers of incompetence or misconduct, it can force them to produce a list of all their clients—all of whom may face further IRS examination, regardless of their personal honesty.

■ *Avoid formal membership in barter clubs.* Members of these clubs trade goods and services on a cashless basis. The club keeps track of all transactions between members. Although no cash changes hands, these trades are taxable like any other profitable deal. Very often, however, they are not reported to the IRS. The IRS can force such clubs to produce membership lists, so that the returns of all club members can be examined.

■ *Answer all questions on the return.* IRS computers generally flag returns with unanswered questions. For example, there is a question asking if you maintain funds in a foreign bank account. Even if you do not, you should answer no to the question.

■ *Fill in the return carefully.* A sloppy return may indicate a careless taxpayer. The IRS may examine the return to be sure the carelessness did not lead to any mistakes.

■ *Categorize each deduction.* Don't place deductions under headings such as miscellaneous or sundry. If you can't categorize a deduction, the IRS may decide you can't prove it.

■ *Avoid round numbers.* A deduction that's rounded off to the nearest hundred or thousand dollars will raise IRS suspicions. The IRS will think the taxpayer is guessing at the deduction's size rather than determining it from accurate records.

Source: *How to Beat the IRS* by Ms. X, Esq., a former IRS agent, who is still well connected, Boardroom Classics, Springfield, NJ 07081.

Audit Angles

Audits are not entirely a matter of chance. While there's no way to eliminate the danger of an audit, you can reduce the risk.

The simple steps:

■ Get extensions and file at the last minute—in the fall. An automatic four-month extension, plus the extra two months you usually get if a second extension is granted, advances your filing date to October 15.

People who file in the fall are less likely to be audited than those who file by April 15. *Reason:* Most targeted returns are selected during the summer months. By fall, most of the year's quota of returns to be audited has been filled.

Caution: Filing extensions do not lengthen the time for paying tax. If you don't pay at least 90% of the tax you expect to owe by April 15, you'll be hit with a penalty and possible loss of the extension.

■ Attach detailed information and substantiation to your return, if you have an unusual or complicated transaction that IRS computers will automatically question. After the computer has selected your return for possible audit, an IRS employee looks it over. You may be able to ward off an audit by explaining the transaction to that person.

Caution: Do not mail originals; send copies only.

Send in full documentation for unusually large deductions, such as large casualty losses. Attach copies of appraisals for substantial charitable donations of property.

■ Answer all questions on the return, including those that don't apply to you. IRS computers automatically flag questions that go unanswered.

■ Fill in the return carefully. The IRS may examine the return to see if carelessness led to mistakes.

If your return is selected for audit, you'll get a notification letter. The items the IRS is interested in are checked off or written in on that letter.

How to proceed then:

Avoid repetitive audits. The *Internal Revenue Manual* says that taxpayers shall not be subjected to needless and repetitive examinations. If you are being audited on items that were examined in either of the two preceding years, and that audit produced no change (or only a small change) in your tax bill, you can request that you not be audited again for the same items. Tell the auditor that you qualify under the repetitive audit provisions of the *Manual*.

Send the auditor:

(1) a copy of the previous year's appointment letter showing which items were chosen for audit,

(2) a copy of the no-change letter, and

(3) a copy of the previous year's tax return.

Try to resolve the issue by mail. If only a few items have been chosen for audit and you can substantiate them, mail in copies of your proof with a covering letter at least 10 days before your scheduled appointment. Give a telephone number where you can be reached during the day should the agent have any questions. If all goes well, you'll get a letter back from the agent, though not immediately, telling you that your return has been accepted as filed—examination closed.

Don't antagonize the agent. Be courteous and businesslike. If you can't keep an appointment, call and change it. If you missed an appointment, call as soon as possible. There may be time to reschedule.

Be prepared to appeal if the audit results in an unfavorable report. There are formal and informal ways to get redress. If the agent has been unreasonable, overaggressive, or clearly wrong about the law, insist on an immediate conference with the agent's group manager. An experienced supervisor may be able to find a way out of an impasse that isn't apparent to a newly trained agent. If you get nowhere with the group manager, you can take your case to the appeals division of the IRS, where the hazards of litigation will be considered, that is, the chance that the government might lose in court if it litigates the case.

Go to court, even when it seems that the law is against you. By filing a court petition, you get an extra pretrial meeting with IRS attorneys. You may be able to work out a better deal with the lawyers than you could with other IRS employees. *Reason:* They are primarily concerned with disposing of cases. A court contest costs the IRS time and money. So if there's no special reason for the IRS to litigate, you may be able to work out a favorable settlement.

The bottom line: Good recordkeeping is the key to winning your battle with the IRS. Be prepared to document your deductions with receipts, canceled checks, and bills marked paid. *The IRS follows a simple rule:* If you spent it, you should be able to prove it. Without proof, you cannot fight. And without good records, you won't be able to convince the IRS to allow your deductions.

Source: Edward Mendlowitz, partner, Mendlowitz Weitsen, CPAs, 2 Pennsylvania Plaza, New York 10001.

The IRS Hit List

Doctors and dentists are high-priority targets for tax audit. *Items IRS agents look for:* Dubious promotional expenses. If the same four people take turns having lunch together once a week and take turns picking up the tab, a close examination of diaries and logbooks will show this. Agents also take a close look at limited partnership investments, seeking signs of abusive tax shelters. And they take a dim view of fellowship exclusions claimed by medical residents. *Other target occupations:*

■ *Salespeople:* Outside and auto salespeople are particular favorites. Agents look for, and often find, poorly documented travel expenses and padded promotional figures.

■ *Airline pilots:* High incomes, a propensity to invest in questionable tax shelters, and commuting expenses claimed as business travel make them inviting prospects.

■ *Flight attendants:* Travel expenses are usually a high percentage of their total income and often aren't well documented. Some persist in trying to deduct pantyhose, permanents, cosmetics, and similar items that the courts have repeatedly ruled are personal rather than business expenses.

■ *Executives:* As a group they are not usually singled out. But if the return includes a Form 2106, showing a sizable sum for unreimbursed employee business expenses, an audit is more likely. Of course, anyone whose income is over $50,000 a year is a high-priority target just because of the sums involved.

■ *Teachers and college professors:* Agents pounce on returns claiming office-at-home deductions. They are also wary of educational expense deductions because they may turn out to be vacations in disguise.

■ *Clergymen:* Bona fide priests, ministers, and rabbis aren't considered a problem group. But if W-2s show income from nonchurch employers, the IRS will be on the alert for mail-order ministry scams.

■ *Waitresses, cabdrivers, etc.:* Anyone in an occupation where tips are a significant factor is likely to get a closer look from the IRS nowadays.

Many people, aware their profession subjects them to IRS scrutiny, use nebulous terms to describe what they do. Professionals in private practice may list themselves as simply "self-employed." Waitresses become "culinary employees," pilots list themselves as "transportation executives." But there's a fine line here. Truly deceptive descriptions could trigger penalties. And if the return is chosen for audit, an unorthodox job title for a mundane profession could convince the agent you have something to hide. Then he'll dig all the deeper.

Source: Ralph J. Pribble, a former IRS field agent, president of Tax Corporation of California, 5420 Geary Blvd., San Francisco 94121.

Audit-Proof Your Cost Of Living

On occasion, the IRS will attempt to reconstruct a taxpayer's income by estimating his cost of living. The IRS does this by adding up all living expenses paid for throughout the year by check then adding to this figure an amount it feels is reasonable for other living expenses it assumes have been paid for with cash. *Advice:* Make sure to pay for expenses such as food, medical expenses, automobile costs, mortgage payments, and credit-card payments by check. This should head off an agent's contention that you had "hidden" living expenses.

Source: Ms. X, Esq., a former IRS Agent, who is still well connected.

Audit Risk Varies Geographically

The IRS district you live in may affect the odds of your being audited. In the Manhattan district, for example, 1.98% of all individual income tax returns filed are audited, whereas in Dallas, the rate is only 1.2%. The following table shows the percentage of returns audited in various IRS districts. It will give you an idea of which areas are the most audit prone in the country.

IRS District	Percent of Returns Audited
Albany	.88
Anchorage	2.48
Atlanta	1.21
Baltimore	.99
Boston	.69
Chicago	.98
Cincinnati	.75
Dallas	1.20
Denver	1.37
Detroit	.90
Jacksonville	1.36
Los Angeles	1.88
Manhattan	1.98
Nashville	1.14
Newark	1.34
New Orleans	1.30
Philadelphia	.82
Phoenix	1.44
Salt Lake City	1.97
San Francisco	2.17

Source: *IRS Commissioner's Annual Report.*

Audits The IRS Forgets To Do

Asking the IRS to transfer your case to another district may be the key to avoiding an audit. Don't expect the IRS to admit it, but transferred cases often fall between the cracks and never get worked on, even though the taxpayer has been notified of the examination. Delays caused in processing the case file between districts, combined with the fact that the case is likely to go to the bottom of the pile when it is assigned to a new agent, may bring help from the statute of limitations. Rather than asking the taxpayer to extend the statute of limitations, as is the usual practice, many agents are inclined to take the easy way out and close transferred cases without auditing them.

Audit risks

Audit Triggers

If you know what makes the IRS decide to audit your return, you should be able to avoid audits entirely, right? Well, yes and no.

Approximately 70% of all returns audited are chosen through a top-secret grading process designed to indicate the probability that an audit will produce money for the government. Every tax return is reviewed and scored by this process, in which a number of DIF (Discriminant Income Function) points are assigned to key items listed on (or omitted from) the return. The higher the DIF score, the greater the likelihood of audit.

The DIF scoring process is a closely guarded secret, but experience indicates a number of red flags that may cause the IRS to scrutinize your return.

Most provocative:

■ Unusually large deductions in relation to income.

■ Unusually large refunds (which you should avoid anyway, unless you enjoy subsidizing the government with interest-free loans).

■ Missing forms or schedules. Always *staple* your return securely after making sure all required elements are present.

Discrepancies, including: Reporting the sale of a dividend-paying stock, but failing to report any dividend income; reporting the installment sale of property, but failing to report interest income; married couples filing separately and claiming the same deductions.

The higher your income and the more complex your return, the greater the likelihood that you'll be audited.

Other factors that could lead to an audit:

■ A taxpayer's past history with the IRS. Some taxpayers may be audited regularly, particularly if a tax deficiency has been found in the first audit year.

■ In any given year, the IRS will *target* certain types of businesses and financial dealings for intensified audit activity (for example, large corporations, small proprietorships, investors in abusive tax shelters, etc.).

Trap: The IRS maintains a list of unscrupulous tax return preparers and audits a much higher proportion of returns prepared by these persons.

Unavoidable:

There is one audit trigger that you cannot avoid, regardless of how scrupulous you are in preparing your return and no matter what your income and expenses may be. It is the Taxpayer Compliance Measurement Program (TCMP) audit, an *entirely random* selection process. If your return is selected by this program, *every item* on it is subject to scrutiny. In a normal audit only certain areas of the return are examined.

Source: Michael H. Frankel, partner and director of the Washington National Tax Office of KPMG Peat Marwick, 1990 K St. NW, Washington, DC 20006.

Charitable Gift Trap

Big charitable gifts of property often trigger audits. Givers must file Form 8283, documenting the value of noncash gifts to a single institution worth more than $500. The Internal Revenue Service matches these gifts against the charity's report of sale proceeds (Form 8282). Any discrepancies between the two reports or the lack of a report from the charity covering the donation may flag the donor's return for audit.

Preparation is half the battle

Prepare...Prepare...Prepare

Stop a revenue agent in his tracks by being thoroughly prepared for an audit. Agents won't waste time conducting an in-depth examination if they get a sense, at the beginning of the audit, that the taxpayer's records clearly substantiate the items claimed on the return. *Real case:* A client knew that the figures he claimed on his tax return could be verified to the penny. However, he didn't want the IRS asking too many questions that might lead to embarrassing and incriminating answers. *His strategy:* He put together a separate folder for each item that appeared on the return. He included in each folder every canceled check and invoice relating to that particular expense. The agent simply browsed through the folders, checked three or four items, and closed the case.

Source: Ms. X, Esq., a former IRS agent, who is still well connected.

Surviving An Audit

Very few things in this world have the effect of bringing the most hardened people to their knees the way notification of an IRS audit can. The letter from the IRS notifying a taxpayer that he or she has been selected for an audit contains language that is far from threatening, yet it strikes terror in the heart of most recipients. Various survival tactics can be used in preparing to do battle at the IRS audit. All of them are legal, but some aren't very nice.

Types of Audits

■ **Correspondence Audit:** Some IRS audits are more thorough than others. The least thorough is a correspondence audit. Here, the IRS seeks to test compliance with perhaps one item on either a regional or national basis. For example, the IRS may send out hundreds of letters asking for verification of rehabilitation credit expenditures. On receipt of this notice, all you have to do is mail in the appropriate documentation to support your deduction.

Technically, this inquiry constitutes an audit. Once it takes place, there is very little chance that the rest of your return for that particular tax year will ever be audited. If the IRS should decide it wants to audit your return at a later date, it must go through a formal "reopening procedure"—which is rarely done. The obvious advantage of the correspondence audit is that if the IRS does not select an area in which you may be vulnerable, it will never know that it could have made other adjustments to your return that might have resulted in more tax.

■ **Office Audit:** The next level of audit is the Office Audit. This examination is handled at a local IRS office. Typically, one or two deductions on your return will be questioned. Without special circumstances, such as suspicion of fraud or gross errors in other areas of the return, the audit will not be extended to other issues. The primary advantage of the Office Audit is that it is generally conducted by individuals who lack the sophistication in tax matters needed to recognize more significant issues. The training and method of operation of the Office Audit level consists of telling the examiner (called a tax auditor) exactly what to look for in a given issue. The audit will be conducted mechanically and "by the book."

■ **Field Audit:** These are conducted by the best educated employees at the IRS, known as revenue agents. They are usually assigned the tax returns of businesses and wealthy individuals. An audit conducted by a revenue agent is usually quite complete, and although it will not examine every item in depth, it will attempt to cover many areas. One of the jobs of the revenue agent is to identify promptly areas with the potential for extra tax dollars and then to spend time developing the tax issues.

The chances of having the IRS uncover unreported income or disallowing deductions that are either personal or otherwise not deductible are more likely at the Field Audit than at any other type of IRS examination. It is unwise to try to handle a Field Audit yourself because the potential adverse ramifications can be severe—even if you think you did everything right! A sharp revenue agent can be quite creative when it comes to interpreting the Internal Revenue Code in the government's favor. Your ability to survive such creativity is enhanced by having an experienced practitioner representing your interests.

■ **TCMP Audit:** The most encompassing type of IRS audit is the TCMP Audit. TCMP stands for Taxpayer Compliance Measurement Program. TCMP audits are conducted to gain a statistical sample of the kinds of adjustments that are being uncovered. The results of these audits are used to reprogram the IRS computers so that in the future they can select those returns most likely to result in additional tax dollars.

TCMP audits are usually conducted by revenue agents. The biggest problem with these examinations is that the agent is required to comment on every item appearing on the tax return, starting with the spelling of your name. This does not mean that every line is audited, but the audit is lengthy and there is greater risk that adjustments will be found that will cost you a lot of money. One of the required audit techniques is the analysis of all a taxpayer's bank accounts for possible monies that were deposited but not reported.

■ **Criminal Investigation:** These investigations, conducted by IRS employees known as special agents, are the most threatening to your personal liberty. The job of the special agent is to gather evidence of the commission of a tax crime. The least serious penalty that may result from a criminal investigation is the payment of some extra tax. The most serious penalty is indictment, conviction and a jail sentence.

The anxiety created by a criminal investigation can be overwhelming. In most cases the subject of the investigation is not a "crook" or "Mafia" character. It is likely to be a professional or successful small businessperson who got carried away rationalizing that some of the money received during the year wasn't really income or, if it was income, that nobody would ever find out if it wasn't reported. The IRS gains tremendous publicity when a local person is convicted of tax evasion. As a result of an indictment of a conviction, the IRS assures itself that the level of voluntary compliance increases.

Survival Tactics

Knowing how the system at the IRS works gives an experienced practitioner an advantage when it comes to representing a client at an audit. Here are some of the truly "inside" things that go on.

■ *Postponing Appointments:* It is possible, though not likely, that the IRS will actually change its mind about auditing you if you have postponed the appointment enough times. The IRS is constantly under pressure to start and finish tax examinations. If the return selected for an audit becomes "old" (i.e., more than two years have passed since the return was filed), the IRS may not want to start the audit. This situation may develop if you are notified of an audit about 15 to 16 months after filing. By the time you have canceled one or two appointments, the 24-month cut-off period may have been reached.

When is the best time to cancel? The day before the appointment. By that time, the next available appointment will probably not be for six to eight weeks.

■ *Best Time to Schedule an Audit:* To someone uninitiated, it may seem ridiculous that one time of the day or month is better than another to have your tax return audited. However, a real advantage can be gained by following some simple tips. Try to schedule an audit before a three-day weekend. The auditor may be less interested in the audit and more interested in the holiday. Another excellent time to schedule an appointment is at the end of the month. If an auditor has not "closed" enough cases that month, he or she may be inclined to go easy on you to gain a quick agreement and another closed case. As for the best time of the day, most pros like to start an audit at about 10 o'clock in the morning. By the time it comes to discussing adjustments with the auditor, it will be close to lunch time. If you are persistent, the auditor may be willing to make concessions just to get rid of you so as not to interfere with lunch plans.

Source: *How to Beat the IRS* by Ms. X, Esq., a former IRS agent, who is still well connected, Boardroom Classics, Springfield, NJ 07081.

Advice From A Former IRS Agent

Good records are the key to success. They should be as complete as possible. But that doesn't mean that you should concede an issue if the paperwork isn't perfect. Under the so-called Cohan rule, you are allowed to use approximations in determining deductible expenses. *Key:* You must establish that you did legitimately incur deductible expenses and that your records are incomplete or unavailable.

Of course, many agents are not candid about the Cohan rule and will try to disallow some or all of your expenses. Don't accept a disallowance you think should be reasonably allowed.

Caution: The Cohan rule does not apply to expenses for overnight travel, business entertainment, or gifts. These must be fully documented to sustain a deduction.

Source: Philip P. Storrer, professor of taxation, California State University.

Preparing To Face The Auditor

Before facing the IRS auditor yourself, the most productive way to spend your time and energy is in gathering and organizing documentation of your deductions and exclusions.

The process includes preparation of schedules of the items involved. In the case of charitable contributions, for example, list dates, amounts, relevant check numbers, and make notations of receipts in your possession. Such preparation will save time during the audit and may encourage the revenue agent to do a spot check rather than tying in all documentation to the amounts claimed on the return.

If you anticipate disputes over certain deductions and exclusions, a valuable added weapon is a memorandum from your accountant. *It should contain:*

■A statement that shows that you understand the law involved.

■A corroborating statement on how and why you fit the particular provision in question or how specific circumstances warrant the position taken on the return.

■Citations of recent relevant court cases.

Source: Ralph C. Ganswindt, partner, Arthur Andersen & Co., 777 E. Wisconsin Ave., Milwaukee, WI 53201.

The Auditor's First Question

"Did you report all your income?" That is the first question a tax auditor is supposed to ask. And for some taxpayers it's a loaded question. How do you respond when you *know* that you failed to report income? The worst thing you can do is lie and say that you did report everything. Lying in response to an auditor's question is a *crime,* separate and apart from evading tax. On the other hand, if you tell the truth and admit that you didn't report all your income, you could be incriminating yourself. *Best approach to this problem:* Get an experienced tax attorney to represent you. Don't try to handle such a sensitive matter yourself.

Source: Ms. X, Esq., a former IRS agent, who is still well connected.

Best Way to Handle An Audit

The best way to handle an IRS audit is to be represented by an experienced tax professional who knows his way around the IRS. *The biggest trap for do-it-yourselfers:* Giving up on an issue because they don't fully understand the nuances of the tax law.

Good news about audits

First-Audit Reprieve

Taxpayers picked for audit do not have to be present for the first meeting with the auditor if a knowledgeable representative is there to answer questions. For a time, the IRS had insisted, especially in audits of business taxpayers who filed Schedule Cs, that they meet with the taxpayer and personally interview him.

When To Ask For An Audit

Most people fear an IRS audit, but sometimes the smart thing to do is to *ask* for one and get it behind you. *Two relevant situations in which it makes sense to ask for an audit:*

■When someone dies, the heirs can count only on sharing the *after*-tax proceeds of the estate. So the sooner the IRS examines matters and settles things, the better.

■When you close down a business, its records and the key personnel who can explain them may soon disappear. An IRS examination at a later date could prove awkward and costly.

Tactic: When you want a quick audit of a return, file IRS Form 4810 to ask for a *prompt assessment* of taxes due. This requires the IRS to act on your case within 18 months, rather than the three years that it normally has to conduct an examination.

Getting A Copy Of Your Audit File

It's relatively easy to get copies of the case workpapers compiled by the revenue agent who handled your audit. The time to ask for your file is after the audit is completed and before you file an appeal. The workpapers will show what information the agent used to come up with adjustments to your tax bill. They'll also show what relevant information the agent did not make a permanent part of the file. *To get a copy of your file,* submit a written request under the Freedom of Information Act with the *disclosure officer* in your IRS district. It takes about six weeks to get the file.

Source: Ms. X, Esq., a former IRS agent, who is still well connected.

Limited Scope

To reduce the backlog of returns that have been selected for audit but not yet examined, some IRS districts permit senior-level revenue agents to *limit* the scope of their examinations. The goal is to get the agent in and out of the audit as quickly as possible by allowing him/her to concentrate on only one or two *significant* items on the tax return. After examining the selected issues, the agent is generally free to close the case. *Note:* Audits of tax returns that reflect losses (those that have been carried back to previous years) are likely to be "limited" audits. *Reason:* In most cases, the revenue agent can determine quickly whether he/she will be able to upset the loss that the taxpayer claimed.

Source: Ms. X, Esq., a former IRS agent, who is still well connected.

IRS audits—myths and realities

The Truth About The IRS And You

A staggering number of misconceptions about the power and workings of the IRS have developed over the years. Even seasoned tax professionals sometimes have trouble separating myth from reality. *Here are some very common fallacies:*

Myth: *Using the IRS preprinted peel-off label to file a return increases the risk of an audit.* **Reality:** Just the opposite is true. Returns that are filed with the preprinted label are processed quickly and routinely. Returns filed *without* the preprinted label are removed from routine computer processing. These returns are more likely to be audited because they are handled by an experienced IRS employee who is capable of spotting problems beyond those the processing clerks look for.

Taxpayer paranoia about the preprinted labels is unjustified. All the symbols on the label are there either to facilitate IRS processing or to assist the US Postal Service. None of the symbols flag returns for audit, not even for Taxpayer Compliance Measurement Program (TCMP) audits. *Bottom line:* Using the label reduces the chance of error in processing your return, prevents refund delays, and certainly does *not* increase your chance of an audit.

Myth: *Filing an amended return doesn't increase the risk of an audit.* **Reality:** It does, though nobody knows for sure by how much. While filing an amended return doesn't guarantee that you'll be audited, it clearly increases the risk. In IRS processing, an amended return is associated with its original return and then scanned by an experienced returns classifier. This person has the authority to initiate an audit on the amendment and/or on *any* item on the original return. If the original has already been audited, both the original and the amended versions are sent to the officer who examined the original return. It's up to that person to decide whether to continue the examination.

Myth: *Nonfilers can avoid prosecution by the IRS by voluntarily filing delinquent returns.* **Reality:** At best, filing returns is only a minor factor in the decision to prosecute. The IRS criminal investigation staff, together with the US Attorney, consider many factors, including: 1) number of years involved, 2) amount of potential tax, 3) age, health, and education of the taxpayer, and 4) publicity value of criminal prosecution.

The one advantage in filing returns in this situation is that it starts the statute of limitation running on *civil*—but not criminal—assessments by the IRS.

Myth: *At least 95% of the nation's taxpayers voluntarily comply with the tax law—as the IRS claims.* **Reality:** The compliance rate is much lower than that, but nobody can give an accurate figure. Since nobody, including the IRS, fully knows the degree of *non*compliance, how could anyone know the rate of compliance? Nonreporting by illegal businesses runs into billions of dollars each year. Deduction padding and nonreporting of undocumented income by relatively honest taxpayers costs the government many more billions of dollars. Apparently Congress is willing to live with this shortfall. It knows that the IRS's enforcement staff—fewer than 100,000—can't approach substantial compliance.

Myth: *The IRS with its computers is Big Brother incarnate.* **Reality:** Far from it. The IRS does keep an electronic file on each and every taxpayer. But only financial information directly related to taxes is kept on that file. The IRS has no information about your lifestyle, travel habits, family affairs, or anything else of that sort. *Reason:* Top IRS officials resist involvement in activities outside of tax enforcement.

Myth: *Auditors don't have the power to negotiate the settlement of cases under examination.* **Reality:** Auditors do have *de facto* settlement authority. Officially, the power to settle cases is in the hands of the IRS appeals division, where hazards of litigation (the chance that the IRS might lose the case in court) are taken into consideration. Auditors are precluded from using hazards of litigation to settle a case. But they find other ways to settle cases under examination—for example, accepting the taxpayer's credible oral testimony, or applying their own knowledge of the taxpayer's occupation or business, etc. *Comment:* This puts examiners in a precarious professional situation. It encourages noncompliance and increases the risk of breaches of integrity.

Source: George S. Alberts, former director of the Albany and Brooklyn IRS district offices.

IRS Envelope Labels–What The Numbers Really Mean

Here's the scoop on the numbers and symbols on the peel-off label the IRS sends with your tax package.

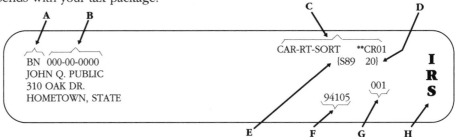

A. Two-letter "alpha code" that is computer shorthand for your name.

B. Your Social Security number. By entering the two-letter code and your Social Security number, the IRS can identify the correct account. The data-entry clerk doesn't have to type your full name and address into the computer.

C. Postal Service home delivery route.

D. Type of package mailed to the taxpayer–1040, 1040A, etc.

E. IRS service center where you filed your return last year–in this case, Fresno, CA. (S29 is the Ogden service center, Kansas City is S09, and so on.)

F. Your postal ZIP code.

G. The IRS's presort mail for the US Postal Service.

H. Certain labels, to help with mail distribution, have either PP, SS, or PL directly under the "S" in IRS. *These letters indicate:*

- ■PP–Package (first label in a package).
- ■SS–Sack (first label in a sack).
- ■PL–Pallet (first label in a pallet).

Source: George S. Alberts, former director of the Albany and Brooklyn IRS district offices.

Secrets of dealing with auditors

How To Handle An IRS Auditor

Prepare meticulously for the audit. Gather all your receipts for the deductions the IRS has questioned. List each, in detail, on a sheet of paper. Also, meticulously reconstruct cash expenditures for which you don't have receipts. Explain exactly how and when you made those expenditures.

By presenting your case in factual detail, you establish your credibility. And credibility is everything at an audit. It will be easier for the auditor to allow nondocumented items if you can show him that you kept some receipts, that you made an effort to comply with IRS rules and regulations, and that you've reconstructed, as best you could, your cash outlays.

T&E Audits

Travel and entertainment is the most commonly audited deduction: *Your goal:* To limit the items the agent examines by persuading him to do a test check of your expenses. Let the auditor choose a three-month period for detailed examination. Or talk him into limiting the audit to items over, say, $100. Make sure you can document all items in the test-check period or in the amount. *Double benefit:* A test check cuts down your work in assembling backup data, and it prevents the agent from rummaging through all your travel and entertainment expenses.

Keep Talking

Don't expect to walk out of an audit not owing a dime. Your objective is to strike the best possible deal. *To get an auditor to see things your way:* Keep harping on the items he says must be adjusted. Keep talking. Don't give up until he reduces the adjustment. Even the most hard-nosed agent will ultimately concede some proposed adjustments if you're stubborn enough. But you must be prepared to give a little, too—to concede items you're weak on, to bargain. Keep in mind that the agent's goal is to close the case and move on to his next audit.

Special Problems

Business audits: If your business is being audited, have it done at your accountant's office, not at your home or your place of business. You don't want the auditor to see your standard of living nor run the risk that an employee will say something to the auditor that could hurt you.

Unreported income. Generally required to be asked at IRS audits is "Have you reported all your income?" Never answer this or other potentially embarrassing questions with a lie. Deliberately failing to report all your income is a crime. So is lying to an IRS employee. To avoid incriminating yourself, deflect the question with "Why do you want to know that?" or "I'll get back to you on that later." The question may not come up again. Another way to avoid answering this question is to not show up for the audit. Then the deductions you've been asked to prove will be automatically disallowed. But you can appeal the agent's disallowance at the appeals level of the IRS. At the appeals level, you're generally not asked whether you've reported all your income.

Special agents. Their job is to develop evidence for criminal tax cases. If they show up at your door, don't answer any of their questions, even seemingly innocuous ones. Tell them to talk with your lawyer. Then retain a lawyer who is knowledgeable in criminal tax matters. *Best:* A former assistant US attorney.

Source: Randy Bruce Blaustein, Esq., Blaustein, Greenberg & Co., 155 E. 31 St., New York 10016.

Doing Business With A Difficult Auditor

You may find yourself dealing with an auditor whose personality just doesn't click with yours. Don't expect that person to come right out and say you don't have a chance of winning. Instead, what you'll find is that every single benefit of the doubt a reasonable auditor would have given will simply not be given. There are two ways to deal with the situation. You can complain to the auditor's group manager and insist that your case be transferred to someone more reasonable. Or, you can beat the difficult auditor into submission by substantiating each deduction, one at a time, and questioning the auditor at every step. If the auditor still considers the deduction not allowable, demand to know why. Even the most difficult of auditors will give up as soon as he/she sees that you mean business.

Source: Ms. X, Esq., a former IRS agent, who is still well connected.

Make The Auditor Your Friend

Your audit usually will progress more smoothly if you present yourself as a friendly, warm, and cordial person. This doesn't mean that you should let your defenses down. It simply means that you should try to make the auditor or agent friendly and sympathetic to your cause. This may be difficult at times, either because of your own anxiety or because the auditor won't reciprocate. You can often overcome an auditor's resistance by embarrassing him/her into being friendly. *Try this tactic:* Say "Why don't you ever smile?" Or smile and say: "If you refuse to be friendly, you can figure out everything on this return yourself...Good luck!" (This ploy works virtually every time.)

Source: Ms. X, Esq., a former IRS agent, who is still well connected.

Hitting The Auditor With Unclaimed Deductions

Many taxpayers are overly conservative in taking deductions. A study by the American Bar Association reveals that a significant number of taxpayers deliberately fail to claim deductions they're entitled to. *Main reasons:* Insufficient records...and fear of being audited. If you are unlucky enough to be audited, here's how to handle legitimate, but unclaimed, deductions. Wait until after the agent has gone over all of his/her proposed adjustments with you. Then, just before you reach a settlement, bring up the new items. *Reason for waiting:* If the auditor knows about your unclaimed deductions earlier, he may be inclined to overcompensate for them by disallowing other items on your return.

Source: Ms. X, Esq., a former IRS agent, who is still well connected.

Helping Novice Auditors

One way to resolve an audit in your favor is to write up the agent's workpapers (the forms he prepares on the audit) yourself. Sounds ridiculous, doesn't it? But it can be done in some circumstances by seasoned tax professionals. Many newly hired revenue agents simply do not have enough experience to know how to set up audit workpapers in a way that won't be criticized by their bosses. If your adviser knows what to put in the workpapers, and what to leave out, he can coach the agent accordingly. Many novice agents are receptive to a helping hand.

Source: Ms. X, Esq., a former IRS agent, who is still well connected.

Don't Be In Such A Hurry

One of the problems tax practitioners face in representing clients before the IRS is that many clients become extremely anxious when they get an audit notice. The client wants to get the audit over with as soon as possible. He begs to be audited. *Advice:* Resist a temptation to rush to meet with the IRS immediately. Time is on the taxpayer's side. Virtually every division of the IRS is monitored in terms of how many months a given case is open. The longer the case is open, the more pressure there is on IRS staff and management to close it...even if it hasn't been fully developed.

Source: Ms. X, Esq., a former IRS agent, who is still well connected.

What Not To Show An Auditor

A favorite technique of tax auditors is to disallow a deduction claimed for a sideline business on the grounds that the activity is really just a hobby. The auditors try to establish their case by asking the taxpayer for copies of returns for the past four or five years. If the activity has produced a loss each year, the auditor will summarily conclude that the current loss is a nondeductible hobby loss. *Helpful:* Avoid falling into this trap by not taking copies of previous years' tax returns to the audit. The taxpayer, in general, has no obligation to provide copies of returns that have already been filed with the IRS. *Also helpful:* Ask the auditor where in the law it says that you must actually show a profit on a sideline business—ever. All that's required is that you *intend* to make a profit.

Source: Ms. X, Esq., a former IRS agent, who is still well connected.

Frustrating The Auditor

One of the most frustrating situations for an IRS agent is not getting all the necessary books, records, and documents to conduct an effective audit. When information is not provided or is provided piecemeal, it is very difficult, if not impossible, for the agent to understand a particular transaction and its significance. An agent has the leverage to disallow a deduction if the taxpayer doesn't provide the required documentation. However, the agent has very little leverage when the information he is seeking is unavailable—or what he does get does not relate specifically to a figure on the tax return.

Source: Ms. X, Esq., a former IRS agent, who is still well connected.

Wrapping Up The Audit

Even after an IRS revenue agent has told you that the audit is over and that he has no more questions, he may still come back with more questions, ones raised by his group manager or by the audit review staff. *A tactic that works in these situations:* Act very annoyed that the case hasn't been closed. Put pressure on the agent to accept oral answers to his questions. *Aim:* To avoid giving the agent time to develop the case further—questions are likely to lead to more questions. You want him to accept your answers on the spot and wind up the audit without having the chance to develop new areas or new issues.

Source: Ms. X, Esq., a former IRS agent, who is still well connected.

Making a deal with the IRS

Audit Strategy

What do you do when the IRS asks for information that's already in its possession? It's not unusual for an IRS agent to ask a taxpayer to provide a copy of his return for the year prior to the one being audited and for the year subsequent to the audit. The agent wants the returns so that he can make comparisons of income and expense items. Even though the IRS already has copies of the returns in its files, the agent has to go to a lot of trouble to get them from the service center. It's much easier to get them directly from the taxpayers. *Strategy:* Tell the agent that you will give him copies of the returns, but only *after* he has concluded his examination and presented you with the items he feels should be adjusted. The agent will probably agree. By not giving copies of the two returns until the adjustments have been settled, you will prevent the agent from making potentially damaging comparisons.
Source: Ms. X, Esq., a former IRS agent, who is still well connected.

How To Handle Consecutive Audits

It's not unusual for an agent, when he's finished auditing one year, to ask for a copy of the tax return you filed immediately after that year. The agent wants to see if a pattern exists–whether you've claimed similar, dubious deductions on both returns. *How to respond:* Before agreeing to show the agent the second return, get him to make an oral commitment to disallow the same proportion of deductions in the subsequent year as he did in the first year. Most agents will go along with this, since it means they'll have to spend less time to complete the case. And the arrangement is virtually certain to save you money—and time.
Source: Ms. X, Esq., a former IRS agent, who is still well connected.

Don't Give Something For Nothing

During an audit, the revenue agent may ask you for a copy of a previous year's tax return. The agent can always requisition the original return from the service center, but that takes months. *Strategy:* Tell the agent you'll make his life easier by giving him a copy of the return, but only if he, in turn, makes a concession. For instance, get him to agree to entirely avoid one of the issues he wants to examine.
Source: Ms. X, Esq., a former IRS agent, who is still well connected.

Second Best Evidence

Just because you can't prove something to the IRS auditor while you're sitting at his/her desk doesn't mean that you should pay more tax right then and there. Taxpayers often show up for audits with inadequate or incomplete proof of their deductions. The auditor's initial reaction is to disallow the deduction, in the belief that the taxpayer would have brought the complete documentation if it existed. *Strategy:* Ask the auditor to tell you exactly what he would accept as satisfactory documentation. If he demands proof that you can't possibly obtain, negotiate for second best, but still satisfactory proof that you will be able to get. Suppose you can't find the canceled checks the auditor wants to see, but you will be able to get an affidavit from the person you paid the money to. Get the auditor to agree that the affidavit will be acceptable proof of your deductions.

Source: Ms. X, Esq., a former IRS agent, who is still well connected.

Helping The Auditor Close The Case

Agents in most IRS districts have heavy caseloads and are eager to get through with your case as quickly as possible. It can be productive to make it easier for the agent by negotiating a reasonable adjustment before he invests too many hours on the case. Give the agent the books and records, and let him work on them for an hour or two. After he has had a chance to see what the records look like, tell him that you're willing to agree to a $2,000 adjustment of whatever item he chooses to disallow, if he'll close the case on the spot. If the agent starts to negotiate about increasing the $2,000 figure, you know you have someone who is willing to make a deal.

Source: Ms. X, Esq., a former IRS agent, who is still well connected.

IRS audit tactics to know

Audit Alert

Since Tax Reform pretty much eliminated tax shelters, what are IRS agents most likely to focus on during tax audits? My guess is that they will renew their attack on hobby losses claimed by businesspeople and professionals. Activities of a recreational nature that reflect only nominal income and large expenses are immediately suspect. Horse racing, dog breeding, sailing, fishing, and farming are the businesses that IRS agents are most likely to suspect as being covers for deducting the expenses of a hobby. *Best defense:* Keep accurate, detailed business records. Be able to document the fact that you operate in a prudent and businesslike manner with the intention of making a profit.

Source: Ms. X, Esq., a former IRS agent, who is still well connected.

How To Beat A Routine Audit Trap

A routine audit procedure used by revenue agents is a bank deposit analysis. Deposits in all of a taxpayer's accounts are added up and then compared with the amount of income reported on the tax return. What if you don't think that a particular deposit was income, but you can't remember the source of the deposit? Ask your bank to supply you with a copy of the check that was deposited. Most banks keep these records for five years. The person who wrote the check can then furnish you with an affidavit explaining the reason for issuing the check.

Source: Ms. X, Esq., a former IRS agent, who is still well connected.

The IRS Contacts Third Parties

An audit technique occasionally used by persistent revenue agents is to contact third parties about information related to a taxpayer's return. *Recent case:* An IRS agent got in touch with a company's vendors to ascertain whether invoices they had rendered, but that were never paid, were real or phony. The vendors all said that the supposed invoices were nothing more than "estimates"...and the services were never performed. The company's deduction for these items was disallowed. Third-party contacts are generally authorized by group managers when the agent has reasonable grounds for suspecting dishonesty.

Source: Ms. X, Esq., a former IRS agent, who is still well connected.

Extending The Statute Of Limitations

It is not unusual for an audit to stretch out beyond the normal three-year limitation period. When this happens, the agent will ask the taxpayer to sign Form 872 consenting to extend the period during which the IRS may propose additional tax assessments. Many times it is in the taxpayer's best interest to give his/her consent, since withholding it will only result in the agent's coming up with an arbitrary assessment in an effort to protect the government's interest. *Strategy:* Agree to extend the statute for only six months rather than the one-year period the IRS normally asks for. This will put a degree of pressure on the agent to close your case. Also, a short extension gives the agent less time to develop tax issues that you would rather not be pursued.

Source: Ms. X, Esq., a former IRS agent, who is still well connected.

When Not To Waive

It's common practice for an IRS auditor to ask you to waive the statute of limitations to give him/her more time to work on your case. If you refuse to sign the waiver, the examiner will generally disallow all the items he/she wanted to audit and issue a Notice of Deficiency. The Notice of Deficiency requires you to file a petition with the Tax Court within 90 days to avoid having to pay the tax until the merits of your case are considered by the Court. *Important:* It may be to your advantage *not* to sign the waiver if there are items on your return that you would rather the agent not dig into at an audit. At Tax Court, you will still have to prove your deductions. But you won't be subject to the kind of probing that can open up other items that you prefer not opened.

Source: Ms. X, Esq., a former IRS agent, who is still well connected.

Dragging An Audit On And On And...

Contrary to what is generally thought, your odds of settling are actually increased if a revenue agent has been holding your case for a long time—over one year. Although tax professionals who intentionally procrastinate can be barred from practice before the IRS, the Service is, for all practical purposes, helpless against tax-payers who procrastinate.

Source: Ms. X, Esq., a former IRS agent, who is still well connected.

Audit alert for companies

Traps To Avoid

There are major audit problems that companies are likely to face *now*. How to handle these problems…

Audit Flags

Most company audits occur after an IRS computer selects the company's return for further examination on the basis of its audit potential. Some examinations occur after something unusual on the return catches the eye of the IRS agent while the return is being processed. In either case, there are certain *audit triggers* that increase the likelihood that a return will be given extra IRS scrutiny.

It pays to know about these audit triggers in advance. With adequate attention, it's possible to minimize current audit risk and future difficulties that will arise if an audit *does* occur.

Tax Reform's audit triggers:

Capitalization rules. Tax Reform rules impose inventory capitalization requirements on many retailers and wholesalers. The IRS is paying a lot of attention here, as well as to manufacturers who are affected by these rules.

The IRS is considering the adoption of these rules by affected companies to be a *change* of accounting method, so these firms *have* to file IRS Form 3115 with their tax returns to report the change. In addition, the IRS may prepare a 10–12 page *questionnaire* that these companies will be required to fill out, to explain just how they implemented the new rules. The answers on this questionnaire may well serve as an *audit guide* for IRS examiners who look at the company's books in future years.

What to do: Have the company's tax adviser carefully work out the firm's implementation of the capitalization rules *now*. Don't make the mistake of putting this unpleasant task off until the last minute and then making decisions in a rush. Mistakes made now may have a *lasting* impact when the current year's return is examined in the future.

Travel, meals, and entertainment. Meal and entertainment costs are only 50% deductible. But many companies haven't set up the bookkeeping needed to break out meal and entertainment costs from travel, lodging, and other related items that *are* still 100% deductible. The IRS is *sure* to look at these deductions on examined returns, and those firms caught without required recordkeeping may get hit with *negligence* penalties.

The Alternative Minimum Tax is going to hit *more* corporations than before, primarily because of Tax Reform's changing tax rates. Companies that don't consider the AMT because they haven't been subject to it in the past can expect that the IRS *will* consider it when they process the company's return.

More Audit Triggers

Other factors that can help trigger an IRS audit of the company's tax return:

■*Large refunds* resulting from loss carrybacks or amended returns. *Every* refund exceeding $200,000 must be reported to Congress's Joint Committee on Taxation, and thus is very likely to be subject to close examination.

■*Income or expenses* that are out of line with those reported by similar companies in the same industry. This doesn't mean that a company shouldn't take a deduction that is unusually large, but it should be *sure* to have the records needed to back it up.

■*Foreign tax credits* and transactions between affiliated companies engaged in international operations. The IRS will want to make sure that such transactions are conducted on fair, *arm's length* terms.

■*Cash transactions* between major shareholders and the company, including shareholder loans, rent paid to a shareholder, large expense reimbursements, and over-large salaries.

■*The size of the company.* The bigger the company, the more likely an audit, although the IRS won't say by *how much* a company's size affects its audit risk.

■*Section 6661 disclosure.* Statements attached to a return in order to provide adequate disclosure for purposes of the substantial understatement penalty will increase the risk of an examination. This doesn't mean, however, that a taxpayer who may be subject to the penalty should not make the disclosure.

Handling The Auditor

The best way to handle problems that arise during an audit is by straightforward dealing with the auditor.

A company that seriously objects to the way an audit is being conducted can meet with the auditor's group manager, and can further appeal to the IRS's local branch chief or district director. The risk, however, is that if the appeals are turned down, the auditor may become personally antagonized by the company's action. And of course, a formal contest at the IRS appeals office or in Tax Court involves delay and incurring the cost of fees for top professional advisers.

Thus, the *smart* thing to do is to develop a good working relationship with the auditor from the start, one that is conducive to the *early* settlement of disagreements. *How to do it:*

■*Starting off.* The company will be informed that it has been selected for examination, and be asked to agree to a time and place for the examination to begin. An auditor will visit the company's premises and usually will want to work there. However, he might agree to work *off* the premises (perhaps in an outside accountant's office) if convinced this would be more convenient and that he would have access to all necessary information there.

■*Providing records.* At the start of the examination, the auditor will give the company an *information document request* (IDR) specifying the records he wants to look at. The IDR should be reviewed by the company's tax adviser, to see what issues the auditor is pursuing. Then the requested records should be provided.

When company officers impress the auditor with their professionalism, the company benefits in *two* ways. If everything seems in order, the auditor is less likely to feel there is something hidden to look for. And, a good relationship will help the settlement of any problems that arise.

■*Day-to-day dealings.* During the course of the audit, it may be best for the company to designate *one* person to act as liaison with the auditor. That person should be a tax professional or company executive familiar with tax matters. His job should be to facilitate the audit by promptly providing all *requested* records and information. However, he *shouldn't* do the auditor's job himself (for example, by *volunteering* information). Straightforward responses to the auditor's questions are all that is required.

■*Extra opinion.* When the company thinks an auditor is making a mistake on a matter of *law*, it can ask him to request *technical advice* from the IRS national office in Washington, DC. The national office will respond with a letter describing the facts of the case and its decision as to how the law should apply.

If at the end of the audit there are unresolved disputes, meet with the IRS auditor's group manager. He/she is likely to be more experienced and be able to see the company's point of view.

If the dispute continues, the company will usually receive a *30-day letter.* Within 30 days, it should file with the IRS appeals office. IRS appeals officers look at *more* than the facts shown on the company's tax return. For example, they consider the cost of going to court against the company and the risk that the IRS might *lose* in court. Thus, the company is likely to be offered *some* kind of settlement here.

Trouble Averters

Of course, the best way to handle trouble with the IRS is to *prevent* it.

When the company is about to enter a transaction with unclear tax consequences, it can ask the IRS for an advance *private ruling* on the matter. This acts as audit insurance. Even if a favorable ruling is *wrong* on the law, the company can still rely on it. *Extra advantage:* If the IRS does have problems with the transaction, the company finds out *in advance* and can take steps to meet the IRS objection.

When the company has *administrative problems* with the IRS bureaucracy (such as forms being lost or tax payments being misapplied), it can get help from the IRS's *Problems Resolution Office (PRO).* The PRO will help only if the company has first tried to resolve the problem through normal channels, so keep records of correspondence and other IRS contacts. But the PRO can be a valuable aid in preventing a small problem from becoming a big one.

Source: Charles Bogen, principal, and Larry J. Abowitz, senior manager, Ernst & Young, 787 Seventh Ave., New York 10019.

TAX LOOPHOLES

EVERYTHING THE LAW ALLOWS

Index